Murdering Masculinities

SEXUAL CULTURES: New Directions from the Center for
Lesbian and Gay Studies
General Editors: José Esteban Muñoz and Ann Pellegrini

Times Square Red, Times Square Blue
Samuel R. Delany

Private Affairs
Critical Ventures in the Culture of Social Relations
Phillip Brian Harper

In Your Face
9 Sexual Studies
Mandy Merck

Tropics of Desire
Interventions from Queer Latino America
José Quiroga

Murdering Masculinities
Fantasies of Gender and Violence in the American Crime Novel
Greg Forter

Murdering Masculinities

Fantasies of Gender and Violence in the American Crime Novel

GREG FORTER

NEW YORK UNIVERSITY PRESS

New York and London

NEW YORK UNIVERSITY PRESS
New York and London

© 2000 by New York University

Library of Congress Cataloging-in-Publication Data
Forter, Greg.
Murdering masculinities : fantasies of gender and violence in the
American crime novel / Greg Forter.
p. cm.
Includes bibliographical references and index.
ISBN 0-8147-2690-9 (alk. paper) — ISBN 0-8147-2691-7 (pbk. : alk. paper)
1. Detective and mystery stories, American—History and criticism.
2. Psychoanalysis and literature—United States—History—20th century.
3. American fiction—Male authors—History and criticism. 4. American
fiction—20th century—History and criticism. 5. Masculinity in
literature. 6. Criminals in literature. 7. Violence in literature. 8. Fantasy
in literature. 9. Crime in literature. 10. Men in literature.   I. Title.
PS374.D4 F67 2000
813'.087209353—dc21   00-009770

New York University Press books are printed on acid-free paper,
and their binding materials are chosen for strength and durability.

Manufactured in the United States of America

10 9 8 7 6 5 4 3 2 1

For my father, Claude, and in memory of my mother,
Eileen, 1937–1973

Contents

Acknowledgments

Many people contributed to this project during its long gestation. I'd first like to thank those friends who offered forms of support that are easier to acknowledge than to repay. Seth Moglen read every draft of each chapter, often more than once and always under pressure, with a loving care and attention that sustained me through good times and dark times alike, and that I've come to think of as characteristic of his enormous generosity. Susan Courtney gave of her time and critical acumen, encouraging my labors, improving my thoughts, and supporting me in vital ways. And Kate Brown offered a range of proposals that made me feel she saw with clarity the things I valued most in the project—things I often could not have learned to say without her help.

Helene Moglen, Danny Kim, Pamela Barnett, and Andrew Cousins each read portions of the manuscript and responded with insight and enthusiasm at times when I really needed them. My family supported me and egged me on, despite being bewildered at times by the snail's pace of my writing. I want especially to thank my brother, Mike, who provided needed material support, read parts of the manuscript, and just in general took good care of me.

My colleagues in the English Department at the University of South Carolina have made it a lively, supportive, and exciting place to work. Besides those already mentioned, I'd like to thank Christy Friend, Nina Levine, Ed Madden, Robert Newman, Bill Richey, Meili Steele, and Greg Wilsbacher, each of whom contributed in ways tangible and intangible. Carl Eby at the Beaufort campus surprised me with his friendship and the mutual overlap of our interests. The students in my graduate class on the American crime novel—Laura Di Prete, Jason Fell, Charlene Monahan-Spearen, Russ Nurick, Andrea Leonard, Brooke Rollins, and Janet Williams—helped me return to the ideas in this book with attentive and newly reopened eyes. Anne Goebel and Eileen Hart provided invaluable research assistance. And Sharon Verba, of the Thomas Cooper Library, tracked down an elusive Faulkner reference.

This book was once a dissertation, and I'd like to thank my committee members—Mitch Breitwieser, Carolyn Porter, and Kaja Silverman—for their individual and collective wisdom. I'm also indebted to Eric Zinner at New York University Press for his editorial insights and commitment to my project, and to the Press's reviewers for comments that helped me improve the manuscript. Others to whom I'm grateful for encouragement, convivial listening, and/or attentive reading are Elizabeth Abel, Alyson Bardsley, Leo Bersani, Bob Bohl, Carol Clover, Robert Corber, Marilyn Fabe, Kristin Handler, Anne-Marie Harvey, Homay King, Jody Lewen, Sarah Liu, James Mellard, Rob Miotke, Mark Muro, Franny Nudelman, Yugi Oniki, Sam Otter, Sam Putnam, Ben Reiss, Becca Steinitz, and Amy Zilliax.

Funding for the early stages of this project came from the Mellon Fellowship Program and from the Department of English and the Graduate Division at the University of California, Berkeley. Summer support from the English Department at the University of South Carolina, Columbia, enabled me to complete the manuscript. In a time of shrinking budgets and diminished grant opportunities for humanists, I'm especially grateful for this funding.

Shorter and substantially different versions of three chapters appeared in the following journals: chapter 1 in *Style*, Vol. 29, No. 3, Fall 1995 (Copyright © 1995 *Style*); chapter 2 in *NOVEL: A Forum on Fiction*, Vol. 29, No. 3, Spring 1996 (Copyright © 1996 NOVEL Corp.); and chapter 3 in *Mississippi Quarterly*, Vol. 49, No. 3, Summer 1996 (Copyright © 1996 Mississippi State University). I'm grateful to the editors for permission to reprint.

Introduction

My mother died the day after I turned twelve: that is the central fact of this book. She died of a tumor, painfully and slowly, and she died at home in an empty room that I could scarcely bring myself to enter. The room was our living room before she got sick. We must once have done some living in it, though I cannot say I really remember. What I can recollect now is this: that afterwards, as she lay dying, her shaven head wrapped round with gauze, her face simultaneously contracted and bloated, her eyes glazed over with drugs that could not hide a pain I did not understand—afterwards, that room was thick with things too scary to confront. In there I knew my mother was dying. I did not want her to die—and yet I wished she would. I felt that my need for a love she seemed unable to express was killing her, and I wanted her to hurry up and go. I thought if only I could love her, could make an adequately caring reparation for my greedy onslaughts upon her attention, then she would recover to be the mother I had always wanted her to be. Instead those onslaughts were now killing her, and death would be her final revenge. She was, I believed, dying on purpose: dying to torment me with her absence, dying to fill me with inexpiable guilt and reproach me for a fantasized omnipotence that destroyed when it could so easily have saved her.

I did not know the words for this then. Even now, I can hardly claim to remember anything of the kind. But I was, at the time, riven with a confusion that blurred the precision of feeling, rendering the most mundane of gestures intolerably conflicted. And so I stayed away. The room and its contents receded into the distance. I banished them from the living house. I pushed them out, out and away, through the French windows that sought to enclose them and into the unkempt yard behind. Now I would have some measure of peace. Now at last I was purified of any affective traffic with death. This, at least, is all I am sure of: I did not even cry when she died.

And yet there is something more to tell—another distant memory, a second secret psychic memorial, without which this first one would seem out of place. Sometime during my mother's illness I began to write a long piece of fiction. I wrote it by hand, in secrecy and alone, on loose-leaf pages that I diligently numbered and accumulated in a green folder. I wrote it without really thinking or planning; not being much of a reader at the time, I can't imagine what prompted me to write or upon which literary sources I drew. Perhaps the models weren't literary at all, but rather televisual. The story was full of action and cars, fast red cars with squealing black tires, and it was equally bloated with unmastered plot and with superfluous, hyperbolic adjectives. I don't know what ever became of the manuscript. Like so much else from that part of my life, it fell insensibly by the wayside—consigned to darkness by some unfathomable yet familial force. I mention it here only because it was, in fact, a detective story, with a masculine hero racing round in that car, confronted everywhere with murder and mayhem, and encountering in the course of his search a host of attractively scary women whose violent threats to his psychic integrity he could counter only with violence.

It's as though I had then already grasped the issues at the heart of this book. As though I had already learned, in a crude and entirely intuitive fashion, that the fragile defenses by which I expelled my dying mother from view, and which were saturated with violent fantasies that confused the boundaries they sought to establish, were profoundly linked to the crime novel. I could no more have said this at the time than I could have given voice to my ambivalence. It was not, indeed, until I'd written the opening chapter of this book that I even remembered having committed to paper my criminal juvenilia. It then became possible to see the ways in which this work is autobiographical. To talk about the crime novel is to talk about myself, to offer a kind of self-accounting. The genre, in fact, is a place in our culture where fantasies of extraordinary relevance to me get a kind of hyperbolic and public elaboration. And it's a genre in which the implicitly gendered content of those fantasies is heightened and rendered explicit: in which it's manhood that defines itself against a femininity whose proximity demands that it be ambivalently repudiated—and in which that femininity often returns, with all the violence of the initial projection, to perforate, shatter, and dissolve the male ego, and so to ruin the self-singularity that (for example) my own conflicted maternal expulsions were intended to consolidate.

This is then a highly personal book whose concerns are also cultural and political. It's a project "about" the American crime novel in a rather idiosyncratic sense. In it, I make use of expressive experiments within the genre of crime in order to tell a series of stories that—I hope it's not presumptuous to think—I'm especially suited to tell, but that are also collective stories that speak to the larger psychic and cultural issues I've begun to describe. The crime novel serves in the pages that follow to mediate between these extremes: between the privacy of a story too personal to be narrated straight and the cultural meanings that exceed but are also embedded within that story. Such mediation has been especially fortuitous in my case. Besides enabling me to discover an idiom that enfolds disquieting autobiographical energies in an academically appropriate form, it has also helped me to tell "my" story through texts alive to its full complexity: texts that counter the misogynist violence of fantasies that they also encourage.

One might, in this light, think of the project as a personal and collective exorcizing of explicitly gendered demons. But "exorcizing" would also be wrong. What's at stake is less a ritual purification than a ceremony of

3

masculine debasement and abjection. My basic claim is that the texts I discuss require men to be defiled: to take back and own up to desires for dissolution and bodily impurity that our culture authorizes them to experience as the external threat of a feminine principle that can (and must) be mastered. For me this has meant, in writing the book, a belated capacity to enter fully into my mother's death chamber. Or rather, to let that room reenter the house from which I once expelled it. To let the scene reenter *me* in a way that—far from making me "whole"—has required me to embrace the psychic disturbance that comes from internalizing desires and fantasies rendered alien through their projection. Such disturbances have a political as well as a personal value. Indeed, the psychic disquiet I'm describing is perhaps the necessary negative prerequisite to positive gender transformation. This, at any rate, is what I shall argue: masculinity may have to be murdered—in order that we might reinvent it.

A good deal of work has recently been done in this area. Most important for me have been the arguments of Leo Bersani and Kaja Silverman, both of whom stress in different ways the relations between what is psychically negative and our constructions of sexual difference. Both insist that, since "femininity" is the name men give to desires for dissolution that they cannot avow, the assumption by men of what's psychically "feminine" can serve to counter toxic male mastery by disturbing the well-bounded form of an ego that is both seat and sanction of violence.[1] The debt that my argument owes to such claims will become clear in what follows. My own work, meanwhile, focuses on the ambivalence surrounding this assumption of negativity—an ambivalence that shows in the strain between my texts' promotion of male toxicity and their persistent struggle against it. The books I examine embody this strain with particular intensity. Belonging, on one hand, to a genre whose commitment to masculine prowess is notorious, they can abject and "feminize" their men only by first imagining them through the normative conventions they inherit. They're thus peculiarly able to register the difficulty of the project I'm proposing. They're able, that is, to help us see the essential sobriety of my claims: to grasp that masculinity cannot be killed without first being embodied, so that there is always tension and struggle, even to the point of textual warfare, the appeal of male power battling and countering the appeal of its repudiation, and repudiation itself, at least for the moment, perhaps asserting its claim upon us largely in the mode of calamity—tragically, painfully, above all, elegiacally. Not the least interest of this mournful conflict is that it's part of what renders my texts resistant to reading itself, in ways I shall be concerned to chronicle.

It is perhaps already clear that psychoanalysis has been central to my inquiry. I've found in Freud's work an invaluable set of speculations about our affective and sexual lives, and have tried to remain alert to the more disturbing impulses in his writings—impulses he himself is often at pains to deny or contain. My project in this sense attempts to extend the revisionary work of a contemporary psychoanalysis suspicious of Freud's official pronouncements: Jacques Lacan, Jean Laplanche, Julia Kristeva, Jacqueline Rose, and Mikkel Borch-Jacobsen, as well as Bersani and Silverman. But this recovery has been, for me, only secondarily a matter of theory. My primary concern has been complexly textual in its impulse. I have tried to show that the books I read, precisely by renouncing the theoretical ambitions by which Freud seeks to stand outside of the disturbing conditions he discovers, can teach us the limits of theoretical speculation by giving an authentically nontheoretical "knowledge" of those states. If the authors of these books know things that Freud tries to unknow, it's because their formal strategies thwart the systematizing and masterful moves that they themselves equate with male power. These are books whose textual modes require male readers to *live* the ruinous negativizing of manhood that Freud knows only as a blinded insight. They're books that beneficently destroy the thematic meanings they construct, not only by way of the psychopolitical ambivalence that I've mentioned, but also through the resolution of that ambivalence. The impulse to self-abnegation defeats the masculine will-to-power, and this defeat, in moving toward the dissolution of structure, is communicable only in an antisystemic experience of breakdown that swaddles characters and readers alike in the darkness of a nonpropositional knowledge.

In this respect, my psychoanalytic aim has been to move the theory toward a form of expression that can honor its most radical insights. I've tried to do this in the pages that follow through a method of mutual implication. The primary texts I examine illuminate psychoanalytic theory just as much as psychoanalytic theory illuminates the texts. The former illumination takes place, moreover, through gestures that ask the theory to "own" those things it cannot logically assimilate, and that therefore seek to revise the very *forms* of psychoanalytic cognition. The texture of my prose is meant in part to help effect this revision. I've sought to avoid as much as possible explicit moments of theorization that are clearly demarcated from textual analyses over which they claim authority, preferring instead a kind of mobility in which the theory takes place in readings that enact, in turn, the breakdowns I'm describing. One effect of this method has been a certain implosive density to the style. It may often be difficult, because of that style, for readers to tell the boundaries between a critic's utterance, a theorist's speculation, a textual statement, and my own interpretation. If such confusion is cause for frustration and a certain loss of bearings, I hope that readers will perceive that this disturbance is a central component of my project's meaning.

But beyond such formal or stylistic effects, my analyses make this hostility to structured sense a major topic of inquiry. I've sought to show how the texts I examine convey their anti-epistemological knowledge in a series of psychically resonant metaphors that say the things about masculinity that Freud can only (un)say, and that thereby give an unparalleled specificity to the forms of male abjection that interest me. Each chapter is loosely centered upon one such metaphor or figure. Chapter 1, for example, examines the function of the corpse in the hardboiled detective novel. I show how Dashiell Hammett's *The Glass Key* uses this figure to particularly disquieting effect, eliciting identifications with a self-shattering pleasure that collapses the distinction between death drive and Eros, as well as the conventional Freudian distinction between masculine sadism and feminine masochism. Man is here, impossibly enough, the psychologically "feminine" compulsion to be a hardboiled corpse. He is the animal who derives enjoyment from the carnal unpleasure of erotic self-destruction. The literally disformulating character of such statements is mirrored in Hammett's third-person style, which reduces the masculine subject to an object deprived of agency and interiority— an object that, by the same token, becomes the target both of sadistically humanized objects within the novel's world, and of the compositional violence perpetrated by the style itself.

Subsequent chapters focus on metaphors more tied to primal bodily experiences, but the function of those figures and the use to which I put them remain essentially similar. I argue that, in James Cain's *Serenade*, metaphors of olfaction trouble Freud's distinction between a male subject of civilized love and the pre-civil violence of feminine narcissism. I show that William Faulkner's *Sanctuary* makes vomit a figure for the psychic state of being "mixed up" in one's feminine objects, a state which Freud suggests men surmount through the function of objective vision, but which Faulkner shows they cannot. I examine the soiling of masculine voice in Jim Thompson's *Pop. 1280*, linking that soiling to an oedipal pathology that conjoins morality with murder. And I argue that Chester Himes's *Blind Man with a Pistol* shows us things that Freud's writings hardly touch upon: that white masculinity is structured by fantasies that deposit excremental impurities in black men, in ways which make it possible to imagine the figural reincorporation of shit as part of the process of undermining that manhood.[2]

In each of these cases, the metaphor functions to trouble both Freud's discursive ambitions and the forms of masculine singularity they support. In each, the attempt to enact this disturbance leads to a remarkable narrative experiment to which I insist we pay attention. And in each, these strategies include an effort to implicate readers constructed as male, making them imbibe the ruinous "object" whose exclusion founds both Freudian system and conventional masculinity.

•   •   •

7

It's in the context of these narrative experiments that I would link my texts to those of our canonized modernists.[3] I've elected not to pursue this connection in detail in this study, partly because the crime novels themselves turned out to demand a level of attention that made extended comparisons unfeasible. It does, however, seem worth making two brief points in passing. First, mainstream modernism is linked to the crime novel by virtue of a shared social genesis. Both are complex cultural responses to a crisis in masculinity that took place in the opening decades of the twentieth century. That crisis was occasioned by increasing demands for social recognition by women, African Americans, and new ethnic immigrants,[4] and was registered in both these forms not just as a threat to male social power, but as a danger to the psychic integrity of masculine identity itself. Second, the canonization of modernism resulted in part from its development of an aesthetic that enabled authors to explore while containing the psychic ruin threatened by these developments. That aesthetic fetishized art as a monument to authorial mastery. While its strategies made it possible to register the self's fragmentation and the disturbing blurriness of its borders, they also included a recuperative moment in which those fragments are formally redeemed by an implicitly masculine authorial will that endows them with unity and significance. Such a gesture transmutes the self's ruins into the splendor of aesthetic objects, whose very status as container of those shards implies an "outside" from which one can have an unimplicated knowledge of them.[5]

The relationship between the texts I examine and this modernist aesthetic is simultaneously intimate and explosive. Though there are, of course, a great many crime novels that respond to the crisis in masculinity with desublimated representations of male violence—openly celebrating the will-to-singularity that our modernists transmute into a more refined discourse of decline and aesthetic redemption[6]—the genre's relegation to the margins of culture opened a kind of experimental space for alternative responses to that crisis. It opened a space in which the commitment to male singularity could be contested. It enabled authors to pursue more fully, without the culturally enforced requirement to ironize or contain them, the desires for masculine disintegration with which my work is concerned. (As we shall see, this is true even of a modernist like Faulkner when he sets out to write a crime novel.) Such explorations self-consciously resist the monumentalizing gestures of modernist aesthetics, just as they do the systematizing moves of psychoanalytic theory. They promote an art of cultural waste by approximating the forms of abjection explored within their representations, rather than seeking, aesthetically or theoretically, to stand outside and above them.

It follows from such comments that this isn't a conventional genre study. I've foregone historical, taxonomical, and synthetic methodologies in favor of close reading, in part because the work of defining the genre has been done expertly by others: John G. Cawelti, Dennis Porter, Julian Symons, Tony Hilfer, Stephen Knight, and Marty Roth, to name a few.[7] But I've also focused on close reading as a way of addressing both the limitations of these scholars and the neglect of more canonically minded critics. Pop culture critics have tended to slight close reading on the assumption that the main interest of crime writing resides in the fact of its popularity. They thus read the genre for its collective capacity to express the fantasies and resolve the conflicts of a pre-given "public," and treat the distinctiveness of individual works as relatively unimportant—except when it signals an innovation in "the formula" that reflects a change in the public at large. Literary critics have, on the other hand, tended to treat crime writing as beneath their notice. They've done so out of a bias against popular tastes that has its roots in the process of modernist canon-formation to which I have alluded. And they've often, as with the texts on which I focus, used the statistical fact of popularity as an alibi for excluding books that they find psychically, socially, and even formally threatening.

In contrast to these tendencies, I insist that these books are important independently of their popularity, and that they're worthy of being *read*—slowly, patiently, attentively. They're books of unusual formal ambition whose originality resides in the way they appropriate generic conventions in order to open up new aesthetic possibilities. The stylizations of these novels, including some we've been taught to find crude, represent attempts to communicate things perhaps inaccessible to more verisimilitudinous representation. And their authors combine this formal inventiveness with a concentrated expressive intensity, enabling them to explore masculinity with subtlety and psychic complexity. For me, these qualities make the books both aesthetically powerful and politically significant in ways that require us to expand our conceptions of the genre's cultural possibilities: to reconsider the generic determinism by which we've tended to associate the crime novel with an unambivalent commitment to male power.[8] My own evaluation is in part a result of the personal history with which I began—a history whose details shaped me in relation to a set of social possibilities: a death, a room, a piece of writing; a constellation of fantasies and sensations whose present insistence is what it means to be "me"; a heightened awareness of the violent gestures that consolidate manhood by rejecting desires that challenge the self's integrity. My readers won't, of course, share with me the exact texture of this history. But I trust it's not too much to hope that they'll find the visions of the texts I read as disturbingly irresistible as I have.

1   Hardboiled Masochism

The Corpse in Dashiell Hammett's *The Glass Key*

"I liked somebody being dead"

Let us begin with the hardboiled detective novel, as this—according to the critical history—is both the first American species of crime novel and the most resolutely masculinist.[1] These two claims are not unrelated. The American character of the hardboiled form resides in part, as critics have noted, in its preoccupation with violence.[2] And that violence typically includes a misogyny by which the male hero defines himself by vanquishing a feminine principle that threatens his "sense of discrete self."[3] The pleasure of hardboiled reading in this sense inheres in our identification with an invulnerable agent of male power and mastery. It results from our imaginative alignment with a man whose mastery includes a capacity to overcome a feminine "outside" that threatens to pierce and dissolve him, as well as a more conventional ability to reduce semantic plurality to a unity by solving the mystery's crime.

Without denying this basic characterization, I want to begin by suggesting that there are pleasures to hardboiled reading that can't be contained within these contours. Critics have often noted these pleasures, though without pursuing their full implication. They've stressed, for example, how hardboiled fiction lingers over linguistic textures and non-teleological narrative elements that are strictly absent from the analytical detective story, and that tend to downplay or even subvert the pleasures of solution.[4] And they've emphasized how the hardboiled detective, far from demonstrating unending mastery, often becomes a manipulated object and even a victim of violence. Tzvetan Todorov thus speaks of hardboiled fiction as "the story of the vulnerable detective." "Its chief feature," he writes, "is that the detective loses his immunity, gets beaten up, badly hurt, constantly risks his life, in short, he is integrated into the universe of the other characters, instead of being an independent observer."[5] Marty Roth suggestively redescribes this danger in terms of a masochistic erotics within the hardboiled form. "Masochism," he writes, "flourishes in hardboiled detective fiction," as "[a]sking for pain is the point of the detective's dares and challenges and his wisecracks."[6] The repeated danger that the dick encounters results in this light from his compulsively repetitive effort to put himself in harm's way. And a final comment, by Gertrude Stein, links this effort more generally to the dilatory pleasures of hardboiled reading:

I never was interested in cross word puzzles or any kind of puzzles but I do like detective stories. I never try to guess who has done the crime and if I did I would be sure to guess wrong but I liked somebody being dead and how it moves along and Dashiell Hammett was all that and more.[7]

"How it moves along," not "how it ends": the penetration of the mystery is here inessential to the pleasure of hardboiled reading. "I liked somebody being dead," Stein says. Such a preference may help refine our sense of the "other" hardboiled enjoyment. For to say "I like somebody being dead" is to say that the end-pleasure of narrative significance is subordinated to what we might call the fore-pleasure of a traumatic violation. It's to offer the disturbing but provocative suggestion that the hardboiled *corpse*—the very thing that provides the mystery and seems therefore most intimately bound up with a temporality of semantic recuperation—is also that which erodes that temporality, dysfunctionalizes pleasure, fixates us on a brute physicality that resists hermeneutic or semantic redemption. To be sure, the detective conventionally manages to overcome that resistance. And, to be sure, he typically does so through gestures of mastery whose incipient misogyny often becomes explicitly violent and central to his success. But inasmuch as the hardboiled novel subordinates the sense of an ending, the scene of the crime might be said to become not just something to be reconstructed and mastered but a scene to whose trauma we're invited to submit. It becomes not merely the impetus for a quest that dramatizes the detective's prowess, but also an initiation into the limits of that prowess: an opportunity to let the mind play over death as one's ownmost destiny.

In this sense the "somebody" one likes "being dead" is not, perhaps, someone else at all. The corpse elicits in us and the dick an identification, a *desire* to be dead. It asks the detective to embark on a journey in which he compulsively courts a violence that threatens his imminent death. And it encourages us to partake of that journey through acts of imaginative identification. To the extent that we enjoy ourselves through this identification, the hardboiled novel begins to subvert the conventionally masculine commitment to mastery, exposing it as a reflex of fear that masks a secret desire: a desire for the renunciation of power in the name of a compulsively repeated submission to the pleasures of masochistic pain.

In order to describe this desire more fully, I want to turn at this point to Freud's late essay, *Beyond the Pleasure Principle* (1920), which offers a searching account of the relations between pleasure, mastery, and submission. A reading of this text can help us explore the masochistic dimension to pleasure in a way that connects it to the compulsively repetitive character of the detective's pursuit of pain. We can do this, however, only by reading Freud in some ways against himself—by suggesting that the hardboiled novel makes visible things about the pleasures of repetition that Freud both sees and seeks to repress.

Beyond the Pleasure Principle attempts at first to theorize compulsive submission in terms of a basic drive toward mastery. "The child cannot possibly have felt his mother's departure as something agreeable or even indifferent," writes Freud in the famous *fort/da* section. "How then does his repetition of this distressing experience as a game fit in with the pleasure principle?"[8] The answer he gives begins as follows:

[O]ne gets the impression that the child turned his experience [of his mother's departure] into a game from another motive. At the outset he was in a passive situation— he was overpowered by the experience; but, by repeating it, unpleasurable though it was . . . he took on an active part. These efforts might be put down to an instinct for mastery that was acting independently of whether the memory was in itself pleasurable or not. (16)

Passivity stands to unpleasure as activity does to the (linguistic) binding of that unpleasure, and to a consequent pleasure-in-mastery. What Freud intuits yet represses in this series is the possibility of a pleasurable compulsion, since pleasure needs to reside with mastery if the term "perversion" is to retain its significance. A pleasurable compulsion would be a perverse pleasure in being unpleasurably "overpowered by [an] experience." It would be a pleasure in masochistic submission to the influx of painful excitation, rather than the incipiently sadistic enjoyment to be had from subduing by binding that excitation. Since Freud sees pleasure as a state corresponding to "a *diminution*" of unbound energy in the mind (8), a repetition that declines to master such excitation—either by discharging it or by psychically binding it—can for him be only a kind of abnormality. The opposition between death drive and Eros will thus turn out to require and enforce the separation of compulsion from enjoyment itself.

For if—as Freud goes on to argue—the compulsion to repeat is the sign of the ego's most radically deathward tendencies, it must be subordinated to this opposition if it is to become conceptually legible. If such repetition is the mark of the psyche's deathly drive to unbind itself, then locating pleasure on the side of compulsion enables an erotics of increased psychic tension in which the ego takes pleasure in its own unpleasurable

14

undoing. Compulsive enjoyment is exactly this enjoyment in the impulse to self-destruction. Neither the satisfaction attaching to masterful binding nor the biologized satiation of an ultimate or complete discharge, such enjoyment is the vexatious pleasure of a compulsively repeated embrace of psychic tension that tends ineluctably toward death. It's the pleasure of a boy repeatedly submitting to the pain of his mother's departure, for no reason more or less than the sheer unmitigated hell of it. It's a pleasure that, far from being masterful, resides instead in the ego's desire to repeat a remembered unpleasure in order self-explosively to submit to it. And it's in this compulsively pleasurable submission that the stakes of Freud's argument start to become clear. The death drive, after all, along with the compulsion to repeat that instantiates it, is meant to lie somewhere "beyond" the pleasure principle, not to inhere secretly within it. To the extent that his argument might therefore fail to separate enjoyment from compulsive repetition, it threatens to transform its intended message—"I seek (nonerotically) my own death"—into its more radically true one: "I like (take pleasure in) somebody (myself) being dead (ecstatically dying)."[9]

And there can be little doubt that the text fails to keep these terms apart. Freud's recourse to "an instinct for mastery," in a passage meant to explain a child's compulsive *submission* to unpleasure, betokens his surrender to an oxymoronic logic that portends a complete theoretical collapse. For the concept of an "instinct" has meaning only if we take it seriously as something to which we must submit. Instincts master us, not we them. The most plausible reading, then, of an "instinct for mastery" is that I am compelled, driven, submitted to (my own) mastery, that in submitting I become master, and in mastering, I give myself up. The pleasure attendant on a will-to-mastery becomes indissociable from the conceptual incoherence of a (masochistically) pleasurable unpleasure.[10] What we give up for the sake of such mastery is the prior and compulsively repetitive pleasure of masochistic surrender itself, and hence the peculiarly repetitive character of Freud's second account of his grandson's game:

These efforts might be put down to an instinct for mastery that was acting inde-pendently of whether the memory was in itself pleasurable or not. But still another interpretation may be attempted. Throwing away the object so that it was "gone" might satisfy an impulse of the child's . . . to revenge himself on his mother for going away from him. In that case it would have a defiant meaning: "All right, then, go away! I don't need you. I'm sending you away myself." (16)

If, as Freud says, "another interpretation may be attempted," we might well wonder why the content of that "other interpretation" resembles so closely that of the first. The movement from explanation one ("it's not masochism, it's a will-to-mastery") to explanation two ("it's still not masochism, it's sadism") is almost no movement at all. The second proposition merely ex-tends and renders explicit the aggression implicit in the "instinct for mas-tery" of the first. Freud's own compulsion to repeat, therefore, the excess of his explanatory ardor, allows us to read in that very repetition a negative af-firmation of the assertion his explanations are designed to disallow. When a footnote describes the child staging his own disappearance in a mirror (15), we're entitled to see in that action what Freud tries not to see, to prevent us from seeing: that this moment marks the disruptive restaging of an originary and involuntary self-abnegation that pre-dates the pretensions of sadistic mastery and well-bound egoic control. The entire project of searching for something "beyond" the pleasure principle now comes into focus as a de-fense against the recognition that there is, in truth, nothing beyond it, and that consequently, the compulsive submission to unpleasurable tension may be not just enjoyable, but sexual enjoyment itself.[11]

How to Be Dead in Style

Let us return, then, to the scene of crime, in order to reformulate our thesis. The pleasure I take in hardboiled reading is in part the pleasure that Freud would deny me: a pleasure in the unpleasure of increased psychic tension that might more properly be said to "take me," in that it entails my compulsory luxuriance in being possessed, broken, and lost to myself. What does this mean? Or—more crucially—what does it look like?

In what follows I explore such questions particularly in the work of Dashiell Hammett, who's both the acknowledged first master of the hardboiled form and a far more eccentric figure than critics have usually acknowledged. His eccentricity is nowhere more evident than in two key elements of his work. First, Hammett was unusually interested in third-person stylistic experiments. He wrote two of his five finished novels in the third person, and this places him in an idiosyncratic relation to a tradition dominated by the first-person voice of a cynical but sentimental detective.[12] Second, only one of his five finished novels (*The Maltese Falcon*) relies for resolution on a full-blown, Blame-it-on-Mame *femme fatale*. Given the centrality of that figure within the hardboiled canon, this fact should seem stranger to readers than it apparently does. My claim is that it's connected to the first eccentricity I've mentioned. For despite the fact that the novel that relies on a *femme fatale* is written in the third person, I will be suggesting that the third-person style provided Hammett with an idiom with which to subvert the masculinism that requires the production and ultimate destruction of that figure. He uses that style to shatter, in ways I shall describe in *The Glass Key* (1931), the fiction of a psychically invulnerable and impermeable masculinity. The style enables him to do so as part of a larger attempt to make men acknowledge that the violence they imagine as the external threat of a dangerous woman is, in fact, the disguised return of an inadmissible pleasure: a pleasure in psychic self-dissolution that I've begun to describe through Freud, and that's deeply at odds with our culture's commitment to masculine singularity and power. Hammett's eccentricity in this sense results from the fact that the hardboiled tradition has sought to repress the dangerous pleasures he offers. Those pleasures nonetheless continue to reverberate within the texts of that tradition, and make it possible to think of Hammett's work as giving us access to the unconscious truth of hardboiled pleasure itself.

Here is how *The Glass Key* opens:

Green dice rolled across the green table, struck the rim together, and bounced back. One stopped short holding six white spots in two equal rows uppermost. The other tumbled out to the center of the table and came to rest with a single spot on top.[13]

Language like this wreaks, to begin with, a kind of epistemological havoc, as it practically disappears in the gesture of its emergence and unsays as much as it says. We can stress as critics often have the "clipped," "bare," "sparse," "lean," "clean," or "hard" stylistic indices. We can even note the observational and practically monosyllabic precision of this language, which seems to record with photographic accuracy the objects on which it focuses. But what's crucial to my mind is the *withholding* character of a discourse that seems, at the same time, so generously attentive to the minutiae of detail that it's almost forced to operate in slow-motion. (We could even read the numbers on the two dice—one giving in abundance, the other reluctant and refraining—as a kind of representational announcement of this parsimonious generosity.) The temporal distention of an event that lasts seconds mirrors in miniature the dilatory fixations of hardboiled narrative as a whole, while simultaneously masking, beneath the strained attitude of its concentration, the informational dearth of its content. Where are we? When? Who's there? Who's speaking? At the extreme, these epistemological uncertainties give way to a kind of ontological murder, which is figured already in the extirpation of human agency from this passage. The dice appear to roll themselves; they're animated with a subjective agency that should not strictly belong to them, striking, stopping, tumbling, and holding in a way that invests them with a human dignity whose very condition, as we shall see, is the stylistic eradication of humanity itself.

But let us begin with the epistemological difficulties posed by this language. We can start by noting that at least *some* of the omissions of knowledge are made good in the subsequent narrative. In an almost cinematic manner, the novel could be said to relay us in relative coherence along its syntagmatic chain, displacing readerly desire from "cut" to "cut" and transforming each "shot" retrospectively into a signifier that makes good the lack of the previous. Thus, when the text moves in the second paragraph to "Ned Beaumont grunt[ing] softly," it begins to fill in the gaps in knowledge broached by its opening passage. Part of the fictive world that the initial close-up omits is conjured into the field of vision by this second shot, in the person of Ned Beaumont. That shot, meanwhile, can't but leave out something else, which it then requires a third shot to provide—and so on. In the very movement of narrational unfolding, epistemological lacks are made good in this way: through the gradual production of a knowable world that, thanks to the recognizable solidity of its contours, confers on the reader a sense of sufficiency, mastery, and knowledgeable control. The gambling room acquires fixed coordinates; the novel peoples it, locates it in larger temporal and spatial networks, embroils it in a plot that endows it with meaning and promises to infuse it with significance. The text's capacity to render its world familiarly mappable in this way—as well as its ability to bind that world in a hermeneutically compliant plot that illuminates it—enables the reader progressively to become an imaginary master of the narrative kingdom. Epistemological desire is thus the desire both of and for realism: a desire for conventions of narrative and verisimilitude that the novel can hardly fail in certain basic respects to satisfy.

And yet the fictive world of *The Glass Key* retains an oddly emaciated look, an eerily evaporative proclivity. We've come a long way from the social density of even, say, a Henry James novel, in part because Hammett only incompletely fulfills the requirements of epistemological lucidity I've been describing. The location of the main action remains unspecified throughout, the historical moment shows up only on the faces of the novel's commodities, and spatial articulations in any given scene are kept to the barest minimum. The text's famously unflinching attention to the "realities" of corruption and violence, as well as its narrational tendency to produce and satiate an epistemological desire, may then betoken a certain "realism," but we need also to reckon the abrogation of that project. Hammett once wrote that "[r]ealistic is one of those words when it comes up in conversation sensible

19

people put on their hats and go home."[14] For all the celebrated objectivity of its vision, *The Glass Key* tends to corroborate such a statement—not just narrationally, not just (as we shall see) by subordinating the sense of an ending, but also and especially "prosaically": through the specific disturbances to the representational function of language effected by its prose style. The eye of that style is too superficial in its grasp to dispel the sense that something yet remains, beyond and animating the representational field, to be seen, mastered, and understood:

A telephone-bell, ringing close to Ned Beaumont's head, awakened him. He opened his eyes, put his feet down on the floor, turned on his side, and looked around the room. When he saw the telephone he shut his eyes and relaxed.

The bell continued to ring. He groaned, opened his eyes again, and squirmed until he had freed his left arm from beneath his body. He put his wrist close to his eyes and looked at his watch, squinting. The watch's crystal was gone and its hands had stopped at twelve minutes to twelve. (36)

The reality effect of a passage like this results primarily from the way it piles up nouns; what's real here is what can be nominally designated, what exists as substance. The style therefore works by juxtaposing only those things— subjects and objects, though we shall soon be confronted with the abolition of this distinction—that can be substantially grasped by the senses. If and when it highlights qualities, these tend to be purely exterior ones (in this case, movement and sound, but also sometimes color, texture, and so on), since this is a style that approximates the real by refusing to register anything but surface. It's a style that moves from object to object with a certain restless but alert rapidity; seeking to reproduce for the reader the "natural" movement of everyday consciousness, it quickly exhausts the thing that it sees, takes it in at a glance, and swallows it whole. We're asked to partake in the peculiarity of this gesture, which brings things into the field of vision only long enough to abolish by registering them. The effect is that efforts to ingest this world are accompanied by an interpretive indigestion that frustrates the will toward epistemological mastery. The very obsessiveness of transcriptive desire turns out to mark the paradoxical failure of mimetic transcription itself.

For the closer Hammett's camera looks (and listens), the less it truly sees (and hears); the greater its focus on the objects it collects, the more it attenuates that linguistic dimension—the significatory—which could alone establish the reasonable grounds for any such collection of objects. Ned Beaumont would seem, for example, to stand in some "meaningful" relation to the ringing telephone, to the stopped watch (with its implied metaphysics and thematics of time), and to the parts of his own body. Either the point of such description resides in its meaning *for Ned*, whose consciousness presumably organizes the scene (it's his head that's near the phone, his feet that touch the floor, his body that's covering his hand, his eyes that read the watch); or else the objects and encounters carry some symbolic/metaphorical meaning that we, as readers, can know, but that Ned either doesn't or can't. Whichever the case, the text appears to be "saying something": it appears to bring together its objects in the name of a legibly thematic intention. If it nevertheless gives us nothing to go on—if the only way to read such a scene is to paraphrase it while imputing affects and motives that the text nowhere explicitly states—this is because Hammett's style performs the double but parallel work of destroying the world in the act of describing it and banishing (or at least minimizing) signification for the sake of its own material extremity. It's as if the passage were simply saying: telephone, ringing, head, feet, eyes, hands, looking, watch, room; as if the very stinginess of its articulations were designed to prevent its world from "meaning" by draining its objects of referential density while refusing to plump them with symbolic weight. The conventional binary of language "or" the world in this sense gives way to a materiality that spurns both the representational and the significatory dimensions of the linguistic sign. For this is a language that isolates and contains, circling its objects and breaking them off from the world, then proceeding to clobber them, flatten them into emaciated thinness, pulverize them, render them astonished and mute. It's a language so committed to the arbitrary and depthless juxtaposition of objects and subjects that their coincidence in one place and time comes to seem accidental: they just "are," in all their brute contingency, there together. And it's thus a language that, far from primarily satisfying the desire to see and know that it produces, epistemologically starves us instead. "To speak, and above all to write, is to fast," write Gilles Deleuze and Félix Guattari in their book on Kafka.[15] When Ned Beaumont says toward the end of the novel that "all the dreams [he] ever had about food ended before [he] got a chance to do any actual eating" (179), he gives the hardboiled version of that argument: to write is to produce a starving text, a text that starves (us). The hardboiled novel, at least in this case, compels a submission to the representational refusal of the realistic feast.

The eye of this style can thus "pull back" or "cut" all it wants to; it can give us belatedly the establishing shots that it at first withholds, can even try to transform non-knowledge into knowledge through a precise temporal ordering of its elements. It continues, nevertheless, to enunciate with a decidedly staid myopia, a blunt and arbitrary parsimony. The world from its vantage is a two-dimensional affair that does not speak, a world composed of empty clues, manufactured evidence, and broken circuits, where accident has effectively absorbed essence and meaning is no more than the spartan byproduct of a predominantly material sign. Only when the text "distorts" that world with narrative, smearing it retroactively with the telos of a hermeneutical desire, does it manage to remand its objects into the custody of meaning. Narrative acts here as a fantasy structure transforming the inert signs of the desire for nothing into the meaningful objects of a desire for something.[16] It takes the voided solidity of the world and literally rediscloses it to us, dressing it up in the meaningful promise of a narrational and redemptive causality. If the primary function of the detective is thus to link the world's objects by way of this causality—to infuse the world with a total significance unveiled at the end of its time—that function remains profoundly at odds with a style that clings to its empty secret long after the narrative secretes. Reading becomes a kind of trauma, interpretation a matter of unauthorized inference. The pleasure of the hardboiled text is bound up with the pain of an interpretive dissatisfaction.

But the depleted character of the novel's universe isn't just due to its informational fissures. It also results from the fact that its style refuses to open a space for interiority, for affectivity—in short, for humanity itself. What makes that style so ghostly, what renders it so bloodless in its apparent solidity, is its evacuation of human agency from the site of the human, and the consequent investment of that agency in inanimate objects and even in the forces of nature:

Wind-driven rain hammered tree, bush, ground, man, car with incessant wet blows. . . .

Wind and rain on [the man's] back pushed him downhill towards the patches [of light]. As he went downhill stiffness gradually left him so that, though he stumbled often and staggered, and was tripped by obstacles underfoot, he kept his feet under him and moved nimbly enough . . . towards his goal.

Presently a path came under his feet. He turned into it, holding it partly by its sliminess under his feet, partly by the feel of the bushes whipping his face on either side, and not at all by sight. The path led him off to the left for a little distance, but then, swinging in a broad curve, brought him to the brink of a small gorge. (123)

It would perhaps be redundant to list the preponderance of active verbs that here take Ned Beaumont for their object, or to point out the radically dehumanizing effect of the first sentence's indifferent and equalizing inventory ("trees, bush, ground, man, car"). Multiplying the sites of sadistic agency, displacing subjective activity onto a rain that "hammers," obstacles that "trip," and bushes that "whip," the passage so thoroughly disperses human being across its landscape that it also effectively abolishes that being. Ned and his world are confused and interfused; he becomes "worldly," his world becomes "human," as the relentless personification of objects marks and enforces an equally implacable objectification of the subject. If the humanized object resulting from this process is not in fact human at all, then neither is the objectified subject that results on the other side. Where "humanity" ceases to coincide with a human form, *the category of the human uncannily vanishes*, losing all possible meaning; it may seem at first glance to lurk almost everywhere, but this is because it in fact resides, simultaneously and just as surely, exactly nowhere. Human qualities survive in such a case only on the side of the object itself, and they're consequently rendered *in*human by the force of their spatial displacement. The human form survives, conversely, in a manner so drained of those qualities we normally attribute to it—agency, interiority, affectivity, for example—as to become unmistakably *dehumanized*.

But this inversion isn't just something that happens "in" the representation; it's above all something performed *by* the representation. The naturalism within the scene is merely the bleeding into content of an essentially formal necessity. Language itself is first and foremost what pummels human being; it's the third-person style that grinds it to a pulp and—as the saying goes—rubs it out. The only omission indispensable to this style is the omission of the category of the human itself. The only thing it cannot abide is an affective, active, and self-conscious subject, who behaves in any way *like* a subject, and we might therefore begin to suspect that the entire point of its omissions and opacities is to render the human as object: to flatten, silence, and blind it ("not at all by sight"); to rip it away from both reference and significance; to reduce humanity to a material register that blots out the difference between people and things by making each a pulpy occasion for the eruption of something that precedes that distinction. Sadistic agency, subjective activity, the use and manipulation of objects that properly belong to human intention: these are placed on the side of the object only as a kind of representational expression of the style's intention to wipe out human being, both within and without its pulverized field.[17] For hardboiled discourse is a sadistic discourse that "repudiates any relationship between speaker and audience"; "its purpose," as Georges Bataille writes of Sade, "is the denial of humanity."[18] In this it is, perhaps in its essence, an utterly impersonal third-person language that seeks to fold over upon and engulf even the human consciousness at its origin. It's a language that can belong to no one because it is characterized by an unending hostility to even the "one" who would own and utter it. Its abduction by such narrating dicks as Raymond Chandler's Marlowe and Hammett's Continental Op marks the attempt of those dicks to

arrogate to themselves a sadistic weaponry—the wisecrack, the deflating sim-
ile—that enables a delusional linguistic mastery in compensation for the psychic unmanning that in fact constitutes their being. In first-person narratives, that is, hardboiled language becomes something like a fetish: an eroticized substitute for a phallic potency that *The Glass Key*'s narration scorns; an
instrument that, in the apparent efficiency with which it binds unpleasurable affect, facilitates the erection of a sadistic armor against the internal and
worldly seductions of a more primary masochistic unbinding.

Return of the Primal Scene

I want now to turn to the novel's content in order to explore how the style
I've described colludes with representational strategies that encourage
masochistic identifications. My claim is that *The Glass Key* at once attempts
to construct a masculine reader and requires that reader to embrace such
identifications; it asks us, that is, to identify with a hero who is himself a
male masochist, and whose thirst for punishment extends beyond those regularly expressive hardboiled set-pieces in which the detective gets beat up as
proof of his virile capacities.[19] There is, as we'll see, something more demonic, something more compulsively repetitive, in Ned Beaumont's persistent pursuit of pain. Identifying with him entails embracing this compulsively repeated pursuit—embracing his desire for a self-shattering pleasure
that men conventionally project in the form of a dangerously feminine so-
licitation of desire, which can be mastered precisely because it no longer appears to issue from within.[20]

Even the briefest description of the novel begins to make my point.
For this is a book in which the detective[21] suffers from a kind of masochistic paralysis, in which he seems erotically transfixed by the prospect of his
own destruction. You "[m]ight as well take your punishment and get it
over with," says Ned Beaumont early in the novel (6). And indeed, his investigative trajectory is marked by a distinctive rhythm, in which masterful activity alternates incessantly with passivity, objectification, and eroti-

cized violation. Having followed a gambler to New York, for instance, with the intention of recovering some money from him, Ned takes a cab that is immediately struck by another taxi, showering him with broken glass and leaving him "huddled" in a corner, "white-faced and shivering," for the rest of his ride (30). When he finally confronts the gambler a few pages later, he's punched in the stomach by a bodyguard, vomits, and spends the rest of the night abusing his body with alcohol (34–36). The middle of the novel is then dominated by a remarkable sequence of punishments: Ned goes to see Shad O'Rory, a gangster and opposing politician, with the apparent intention of tricking him, but is instead tricked himself, savagely mauled by a bulldog, and beaten mercilessly into unconsciousness. When he wakes up, he repeatedly behaves as if he's in control of a situation in which he's clearly a prisoner; so his acts serve only to inspire the goons to beat him over and over again, in a manner that Hammett goes out of his way to eroticize.[22] Lastly, Ned initiates a second showdown with Shad over the suicide of a newspaper editor; he's immediately forced to flee from him, running "through brush that [tears] his hands and face [and] clothing" (137), only to end up back at the house, where the new widow screams at him and slaps him unconscious (140).

There's hardly for Ned a gesture of mastery that doesn't lead to him being mastered. The very telos of acts of mastery seems, in fact, to be the submission to pain. And in between these bouts of suffering—punctuating the rhythm I'm describing, if you like—Ned remains extraordinarily passive for a detective in a genre that's meant to be defined by its proclivity for action. He in fact *does* almost nothing in the novel. If his boss, Paul Madvig, insists that he "want[s] action" (65), Beaumont spends enormous amounts of time in bed—sometimes his own (16, 76), sometimes the hospital's (94–116), sometimes the one in which he's held prisoner (87–93)—and his characteristic posture is one of a thoughtful and attendant lounging:

He pulled the covers up to his neck, clasped his hands together behind his head, and stared with dissatisfied eyes at the etching that hung between his bedroom-windows.

For half an hour he lay there with only his eyelids moving. . . .

He took a cigar from a box on the table and sat in a wide red chair. His feet rested in a parallelogram of late morning sun and the smoke he blew out became suddenly full-bodied as it drifted into the sunlight. He frowned now and chewed a fingernail when the cigar was not in his mouth. (16–17)

As regards the novel's central murder, this is about all the detecting Ned Beaumont ever does. He even hires a private detective to do most of his legwork, and his solution of the crime seems finally no more than divination, a matter of waiting for it to come to him and for the right moment to spring it. (When the killer's daughter asks, "How long . . . have you known . . . about father?" Ned replies, "It's been in the back of my head for a long time" [209]). Such a procedure links Ned to the "effete" detectives against which the hardboiled form is supposed to have revolted, rather than to the hypermasculine heroes by which the genre is conventionally defined.

Two points need especially to be stressed here. First, Ned doesn't just submit to violence "accidentally"; he courts it, pursues it—in short, *desires* it. He is, in fact, a kind of male masochist, as the novel makes clear through the charmingly sadistic glee with which he's greeted by Jeff Gardner, one of the goons who beats him. When Jeff encounters Ned late in the novel, long after the extended scene in which he beats Ned at O'Rory's, the homoerotic sadomasochism of their relation could hardly be much clearer. Jeff's "reddish small eyes glisten" and he exclaims delightedly: "Well, blind Christ, if it ain't Sock-me-again Beaumont!" He clamps his arm around Ned's shoulder, buys him a drink, and calls him "sweetheart." Ned, he tells his comrades, is "the swellest guy I ever skinned a knuckle on," because, Jeff says, "he likes it. He's a . . . God-damned massacrist, that's what he is" (185–86). This cluster of statements suggests not only that Ned takes pleasure in being beaten. It also shows that he does so by occupying a passive and conventionally "feminine" position in relation to Jeff's sadistic masculinity—the position of "sweetheart" here making clear how masculinity is associated with power at the cost of a masochistic femininity that the book asks Ned to assume.

Second, this feminizing pleasure in pain isn't just something attributed to Ned by another character. It's a pleasure that the novel itself ascribes to him, or at least encourages us to ascribe to him through the peculiarities of the third-person style. Here, for example, is the scene in which Ned discovers the body that sets the mystery in motion:

Ned Beaumont took his hands away from the dead man and stood up. The dead man's head rolled a little to the left, away from the curb, so that his face lay fully in the light from the corner street lamp. . . .

[Ned Beaumont] was breathing through his mouth and though tiny points of sweat glistened on his hands in the light he shivered now and turned up the collar of his overcoat.

He remained in the tree's shadow with one hand on the tree for perhaps half a minute. Then he straightened abruptly and began to walk towards the Log Cabin Club. He walked with increasing swiftness, leaning forward, and was moving at something more than a half-trot when he spied a man coming up the other side of the street. He immediately slackened his pace and made himself walk erect. (13–14)

The style's fixation on the surface in this scene produces once more the indeterminacies I've described. It renders Ned's inner life opaque by making him the visible object of a "camera" that appears to be strapped to his shoulder: a narrative "eye" that never lets loose its hold, that follows him throughout the novel but registers only his external functions, and that seems so fully attached to his body that it constantly risks the annihilations he faces while rendering him little more than a kind of unintelligible object. The *narrative* significance of this scene, in other words, may alert us to the fact that something affectively intense is happening "inside" Ned—but the refusal to go beneath the body's surface makes it impossible to know the meaning of those affective intensities.

Still, the scene invites us to speculate. It does so by putting in play two sets of apparently incompatible meanings, between which it then invites us to choose while itself refusing to adjudicate. The choice, it seems, is between Eros and trauma. The outbreak of sweat that Ned experiences, the increased rate of respiration indicated by "breathing through the mouth," the ever more rapid movements that lead up to erection, the orgasmic "shiver," the pallid lips, the sense of being so overcome that one needs support to remain standing—these seem to me equally legible as pleasurable excitation or traumatic disruption. They could just as well betoken an experience of erotic arousal as one of fear, horror, or nonsexual trauma. My claim, however, is that this choice is in fact no choice at all. Precisely because the rest of the novel will show Ned so willfully pursuing a course that threatens to turn him into a corpse, we can think of this moment as one in which he begins by identifying with that corpse, and takes such pleasure in the danger of that identification that he seeks perpetually to repeat it. The discovery of the body thus turns out to be not erotic "or" traumatic—it is erotic *and* traumatic. The novel's disinclination to decide between options encourages us to equate them, so that what Ned feels in discovering the corpse can be read as a painful psychic effraction that's also a form of erotic pleasure.

We might, in this context, interpret the passage as a displaced reprisal of the primal scene—that scene of parental coitus that Freud has theorized as traumatizing the (male) child who witnesses it, because the child misunderstands the sex act as one of paternal violence toward a mother with whom he also identifies.[23] Several critics of detective fiction have already made this connection. Geoffrey Hartman argues, for example, that such fiction offers us "one definitively visualized scene to which everything else might be referred." Hartman links this scene himself to the Freudian primal moment, suggesting that detective fiction "allow[s us] to triumph" at a secondary level "over [the] passivity" of that moment, since the detective's solution of the crime renders it the visually masterable origin of the novel's disruptive events.[24]

Geraldine Penderson-Krag makes a similar claim in her attempt to refute suggestions concerning an "identification with the victim" in detective fiction. For her, crime stories allow the reader "a sadistic return to the primal scene." That scene is figured by the initial murder (committed offstage, experienced in its traces, arousing anxiety, desire, and curiosity), whose

traumatic disruptions the reader is now able to bind and master through repeated readerly returns to that scene.[25] Reading such fiction is thus once
again the means for overcoming trauma. Though Penderson-Krag doesn't say
so explicitly, her argument implies that the pleasure of that fiction resides in
the way it helps a reader whom it addresses *as male* surmount a traumatized
and unmanning identification with the maternal "victim" of primal violence. And since the primal scene is here the scene of primal crime, the maternal victim within that scene can only be located at the site of the corpse.
The male reader comes now finally to see, at the deepest level of his psyche,
that *he* is not that "corpse"—not the passively feminine recipient of an erotic
paternal violation—but is himself a masculine heir to the father's sadistic
legacy. The reading of detective fiction is thus intended to facilitate the male
reader's repudiation of a masochism that's perhaps constitutive of all subjectivity, by helping him project his deathly desire onto an object that's experienced as "feminine" precisely inasmuch as it seems to embody that repudiated desire for death.

It should by now be clear that things work rather differently in *The
Glass Key*. Though the corpse is not in this case female, and though it would
be a mistake to take the Freudian analogy too literally, it does seem useful to
think of the moment when Ned Beaumont discovers the corpse as one in
which Hammett stages the possibilities opened by the primal moment:
masochistic surrender through an identification with the victim of violence
on one hand; masculine triumph through a repudiation of that identification on the other—a repudiation that enables the assumption of paternal
power and mastery. What critical arguments miss in this light is the libidinal
idiosyncrasy of *The Glass Key*. The primal scene here issues less in a kind of
triumphant demystification than in a traumatized emulation of the condition of the corpse. That emulation is in turn feminized by Ned's association
with the masochistic position of sexual object or "sweetheart." And the
novel in this sense helps us revise even Freud's conception of the primal
scene. For Freud, too, tends to insist on mastery at the expense of erotic submission. He writes in his "History of an Infantile Neurosis" that the Wolf

Man "assumed to begin with that the event of which he was a witness [the primal scene] was an act of violence, but the expression of enjoyment which he saw upon his mother's face did not fit in with this; he was obliged to recognize that the experience was one of gratification."[26] Eliding the fact that the facial "expression of [sexual] enjoyment" is at its most intense indistinguishable from agony, Freud equally forgets that, even on his own account, the primal scene makes no sense unless we understand it as an aggressive scenario in which the appeal of the mother's position lies in its promise of potential enjoyment in the form of a ravaged submission. The Wolf Man's desire assumes "pathological" proportions because it persists in an identification with the mother, even after he understands her pleasure as indissociable from the violence of "castration."[27] Gratification and disintegration are in this sense inseparable. To derive satisfaction is here the same thing as to embrace an unmanning self-violation.

If Freud's text sometimes fails to remember this, *The Glass Key* rarely forgets it. Ned's compulsive submission to pain replays an originally perverse primal moment, in which he takes pleasure in such a submission and seeks to repeat and recover it. The subtraction of the father from that moment, meanwhile—the reduction of the corpse's discovery to a dyadic event that eliminates any locus for normative identification—allows an intensification of pleasure in the image of what the father can *do* to Ned: penetrate him, unman him—at the limit, kill him.[28]

It follows from this that the third-person style stands in a still more remarkable relation to questions of psychological significance. It's on one hand hostile to interiority, in the way I described in the previous section. But it nonetheless invites forms of psychological speculation that yield *anti*-psychological answers. The staging of the body's discovery as a primal scene is not about tracing the psychic genesis of a character. It's even wrong to say that Ned "experiences" any of this, if by that we mean to render him comprehensible in terms of a deep-psychological past. Character is here superficial and atemporal. It has no hidden secrets, is haunted by no ghosts. It exists only within the opacity of its immediate and illegible manifestation. The invocation of the primal scene is merely the book's way of giving content to an essentially contentless and atemporal mode of being. It's a way of saying that this is a "character" unleashed from the binaries that structure character, liberated from depth and psychological memory by the identity of pleasure and pain, the collapse of masculinity into "feminine" submission—and the indistinguishability of oedipal formation from pre- or even anti-oedipal forms of psychic mobility (a perverse primal scene subverts the normative force of the oedipal narrative). Character is here the occasion for playing out the masochistic self-shattering of character itself.

The effect of this shattering can perhaps best be gauged by comparing *The Glass Key* to the first-person novels of a figure like Raymond Chandler. My guiding speculation in this comparison is that, in first-person hardboiled narratives, there are two completely different scenarios for male desire and identification—a normative one featuring the detective, and a perverse or "feminizing" one featuring the corpse—but that *The Glass Key*'s third-person strategies tend to collapse the two, absorbing the first into the second and making the male reader's masochistic encounter as inescapable as the criminal's capture. First-person narratives could even be said to enforce a regime of identification that disavows the knowledge of male masochism that *The Glass Key* requires us to confront.

The pathos of Chandler's novels, for example, resides within a masculine consciousness whose cardinal imperative, as Martin Priestman notes, is *noli me tangere*.[29] Marlowe retreats again and again into the rich elaborations of his interior life, into a private discourse of sentiment and of a doomed desire for human connection, precisely from the knowledge that to touch is to *be* touched, and that to be touched is to risk being brutalized, violated, penetrated by force and by sexuality. Contact in fact becomes possible in Chandler only on condition of its extreme neutralization: "If I touched you," says Marlowe to Merle Davis in *The High Window* (1943), "it was just like touching a chair or a door. It didn't mean anything"; or again in *Playback* (1958), after one of only two sex scenes Chandler ever allows his hero, the lovers banter with each other to the touching tones of "I don't love you" ("Why would you?" replies Marlowe. "But let's not be cynical about it") and "I hate you."[30] Human touch becomes the stirring occasion for a self-protective and insular retreat into objectification, irony, and masculine sadism. Marlowe moves in the direction of his world—touches and even "connects" with it— only in verbal and physical assaults designed to master the unending threat of a universe that unmans by brutalizing him. It's therefore no wonder that the books divide that threat rigorously between violence (cops, criminals, doctors) and sex (women and effeminate men). The division signals an attempt to stave off the recognition that the two are in fact one, and here we arrive at the centrality in Chandler's work of the *femme fatale* that, as I noted earlier, remains in Hammett significantly tangential.

For the *femme fatale* signals the eruption of a seductively excessive and dangerous pleasure. With her, the submission to sex *is* the submission to force because in fucking you—in the very act of fucking you—she also invariably fucks you over. What she holds out and promises as an erotically cathectable scenario is the possibility of an impossibly thrilling identification with the image of one's own death. Precisely because she refuses "to cede her desire" and so "fully [assumes] the death drive,"[31] the danger she poses is one of a pleasure in the explosive intensities of self-violation, of taking as one's own a "frenetic enjoyment"[32] whose augmentations of psychic tension are nothing short of self-annihilating. In desiring her, then, the dick *desires*—period: it's a pure and object-less desire for what he would most like to be: dead. The *femme fatale* provokes a wish for the pleasurable identification with a corpse. And it's exactly to protect himself (and us) against such a wish, which figures the coincidence of the threat of sex and the threat of violence, that the dick so completely disappears behind his "I," his masculine consciousness. The body of the detective shows up in Chandler's work only in order to be penetrated and ravaged; thus it seeks to make itself localizable only in its ultimate lack of locale, its virtual and eerie withdrawal from the spaces—geographical, gendered, class, even (in *Farewell, My Lovely*) racial—that its investigative quest maps. Marlowe becomes for us an identificatory possibility just to the extent that he fully identifies with his own investigative function.

He remains "ideal"—an ego ideal—exactly insofar as he remains above all a private and disembodied *eye*. For in this he steers us, however circuitously, toward a vanquishing of the *femme fatale* and the narrative pleasures of solution, away from the enjoyments of *dis*solution that entail succumbing to the *femme fatale*, and he thereby enables us to keep at bay the endlessly seductive image of all those beaten, bloated, penetrated, and bruised victims of an irresistible violence.

Things are once more significantly different in *The Glass Key*. To say—as I've said—that the detective is in this novel victimized by the third-person style is to say that the book declines to dissolve the male body into an investigative ocularity. It chooses instead to specularize the body in its unmanning, to satisfy what Theodor Reik has called the "demonstrative" function of masochism. "We know," writes Reik, "that it is a psychological necessity for masochism to have witnesses. . . . The masochist does not hide his misery; he shows it to everybody, he propagates it. He seems to wish the whole world to hear him. . . . He does not cover his defeat as best he can. With its assistance he shows off as best as he can."[33] Though one should perhaps attribute this exhibitionism more to the novel than to Ned himself, it's clear that *The Glass Key* embraces the risk that Chandler routinely surmounts. It makes Ned Beaumont visually available on nearly every page, and subjects him to the violent consequences of that visibility. His submission to the eye of the style, in this sense, goes hand in hand with his specular subjection to the gaze of those who ravage him—with his repeated efforts to be seen to suffer by provoking the sadistic ocularity (Jeff's "red" and "glistening" eyes [185]) by which his enemies find and beat him. One might even suggest that Hammett makes the Marlovian tactics of defense unavailable to the third-person style, in order to effect a reinternalization of the masochistic and self-specularizing desires that are habitually projected out as a feminine threat to the dick's sense of self.

My point here is not that Marlowe never gets beat up while Ned Beaumont does. A certain amount of bodily pain goes with the territory, and both detectives in some sense "know" it. But where the physical

workovers Marlowe receives consistently give way to a more or less immediate and complete resumption of masculine power, *The Glass Key* prefers
to defer that resumption indefinitely, to keep its dick on the perilous brink
of existential obliteration.

When, for example, in Chandler's *Farewell, My Lovely* (1940), the rack-
eteers imprison Marlowe after drugging and beating him, he screams "fire"
to lure his jailer and then beats him to make his escape.[34] But when Ned
Beaumont finds himself in much the same position, he tries, first, to slit his
throat, then *builds* a fire that almost kills him, and lastly jumps in darkness
from a high window that lands him in a hospital bed for almost a third of
the novel. Marlowe's *physical* escape results from an *imaginary* fire, and is at
the same time an escape *from* the physical; to vanquish both his opponents
and his circumstances, he ascends to a realm of imaginative cunning that
marks his body's re-erasure from the page and the assertion, once again, of a
somatically unencumbered consciousness. For Ned Beaumont the case is
quite the contrary. Not only does the eye of the third-person style keep him
before us as an objectified plaything whose capacity for volition remains radically in question; the fact that he actually starts a fire also points to a disturbing will toward the annihilation of consciousness, a desire to become a
corpse displayed for the delectation of our scopic pleasure. Ned's is a body
that exists to be seen and beaten, seen *to be* beaten. It's a body that's "feminized" precisely inasmuch as specularity and masochism are assigned by our
culture to an abhorred femininity, despite the fact that, as I've suggested,
they may be constitutive elements of human subjectivity itself.

The dangers this strategy poses to male readers are perhaps evident
enough. Far from serving merely as a conduit for the enjoyment of mastery
and narrative solutions, Ned Beaumont also opens up the text in order to
summon us to drown in it. His beatings require us to identify with a man
who compulsively seeks his own death. They circle back again and again to
a primal and nonprogressive scene of "feminine" self-destruction, through
which Ned seeks to repeat the pleasurable pain of identifying with a corpse.
And they thereby ask us to partake of a "movement" that resists the drive to

35

solution—to fixate upon an anti-narrational moment of psychic trauma—in much the same way that the incantatory repetition of Ned Beaumont's full name (Hammett never simply calls him "Ned") serves as a kind of dadaesque fixation that retards and erodes developmental kernels. "Formally speaking," Deleuze writes, "masochism is a state of waiting; the masochist experiences waiting in its pure form. . . . [He] waits for pleasure as something that's bound to be late, and expects pain as the condition that will finally ensure (both physically and morally) the advent of pleasure."[35] This is, I'd suggest, a precise reformulation of the reading experience I've been describing. The narrative pleasure of *The Glass Key* comes "late," and always at the cost of an expected pain. We cannot access that pleasure without first suffering through a reading that threatens to destroy us en route to the end. But we need I think to add as well what even Deleuze seems unwilling to say,[36] that an exquisitely different pleasure inheres in being conned into this waiting, in being brought back over and again to the transfixing nightmare of a psychic unmanning that shatters us into the book's primal scene.

"A God-damned massacrist"

And yet the novel closes, narrative pleasure arrives—in short, "Sock-me-again Beaumont" solves the crime. The fact that Hammett has him do so is in part a result of the author's historical position at the beginning of the hardboiled form, and we shall see, in chapter 4, that a later figure like Chester Himes can imagine a hardboiled ending that offers almost none of the pleasures of closure. For now it's important merely to note that *The Glass Key*'s resolution is in part the fulfillment of an alternate impulse within the novel— an impulse that's at odds with the one I have been tracing, and that's at once more masterful in its thematics and more teleologically inclined in its narrational strategies and intentions. In this section I describe this impulse as a way of marking the political limits of masochism in *The Glass Key*, but also in order to specify the value of what the novel has to offer.

One way to do this is to stress the complexly oedipal character of the novel's plot. That plot is comprised of two interlocking triangles that reinforce and complicate each other. The first of these is structured around Paul Madvig, Janet Henry, and Senator Henry. Its meaning pivots upon the attempt to break with a paternal generation (the senator's) that's imagined as at once effete and oedipally murderous. The novel encodes Senator Henry's effeteness through his membership in a political "aristocracy" whose gentility allies it with "women's clubs" (11)—an aristocracy that remains sentimentally attached to outdated codes of honor and speaks in a refined, nonvernacular diction that the novel implicitly contrasts with the language of its more manly men ("Please remain, Mr. Beaumont. I shall not be long. . . . It is on what you told me that I'm acting now" [200, 201]). At the same time, these less than manly attributes are fused with a kind of phallic violence. The senator is at the end revealed to be the murderer of Taylor Henry; he's the man who killed his son with a walking stick in order to further his political ambitions. He is in this sense doubly indicted by the narrative movement of the novel. He at once represents a castrated manhood with which *The Glass Key* seeks to break, and a toxic paternality that murders its sons in a way that threatens the transmission of paternal power itself.

In the context of this first triangle, then, Paul represents the possibility of moving from a genteel yet violent patriarchy to something at once more populist, more intergenerationally pacific, and more masculine. This transition can be effected only through the transmission of the daughter (Janet) as object of sexual desire, which perpetuates through marriage the homosocial pact that the murder of the son prevents. The novel complicates this movement, however, by superimposing a second triangle upon the first one: Ned-Janet-Paul. This triangle opens the novel up to a third generation, introducing a temporal rift that figures Paul as an intermediary style of manhood between the senator's and Ned's. Such a disjuncture effectively rewrites the central struggle in the novel as one between Ned and Paul. And the terms of this struggle are, once more, implicitly oedipal in character. They entail in part a battle over Janet as object of desire. But they also entail, perhaps more importantly, a movement from Paul as old-style gangster whose aspirations toward political legitimacy expose how he's out of touch with male power, to Ned as a younger, more contemporary figure whose forms of masculine knowledge enable him to gain ascendancy over Paul.

There are several components to *The Glass Key*'s efforts to mark Paul's masculine inadequacies. We can note, to begin with, the peculiar way in which his phallic power is itself inseparable from symbolic castration. He is on one hand Ned's literal superior and clearly also a paternal elder; and yet he repeatedly turns to the younger man for advice about clothes and women. He makes all the wrong political decisions, and is generally found sitting impotently behind his desk, his knowledge of the killer's identity rendered useless by his political imperatives. Whenever Paul does, in fact, start brandishing about a phallic manhood, the novel quickly exposes it as the source of his difficulties, not their solution. The "cyclone shot" that's "[his] kind" of "fighting" and entails "going in with both hands working" (65) causes a gang war that loses him the election; and his clumsy assertions of masculine prerogative work more to repel than to attract his beloved, as they lead to her brother's murder and to her conviction that Paul is the murderer. The book thus imagines Paul as a patriarch from whom all manly substance has been drained. The more he tries to "act like a man," the more the novel degrades and punishes him; the more he seeks to master his world through the assaultive gestures of manly assertion, the farther he places the things he desires definitively out of reach. To identify with the paternal function thus offers none of the rewards that it should, since it is Madvig's excessive identification with this function that *The Glass Key* codes as problematic, and that it therefore feels the need to interrogate, to challenge—and even to repudiate.

The novel goes on to link this inadequacy to a failure in class adaptation. Paul's style of manhood was once, in this sense, sufficient, powerful, effective: "I don't know anything about your kind of fighting," he tells Ned. "All I know is when you got somebody cornered you go in and finish them. That system's worked all right for me so far. . . . I came up from running errands for Packy Flood in the old Fifth to where I'm sitting kind of pretty today" (73). Part of the novel's burden is to show that this "system" doesn't work any longer. Precisely inasmuch as Paul seeks to wed his working-class manhood to the book's aristocracy, the physical strength and indomitable will that used to mean male power for him now turn out to signal power-lessness, failure, and political defeat. Real power lies, at least in part, in the genteel style of Senator Henry's generation—a generation that may be on the decline but nonetheless continues to dominate the realm of "legitimate" pol-itics. That generation thinks of Paul as "a lower form of animal," a creature with whom one might make alliance but whom one can discard at will be-cause "the rules [don't] apply" to him (9). The price of masculine upward mo-bility is thus an ensnarement in genteel institutions that are by nature emas-culating, so that the only effective form of manhood will turn out to be one unencumbered by institutional alliances of any kind.

This is, I think, what Ned represents within the narrative I am tracing. Unlike Paul, he's young enough to afford the luxury of believing in nothing (177). He has no permanent loyalties, no lasting affiliations, and seems to *want* almost nothing at all, except to gamble, perhaps to lose, and certainly to enjoy the pleasures of pain that he courts with such assiduity. This free-dom from wants and dependencies grants him a certain mobility within the power networks that have caught Paul up like a fly. And this mobility, in its turn, enables Ned to gain a knowledge of modern masculinity that Paul es-sentially lacks. Ned knows, for example, that becoming beholden to senators is bound to put you at the mercy of the "women's clubs" I've mentioned, as well as to make you vulnerable to charges that things were "different in the old days before you put in with the Senator" (11). He sees that "what was good enough for the old Fifth" is not "good enough" today, that where it used to be appropriate to "finish" an enemy once you had him cornered, you need now to leave him a way to save face, or else risk open declarations of war that spoil your political ambitions. Finally, Ned's familiarity with the po-lite society that he simultaneously scorns—with the manners and doings of the likes of Janet Henry, who appears regularly on the society page—helps him avoid the class humiliations to which Paul is continually subject. At one point, Ned tears up and rewrites a letter he has carefully composed to Janet, all in order to remove a split infinitive that Paul would hardly have noticed (103–4). He later greets Paul's mother in the hospital by kissing her sociably on both cheeks ("Do stop it," she retorts. "You're worse than the Airedale Paul used to have" [111]). And he lets Paul know that he "oughtn't to wear silk . . . with tweeds" no matter how much he "like[s] the feel of silk" (62), and that he shouldn't give gifts to women without being sure that they'd like to receive them from him (10–11).

Above all, however, the generational difference in this second triangle is between Ned's passive masochistic proclivities and Paul's incapacity to relinquish his desire to dominate through brute force. Ned is the novel's preferred masculinity, at least within this alternate impulse, because he knows that in order to be manly in the modern world one must renounce the thirst for power that embroils one in effeminizing institutions, just as one must learn to submit to pain rather than seeking to dish it out—must come to see that it's precisely in "taking it" that one is able to vanquish opponents by doing little more than outlasting them. This is, in my view, what the novel means when it has Paul speak of Ned's "kind of fighting." Ned does battle by masochistically submitting, not—like Paul—by aggressively asserting. His masochism signals the stubborn elasticity of an apparently unconquerable toughness, an existential resilience that seems to make it impossible ever to "croak him" (88). Ned therefore not only survives but does so in a manner that enables him to win the battle over Janet. And this suggests that we should read the book's ending—where Ned and Janet get together—as an oedipal triumph in which Ned's masochistic tendencies usurp the place of what the novel codes as Paul's normatively phallic but obsolescent masculinity.

In light of these comments, one might well wonder if there's anything we would want politically to value in the masochism of *The Glass Key*. If that masochism can be read as a moment in the narrative of male power, how can it contain the liberatory potential that my argument ascribes to it? Does embracing it alter men's relations with women at all? Does it entail the renunciation of male power, the abdication of patriarchal privilege, or merely the clothing of power's iron fist within the velvet glove of powerlessness?

These are by now familiar questions within gender studies and feminist circles, and I don't mean to revisit them in detail. Suffice it to say that a range of critics have recently cast suspicion on arguments for the politically progressive value of male masochism. David Savran argues, for example, that a certain type of masochistic sexuality that Kaja Silverman has called "reflexive masochism" has itself become the dominant mode of white male power in the post-Vietnam era.[37] Tania Modleski has similarly suggested that "masochism in the *guise* of powerlessness is . . . frequently the luxury of empowered beings, [as] social power and sexual humiliation may coexist quite easily."[38] Finally, Nick Mansfield advances the suggestive thesis that "[m]asochism presents a model of a power that can strengthen itself by self-renunciation, that can advance itself by acts of self-denial, even self-mutilation." The masochist's "appropriation of, or identification with, the feminine . . . is never at the expense of his masculinity, and is never simply undertaken because he understands femininity as more implicitly passive."[39]

I find these critiques timely and necessary, a salutary corrective to the ebullient optimism with which many of us embraced theories of male masochism in the late 1980s and early 1990s. And yet it seems to me that they often mirror the problems they seek to correct. For where figures like Kaja Silverman and Leo Bersani sometimes sound as if they think male masochism, at least in some of its forms, is inherently progressive, Savran, Modleski, and Mansfield come close to saying that it cannot ever be progressive.[40] This is especially true in the work of Mansfield and Modleski, where masochism becomes in essence defined as a stealthy ruse of power. Thus the globalizing confidence with which Mansfield uses the word "never" in the passage quoted above. And thus the fact that, despite her laudable efforts to temper her more tendentious claims, Modleski fails to adduce a single instance of feminization or male masochism of which she herself approves.

My own sense is that there are in fact times when the renunciation of power does *not* entail its disavowed perpetuation. Even if masochism has indeed become a dominant form of male power, it isn't always so in practice. It is at least possible to "mean it" when one renounces power in order to embrace a sexual self-shattering—and possible to carry this hostility to the male self into one's broader gender relations.

This, at any rate, is what I want to suggest about *The Glass Key*. The alternative narrative I've traced in this section does not supplant the more radical one that the bulk of the chapter has chronicled. It signals, rather, a conflict in Hammett—one by which he tries but fails to recuperate masochism for normative ends. This conflict is both crystalized and resolved in the tension between two metaphors that the novel uses to think about masculinity. The first of these Hammett puts in the mouth of Jeff Gardner. When Ned shows up at one of Shad's hideouts toward the end of the book, Jeff turns to another goon and says: "By Jesus Rusty! . . . little Rubber Ball has come back to us. I told you he liked the way we bounced him around" (124). Despite the offhandedness of this remark, I think we're meant to take it seriously. For a masochist who's a rubber ball is not just one who repeatedly returns for more; he's also a masochist who always regains his shape, who's never quite bent *out* of shape, whose very assumption of an eroticized death drive goes hand in hand with an undying ability to recover and bounce back. It's this resilient and rebounding masochism that leads in this novel to masterful solution, and that later hardboiled writers and their critics adduce as proof of the dick's manliness. It's this that enables Ned to get the girl, that lends him the veneer of a hero in a novel that's not only deeply anti-heroic, but anti-egoic as well. And it's this style of masochism that transforms gambling from a loser's rut into virile victory, enabling Ned to walk "tall" and "erect" (49), to "take [his] tail out from between [his] legs and feel [like] a person again" (23–24)—rather than being "kicked around" and forced simply to "stand it" (23, 6).

But the novel's title contains a metaphor that cannot be assimilated to this one. The title refers to a dream that Janet Henry recounts toward the middle of the novel. She and Ned are lost in a forest, tired and hungry, when they come upon a house through whose window they see "a big table piled high with all imaginable kinds of food." The door is locked, and when they finally find the key and open it, they discover hundreds of snakes they hadn't seen before. The dream apparently ends happily; they trick the snakes into coming out, then go in and eat the food (178). But Janet later corrects herself:

> "In that dream—I didn't tell you—the key was glass and shattered in our hands just as we got the door open, because the lock was stiff and we had to force it."
>
> He looked sideways at her and asked: "Well?"
>
> She shivered. "We couldn't lock the snakes in and they came out all over us and I woke up screaming." (211)

Such a revision turns the dream into a metaphor for the novel's vision of masculinity: the incipiently sadistic assertion of mastery (inserting the key, surmounting danger) leads only to defeat and to the shattering of the masterful agent. The effort to unlock the door to the mystery is inseparable from a disintegration that opens one up to the forces of an explicitly phallic chaos ("hundreds and hundreds of snakes" [178]). Ned, in other words, is the glass key: a phallic aggression perpetually destroyed by the invasiveness of its masterful gestures.[41] To the extent that the key could be said to have a conventionally sexual connotation, its shattering suggests not just Janet's anxieties but Hammett's sense of how male sexuality entails the pleasurable detonation of the self in the act of sexual mastery. And to the extent that the title implies that the book is itself a kind of "glass key," Hammett is making a joke about our efforts to "use" it to unlock the mystery: we cannot but try to use it in this way—and it can't but shatter in our hands when we do so, giving us access to the solution's secrets only at the cost of a reading experience that breaks us apart and submits us to pain in the act of gratifying our epistemophilic urges.

Furthermore, the dream in which the key appears suggests that we ought to privilege this metaphor by interpreting the novel's ending through it. If that dream reflects upon the effect of unlocking the door to the book's mystery, and if the effect of that unlocking is to shatter the one who solves the crime into bits and pieces, then the novel's conclusion becomes one in which Ned's demonstration of mastery is inseparable from his psychic destruction. That destruction is not hard to find in the novel's closing pages. The heterosexual coupling that the solution enables is marked by an extraordinary lassitude, in which Ned agrees in complete passivity to take Janet to New York with him, without once indicating that he loves her or even expressing a desire for her ("I'll take you if you want to go," he says [211]). The novel thus ends less in triumph than on a note of loss and disconnection: Janet despairingly "look[s] at Ned Beaumont" in an effort to claim the definitive transfer of his allegiance to her from Paul Madvig; Ned, for his part, "stare[s] fixedly at the door" through which Paul has just left for good (214). The book in this way suggests Ned's continued fixation upon a paternal object to which he remains subjected in triumph. It suggests that the second triangle I've described is less oedipalizing than it appears, that the triangulating introduction of Janet disturbs a prior male/male dyad,[42] and that the erotic charge of the triangle remains the desire to be beaten/loved by the father that Freud describes in "'A Child Is Being Beaten'"—a desire for eroticized violation that's displaced onto other men in the novel, but whose origin in Ned's passion for Paul is clear from the way his beatings so often result from an almost madly self-punishing loyalty to his boss.

It is, to my mind, enormously sad that the ending is marked by such disconnections—that Janet gets Ned but not his desire, and that Ned will perhaps be permanently scarred by the unmournable loss of a sadomasochistic and homoerotic attachment. At the same time, it's my contention that the negativity which produces this quandary is responsible for what's politically most promising in the novel. It accounts, for example, for *The Glass Key*'s surprisingly positive representation of Janet. That representation is almost unparalleled in hardboiled fiction of the 1930s and 1940s. Janet is unusually well-rounded and complex for a female character in such fiction, with motivations having to do with her own self-respect and desire to be loved, rather than with insatiate greed and a sexually predatory destructiveness.[43] She dislikes Paul from the start because she knows that he's basically trying to buy her. She refuses to be the sexual pawn into which her father tries to make her, suggesting an implicit critique of how men produce the *femme fatale* by manipulating female sexuality in ways that unleash it as the fantasy of a force against which men must defend themselves.

The novel, furthermore, invites us to link this feminine complexity to Ned's masochistic self-shattering. What enables the richness of *female* character is the disintegration of *masculine* character; the masculine assumption of self-shattering desire liberates the novel from the need to invent an unambivalently bad femininity that threatens the male subject from without—and which he must both possess and destroy in order to protect the sanctity of his borders. The darkness of the novel's ending is thus perhaps its greatest strength: it insists upon the psychic costs of reconfiguring heterosexual love, suggesting that we may have to pass through moments of dysfunction, negativity, and—for men—psychic death, before we can arrive at anything like an intersubjective gender relation.

Deadly Is the Female Animal

Smell in James Cain's *Serenade*

"Do I, for God's sake, sound like that?"

There's something fishy in the work of James Cain, something that doesn't smell right. I mean this, first of all, as a metaphor, though I propose to take that metaphor seriously. And I mean it to crystalize what the more discriminating among Cain's critics have sensed for some time: that central to the experience of reading him—central to the fascinated revulsion that so often greets his work—is a disagreeable and depressing sensation of having been "had." Cain seems somehow always to be cheating, to be playing dirty. The goods he delivers evaporate behind their thin glitzy wrappers, leaving only an overpowering scent of sulfur and sleazy sex. His effects grip and seduce us, sometimes even to furious abandon, but they also invariably muss us up, since they are, in the end, dirty little tricks, cheap and sensational effects, shams—by no means the real thing at all. "The list [of ingredients that made Cain's first novel a success] must always include a large item of trickery," writes W. M. Frohock in his book about violence in American fiction.[1] Or again, from Joyce Carol Oates's essay on Cain: "The freedom of women and money and power, and the promise of adventure. . . . These are his tricks, his gimmicks."[2] Trickery, gimmicks, "legerdemain"[3]: it's almost impossible to talk about Cain without acknowledging this fakery, the ersatz dimension to his work. So that when I open by evoking something fishy, I mean in part to make that acknowledgment—to insist colloquially that Cain is "up to no good"—and to assert that ultimately, for me as for others, this "no good" can't but show: the writing may be able to "perform dazzling tricks but it cannot quite make us believe in them."[4]

The reason for this is that Cain's "no good" has, to begin with, aesthetic connotations. Oates writes that he "never manages to become an artist" because "there is always something sleazy, something eerily vulgar and disappointing in his work" (110). Cynical and exploitative (110), neither "poet" nor "philosopher," he is "in the end . . . simply an entertainer"; and an entertainer, of course—if he's to be a good one—must possess "an uncanny knowledge of the perversities of his audience, [and of] the great range of their vulgarity" (114). This is the subterfuge, the artifice of Cain's "art": "masterful and intelligent" in itself (114), it understands and exploits the vulgarity of "mass man" (124), who pants only after crude entertainment and finds it only in the rankest of places: in a sexual violence that brutalizes humanity, in the shocks of action and the twists of plot, in the indelicate obviousness—the flash and excess—of mass art. *To entertain on a mass scale is itself to trick*; it's to take artistic shortcuts that drag the reader through filth and mud, renouncing all high subtlety in favor of the basely obvious, the excessive, the grossly sensorial. "[T]he vulgar degrade all notable qualities," Oates continues, "especially that of subtlety. What is not exaggerated will be passed by" (120). Cain is thus driven to excess—driven to cheat: it amounts to the same thing—by his desire to satisfy the insatiable brutishness of the vulgar herd.

It goes without saying that the vulgar themselves, being on this reading always already degraded, know and demand nothing but trash, and they consequently remain blissfully unconscious of anything sweeter-smelling. For them, the trick precisely *doesn't* show, and the danger of befoulment thus threatens only "us": the non-vulgar who, gradually becoming hip to the

trick, finish Cain's books with a shuddering sense of having had foul and polluting contact with something like lower life forms.[5]

It's important, then, to be clear about this contact, to familiarize ourselves with these forms. Oates's essay betrays such a slumming sensitivity to
the pleasures of vulgarity that the source of her disgust becomes hard to
grasp. We still need to ask: with what exactly do the crudities of Cain's art put
"us" in contact? And here the answer is startling in its simplicity, crude in its
very obviousness: if Cain inspires an aesthetico-moral nausea, if his work induces in critics an aversion that can only be adequately expressed in disgust,
this is because his books address us as though we were ourselves vulgar, placing us in the uncouth minds of their narrators and asking us, incredibly, to
feel at home there: to find in those minds our own vulgar selves, debased in
and as mass man.[6] Frohock both makes and misses this point when he says
that *The Postman Always Rings Twice* "is thoroughly immoral . . . not so much
because of the unpraiseworthy behavior of the characters as because of the
unpraiseworthy behavior of the reader" (21). The danger his essay actually
describes is of a devolutionary identification so complete as to nullify such
distinctions:

The one fact the reader had become most convinced of was that Cain's hero [in
Postman] *was the kind of man who could* not, *in any circumstances, have written
a story, and discovering that one has been enthralled, instead, by the* in extremis
*jottings of a writer who could have made his living any time writing for M-G-M
was like being caught by the rising house-lights wiping one's eyes after a particularly bathetic movie. (14)*

The trickery here consists in our having been made to believe in our civilized
superiority to the murderously unpraiseworthy, only to have that compla-
cency shattered by the shock of excessive likeness. Frank Chambers, it turns
out, has *written* the narrative we're reading; the very thing we were most
convinced he couldn't do, that we needed most to believe was beyond him,
he has in fact done. And if a "mad dog"[7] like Frank has the capacity for
so supreme an act of civility, who's to say which of his vulgar atrocities I

mightn't myself be capable of? The fantasy governing this discourse of disgust is one that links illiteracy to an asocial will that's at once pre-individuated ("mass"), inhuman ("animal"[8]), and altruicidal (Cain's heroes, as we know, carry destruction immanently within them); so that when it turns out that the mad dog can write, the resulting terror is that I myself, literate though I am, might be caught when the lights go up convulsed on all fours, mingling and putrefacting my unique civil self in the undifferentiated and murderous will of mass man. Cain's texts demand that we partake of this movement, this effacement of the boundary separating our pacifically socialized selves from the unnameable *that*—undifferentiated, animal, internecine—that must be thought to "precede" the self. Frohock may figure this process sentimentally, but such a figuration need not deter us. "There is no doubt . . . that brutality brutalizes and sentimentality is but one form of brutality."[9] Caught with one's pants down, down on all fours, or caught "wiping one's eyes after a particularly bathetic movie": the difference is in the end negligible, since both images capture the humiliation attendant upon an excessive and dehumanizing identification. The sentimentalist becomes a kind of weepy grotesque who effaces human complexity with an affective exaggeration that mimics the emotional fraudulence on screen. The brute, in perfectly symmetrical fashion, enjoys fantasmatically his affective reduction to an animal (in)humanity, seeping creepily into an identificatory mire where "I" is "Frank" and Frank is me and the "emotional . . . stunted[ness]"[10] leading one of us to murder can only be my own.

We shall have momentarily to turn to Cain and flesh out this skeleton of animalized man, as well as of the mechanisms that animalize him. For now, let's just note that he indeed smells, this brute, that stench is both his preferred milieu and a perfectly proper trope for understanding him. Raymond Chandler could hardly be more explicit in his 1942 letter to Blanche Knopf:

I hope the day will come when I won't have to ride around on Hammett and James Cain. . . . Hammett is all right. I give him everything. There were a lot of things he could not do, but what he did he did superbly. But James Cain—faugh! Everything he touches smells like a billygoat. He is every kind of writer I detest, a faux naif, a Proust in greasy overalls, a dirty little boy with a piece of chalk and a board fence and nobody looking. Such people are the offal of literature, not because they write about dirty things, but because they do it in a dirty way. Nothing hard and clean . . . and ventilated. A brothel with a smell of cheap scent in the front parlor and a bucket of slops at the back door. Do I, for God's sake, sound like that? Hemingway . . . got to be pretty damn tiresome, but at least Hemingway sees it all, not just the flies on the garbage can.[11]

This is disgust at its most confident, its purest, its most imperious. No manifest ambivalence clouds the issues, no delicacies curb the expression of a passionate loathing, and the passage thus has at least the virtue of honesty in its display of revulsion. Chanting the familiar refrain, it tells us again that Cain plays tricks: he's a "faux naif," not a genuine innocent; a "Proust in greasy overalls," rather than the real article. But it also insists that those tricks stink, making thereby disturbingly legible the unconscious logic in Frohock and Oates and suggesting we take as literally as possible the olfactory metaphor with which I began. Cain's crafty "way" is crafty *because* "dirty," with "[n]othing . . . clean and . . . ventilated" about it; if "[e]verything he touches smells like a billygoat," if he is, for Chandler, no Proust, this is because the stains on his overalls mark him already as a feculent creature who deals in "slops" while attempting to mask their aromatic filth with the smell of a cheap stylistic perfume. The essence of Cain's trickery resides in the doctored *fetor* he transmits in this way—as a potential for malodorous contamination. To read him is to risk both smelling "like a billygoat" and developing a wayward taste for that smell. The explicit reference to sex, moreover, in Chandler's disgusted denunciation, suggests that what is at stake in Cain is an aberrantly "erotic" impulse that's inseparable from the mimetic dangers that Frohock and Oates have helped us define.

Chandler himself tends more to enact than to reflect upon this conjunction. I want, therefore, to turn for a moment to Freud's essay "The 'Uncanny'" (1919), which offers a remarkable theoretical account of the relations among sex, identification, violence, and smell. One of my claims will be that Cain knows things about these issues that even Freud is at pains to deny, and that this denial has everything to do with the theoretical ambitions by which Freud seeks to surmount a condition that he shows to be—precisely—insurmountable. Nevertheless, Freud's essay can help us provisionally to grasp the nature of the critics' fears and repulsions, and in particular, to bring into focus two points that Chandler's disgust intuits.

First, the rankness of "mass man" in Cain—the deathly reek of his inhumanity—is not just an "exterior" threat to an otherwise odorlessly pacific subjectivity, but is in fact immanent to that subjectivity, the very air it breathes. "Do I, for God's sake, sound like that?"—what does this mean if not, at least in part, "Oh my God, *I sound like that!*"? And does not the question therefore announce the implacable bind of a mimetic rivalry, where hatred is born of a sense of resemblance to a double (Frank Chambers, James Cain) whom I must repudiate if I am ever to be "myself"? To "sound like that" is to sound putrid, vulgar, indistinguishable from the mass. It's to be so mired in the vulgar other that the two of us remain a kind of muddy mass that is as yet unable to identify itself—no longer an other, not yet an "I," but simultaneously both of these, and therefore neither. And it is, of course, to the disconcerting return of just such a condition that "The 'Uncanny'" traces the violence of this kind of specular relation.

Once upon a time—the essay suggests—in the "narcissistic," "animistic," or "savage" prehistory of the civilized self, "the ego had not yet marked itself off sharply from the external world and from other people."[12] Exterior and interior were then as one; to wish was fantasmatically to fulfill that wish; and the ego, in all its "unrestricted narcissism" (240), was at once everything because it had not yet learned its difference from others, and nothing since, properly speaking, it could not really have been itself until the institution of a boundary between inside and outside. The ego begins as a kind of mass ego, a pre-egoic being-(in)-objects; it stands at the outset in a *familiar* relation to all that is not it. Once this initial state has been "surmounted" (249), however, the return of the familiar in the figure of the double can breed in me only an instantaneous loathing, an unmitigated and everlasting contempt. I now encounter, exteriorized and alienated, what I once lived as my ownmost "identity." The double calls me back again to a teeming intimacy with the not-me, but the renewal of that intimacy can only be uncanny since I now see "myself" outside myself, in a self-image that I must also recognize as "someone else."[13] An alien self(-image), then, an intimate stranger—this figure confronts me as "the uncanny harbinger of death" (235). He wants nothing less than to drag me once more into that identificatory muck from which I've come, causing me to cease to be (myself) and dissolving me again in a primordial mass that's "vulgar" in that it cannot say "I," "primitive" in its confusion of thought and deed, naively murderous in its magisterial assimilation of all difference to itself. "Do I, for God's sake, sound like that?" This means as well: "I do not sound like that," "I must not sound like that." The ego can't but violently assert itself in the face of a debasing identification it must already have made. "I" am Raymond Chandler, "you," James Cain. Or better still: I simply *am* (the cultured, sociable, individuated self), while you, James Cain, *are not*. The mimetic double must be furiously dismissed in order that I might remain—myself.

This, then, is the first thing Freud helps us to see: that if Cain provokes in his readers a disgusted self-assertion, it's because his texts seek to degrade and primitivize the civilized self by reamassing it with its primordially familiar "others." The game—once launched—is a deadly one; it takes two to play it, and we shouldn't therefore be surprised to find that Cain seeks also to escape the mass he simultaneously drags us into, waging an eternal war with his doubles ("Hammett," "Hemingway," "Chandler") over the absolute sovereignty of his voice.[14] But let's not concern ourselves with this war here; we need, for now, to linger a moment longer with the Freudian uncanny, in order to bring out the second point that it helps us to find in Chandler's response.

Freud continues: "It often happens that neurotic men declare that they feel there is something uncanny about the female genital organs. This *unheimlich* place, however, is the entrance to the former *Heim* [home] of all human beings, to the place where each one of us lived . . . in the beginning" (245). *Unheimliches Heim,* familiar strangeness: the female genitals are here the portal to an originary and dissolutionary mass (of) being. They are, in short, the synecdochic representation of a place where the ego *really was* in the other, and we can thus begin to speculate about why Chandler's revulsion takes such an explicitly olfactory form. For aren't these genitals also a site for the male psyche's fantasmatic and proverbial aromatic investment? Do they not, according to a disgusted misogyny, "smell fishy"? And isn't the danger of succumbing to Cain's tricks precisely the threat of being brought back *there,* to the fantasmatically violent reek of a place that was once "me," to a smell that's become the imaginary medium of an original being-in-objects?

The logic of the double is an olfactory logic in that the referent of the resemblance I now see is the odor I attribute to the "object" I once was. It is, accordingly, the reminder of that smell that enrages me, drives me to murder. If the double appears to be taking "my" place, this is because that place is itself a return of the site where we were once identified in the overpowering indistinction of its smell. Out of that indifference a male subject has been born; a masculine ego now quite confidently says "I." But it does so without being able to deliver itself from the odor of that place where it was not yet itself, without ever escaping the naive bellicosity of its own prehistory as a mass that let neither subject nor object "be" (itself). Smell is in this sense the relic and promise of an inescapable violence.[15] And it's smell, accordingly, that makes Cain guilty of the double dirtiness that Chandler intuits: first, because the reek of his work is invariably the reek of the genitals, and we know that to write about them is to "write about dirty things"; but, second, because by writing about those things "in a dirty way," he makes sex *smell too much,* confusing it with waste and shit and bemiring us in something completely offensive: not a sociable sexuality, not a lasting and relatively odorless opening onto others, but a violent sexual amassment, briefly enacted and frenzied—fundamentally non-socializable—and governed above all, as we shall see, by the animal convulsiveness of the sense of smell.[16]

Narcissus Odoriferous

The violent smell of (violent) sex, the overpowering and murderous scent of a primordial "object relation": this is where the trail has led us so far, and we may as well succumb at this point to the crudity of that Cainian place. Nothing is to be gained by delicacies in a matter so indelicate. Let us simply assert what should by now be starting to come clear—that Cain's characters make love with their noses. Here they are, doing what they do best:

She was so close I could smell her. (Postman, *7)*

I didn't look at her. But I could see her dress. . . . It . . . was a little bit rumpled now, and mussy. I could smell her. (Postman, *8)*

From then on, I began to smell her again. (Postman, *13)*

A whiff of her smell hit me in the face, and I knew she was standing right beside me.[17]

Her dress slipped up, above her knees. . . . I didn't look, but I could smell her. (Serenade, *31)*

Her head touched my coat, and as it did I could swear she inhaled, as though sniffing what I smelled like.[18]

She started unbuttoning my shirt . . . nuzzling into my armpit. . . . After some moments of that she seemed to wilt . . . and began whispering to me, " . . . Burl Stuart . . . stinks. Maybe . . . he smells nice to others, but to me he smells like feet. . . . But you . . . have a heavenly smell. . . . You smell like grass, grass that's just been cut." (Cloud Nine, *43–44)*

It would be pointless to extend the catalogue further, as these examples already exhibit a monotony that tells us what we need to know. Love, these excerpts say, is *blind* ("I didn't look," "I tried not to look," "eyes closed," and so on). It strikes not so much the eyes as the nasal passage, is both stimulated and sustained in an olfactory tremor that's all the more damning for being irresistible, all the more binding because it operates in a medium beyond the self's control. The Cainian subject gets turned on by way of a sense it can't turn off. Where vision, here, marks at least the possibility of libidinal voluntarism—the sight of Cora's lips may make Frank "want to mash them in" (*Postman*, 4), but he can always try to quell his violent passion by looking away—smell is what invariably defeats such intention, eclipsing it in an odoriferous cloud that opens the self onto the other only in the mode of a fatal enslavement.

For on this point we must insist: however depraved or "unenlightened" he might seem, Cain partakes of a long tradition in Enlightenment thought that classifies smell as the sense of unfreedom. Smell "interfer[es] with individual freedom," writes Kant, because "other people are forced to share a scent whether they want to or not."[19] It does violence to the sanctity of the self by opening it, exciting it, *agitating* it, independently of subjective intention. It makes stealthy use of a vital necessity—one must, after all, breathe—to infiltrate and conquer individual autonomy with a coerced olfactory "sociality": one "shares," but involuntarily; one connects with others, but only by way of an irresistible compulsion. And smell performs this tyrannical violation, at least as Cain wants us to see it, in the name of an erotic fatality. "I didn't look, but I could smell her," "A whiff of her smell hit me in the face": the odor that blinds and binds me is almost unfailingly the odor of the sexual other, an indomitable sexual effluvium that binds me *to* that other and that leads inexorably, through this subjection, to crime, social transgression—a virtually ontological destructiveness.

This is the famous "fatality of passion,"[20] the libidinal bind of Cain's work. It's important to have it before us at the outset, though I shall trace it in proper detail only in the following section. For now, what's crucial is merely to note that this fatality also includes a sense of promise and possibility, as love appears to offer a way out of an unrepresentably prior condition. Without, that is, the hero's immediate investment in external objects, there would here be neither self nor world since in Cain the universe clearly "extends no farther than the radius of one's desire."[21] It's desire and desire alone that makes the narrative world "show up," bringing its objects into a dreamlike focus and elaborating the rhythm of its unfolding. The opening of a Cain novel is thus typically also the "opening" of its hero; it recounts the broaching of an egoic envelope in a momentous but apparently adventitious encounter, marking the birth of an object orientation that's also the condition of the self's emergence:

I was in the Tupinamba, having a bizcocho and coffee, when this girl came in. (Serenade, *3*)

Then I saw her. . . . Except for the shape, she really wasn't any raving beauty, but . . . her lips stuck out in a way that made me want to mash them in for her. (Postman, *4*)

A woman was standing there. I had never seen her before. She was maybe thirty-one or -two, with a sweet face, light blue eyes, and dusty blonde hair. She was small, and had on a suit of . . . pajamas. She had a washed-out look.[22]

The centrality of vision in these examples already suggests that, however disastrously it will end, love begins by representing the promise of libidinal normality. The urgency of this promise is conveyed by the almost metaphysical sense of necessity contained in the repetition of such encounters. For the Cainian hero, like it or not, *cannot not love*; despite the measured offhandedness of the tone, despite a casualness that makes it all seem fortuitous, the sheer numerical insurgency of these moments indicates that for Cain there's no alternative to a love-bond that literally makes his world "go round." The other *abrupts*—the hero invests himself—the narrative world unfolds. Such a sequence is primal, foundational, structurally and ontologically indispensable. Everything appears to follow from it—nothing seems to precede it—because the entire point of the encounter with the other is to banish all that comes "before" into the depths of novelistic prehistory, while liberating the hero from a loveless past into a present saturated with (object) love.

Prior to that liberation—prior, in short, to object love—there's only the splendid solitude of narcissism. "*I* was in the Tupinamba," "Then *I* saw her," "*I* had never seen her before": in the repressed beginning before these beginnings, the "I" exists alone, unbonded, in a "relation" to "itself" and a nonrelation to others which requires that the subject be freed into love—in order to save it from a state of war. For what, after all, can this narcissism be if not that condition we noted earlier, where ego and object annihilate each other in an identificatory amassment that knows no bounds? "[I]n the last resort," writes Freud, narcissism must be sacrificed and "we must begin to love in order not to fall ill."[23] The openings of Cain's books enact just this sacrifice, and Cain knows full well that the name of the sickness that narcissism threatens is violence, unending warfare—an identificatory belligerence that respects no difference and that the bonds of love are meant to cure.[24]

And yet, try as he might, Cain seems unable to speak this name. No sooner does he begin to imagine a moment prior to object love than he ends up saying something very much like "love" after all. "You have been with a man" says Juana to John Sharp in a crucial scene of *Serenade*; "I speak of man you love."

> "*Oh, I'm a fairy, is that it?*"
> "*Yes.*"
> "*Well, thanks. I didn't know that.*" (141)

The truth, of course, is that he did know it, that "[e]very man has got five per cent of that in him, if he meets the one person that'll bring it out" (144), and that Sharp has, before the novel's "present," met just that person in Winston Hawes.

The "illness" the novel sets out to cure thus seems quite manifestly a "libidinal" one. Cain's opera-singer hero has made an unacceptable (because) homosexual object choice, which is absolutely primary in his psychic development, even if it's revealed to us only when Hawes uncannily resurfaces more than halfway through the novel. At that point, when Sharp lifts up the telephone receiver to find Winston on the other end, "homosexuality" would seem to become the name for all that ails him. We now discover that his "unhealthy" attachment to Winston led to a fantastic debilitation of masculine prowess whose primary sign is the ruined voice with which we find the hero at the book's beginning. "Hoaney," Juana continues,

these man who love other man, they can do much, very clever. But no can sing. Have no toro in high voice, no grrr that frighten little muchacha, make heart beat fast. Sound like old woman, like cow, like priest. (142)

The crudity of this homophobic "theory" is staggering, but let's at least make sure we grasp its implications. The passage says that homosexual desire is incompatible with the vocal art because it makes men's high notes sound too *tame*. It takes away their masculine *"toro,"* the *"grrr"* that's the mark of a healthily dominative relation to the other sex, and replaces it with the lamentably mild and effeminate sounds of "old woman," "cow," "priest." If gay men are nonetheless said to be "clever"—if they can, nonetheless, "do much"—this serves merely to extend offhandedly the indictment of a "sexuality" that's here imagined as a fundamentally virulent form of disorder.

For Winston's "cleverness" is part and parcel of an excessively cultured "homosexual" disposition that the novel reads as the flaccid cause of a pervasive cultural decay. Suspiciously rich (127), fundamentally dilettantish, he doesn't really "care about art . . . as something to look at and feel," but wants instead "to *own* it" (127). He wants, in short, to make "a whore out of [music]" (127). Though "[y]ou can't," as Sharp insists, "own music the way you can own a picture," you can at least "own a big hunk of it"—can own, for example, "the singer" who sings for you (128), and it's in this sense that the relation between homosexuality and artistic prowess must be understood. The homosexual bond is a bond of unfreedom that ruins the artist by *buying* him, financially subjecting him, pimping him—making him, in short, "depend . . . on [the other] like a hophead depends on dope" (131). While Hollywood may thus be thoroughly "homosexualized" in that it, too, thinks "singing is . . . something you buy" rather than something that's "good for its own sake" (99), Winston is at the origin of even that decadence since he seems himself to own Hollywood (135). Furthermore, the novel codes his pandering as still more iniquitous than the studios' because he pimps art, not for the money, but for the narcissistic profit of his own febrile and excessively refined pleasure:

You went to his concerts, but you didn't sit out there at his rehearsals, and see him hold men for an hour overtime, at full pay, just because there was some French horn passage that he liked, and wanted it played over and over again—not to rehearse it, but because of what it did to him. *And you didn't walk out with him afterwards, and see him all atremble, and hear him tell how he felt after playing it. He was like some woman that goes to concerts because they give her the right vibrations . . . or have some other effect on her nitwit insides. (127–28)*

It's this feverish and feminine self-absorption, this prostitution of art for the vibratory enrichment of one's overly cultured and "nitwit insides," that threatens the sexual and artistic prowess of the individual artists Winston "owns." Bound over by his cash and his emotional paternalism—"you're in trouble," Hawes says; "Tell it to Papa" (132–33)—those artists lose all masculine autonomy to become instead the feminized shadows, the instrumental whores, of an internal and erotic operatic gratification. The gay man's passion for cultural "capital" in this way pimps the "straight" male artist for the sake of expanding its narcissistic territory. The result, of course, is nothing less than the emasculating "blindness" of death (57). "Something in me had died" says Sharp of his vocal "crack up" (57), and "my voice" had not "one particle of life [left] in it" (48–49): the bond of gay love is an unbonding bond that portends the death, the radical destruction, of at least the "dependent" partner in that contract.

What Cain reviles as "homosexual love," then, is not in the first place libidinal at all. The danger he's describing consists in a bond that abolishes the other's autonomy; it threatens independence because it reduces the other to a function of the ego's enjoyment, and this means that the danger of gay bonds resides in their status as *identificatory attachments*:

[L]ittle by little, he began making suggestions. Then I began dropping in on him in the morning, and he'd take me through some [vocal] things I had been doing wrong. . . . Then he began to take my acting apart, and put it together again. . . . He made me learn a whole new set of gestures, done naturally, and he made me practice for hours singing sotto voce *without using any gestures at all. . . . I got so I was with him morning, noon and night, and depended on him like a hophead depends on dope.*

Then came my crack-up, and . . . I had to leave Paris. (130–31)

What's perhaps most extraordinary about this passage is the way it starts by sounding the note of sexual seduction ("he began making suggestions") and ends by describing a mimetic transformation. The seduction might even be said to reside in a "coaching" that identifies the other with the self. Sharp conforms himself to the dictates of Winston's imagination, "learn[s] a whole new set of gestures" and an entirely different style of singing, precisely as the mark of his submission to the homosexual's predatory wiles. The gay "proposition" in this sense seduces by making one over in the image of another. If the bond it induces causes Sharp to lose his manly voice, this is because that bond entails a relation of "being" rather than a strictly "sexual" possession. In fact, it rewrites "having" *as* "being," transposing the theme of erotic possession into the key of the subject's *dis*possession: to possess him is to kill *him* ("Something in me had died") by making him "be" me; it's to love him to death in the name of my imperious narcissistic dilation, to ventriloquize in "his" place by bequeathing him "my" gestures and assigning him "my" priestly and bovine—my thoroughly effeminate—voice. "Do I, for God's sake, sound like that?" The answer is in Sharp's case "yes," since the eroto-mimetic bond I'm describing is a (non)bond of (de)subjectifying hypnosis. John sounds like "that" because *he is that*, because, "hypnoti[zed]" by Winston's "live [conductor's] stick" (129), he dies into the other(-subject) so completely that the other no longer appears as another, does not in fact "appear" at all, but is lived immediately as his ownmost self. The hypnotized person "executes . . . the order of the hypnotist *without seeing or knowing that an order is involved and* *that the order is addressed to him,"* writes Mikkel Borch-Jacobsen. "He does not [merely] submit himself *to* the other, he *becomes the other,* comes to be like the other—who is thus no longer an other, but 'himself.'"[25] Bound, then, by this hypnotic bond, Sharp must perish as an autonomous being to be reborn as a subject-object, a mass (of) being: an other self (which is not other, and which has no self) whose injunctions he now executes and whose voice he now mimes—blindly, madly, *somnambulistically.*

Let us be perfectly clear, however. If the gay man augurs my masculine death by making me "be" (like) him, it's equally true that, in becoming him, I myself am transformed into a feminine and hypnotizing assassin. I am (in) him and he is (in) me; perishing into this collectivity of being, I can't but be united with its blind and dumb fury, can't but be reborn as the other who murders (me). The novel, moreover, links this transformation to an animal form of regressiveness:

I wanted to shut it out, the whole horrible thing [Juana] had showed me, where she had ripped the cover off my whole life, dragged out what was down there all the time. . . . But one thing kept slicing up at me. . . . It was the fin of that shark. . . . I kept telling myself she was crazy . . . that Winston had no more to do with what happened to me in Paris than the scenery had. But here it was, starting on me . . . the same way it had before. . . . I closed my eyes, and I was going down under the waves, with something coming up at me from below. Panic caught me then. (144)

The feminizing Winston is also this panic-inducing shark,[26] and so of course is Sharp, since to be swallowed up in this fantasy is to be nothing less than incorporated: to be made fantasmatically a corporeal part of a bloodthirsty and man-eating monster. Devoured by the other, I'm dragged "down" to its prehistoric depths, intestinally worked over, ingested and reassimilated to a bellicose and pre-egoic animal (in)humanity. This transformation marks both the death of the subject and its regressive rebirth as a beastly automaton whose murderous mission the subject now mimes. (The animal is of course no more free from this mime than the hypnotized person, since it remains enslaved to an instinct whose imperious command—"Eat!"—it

61

doesn't even know it's obeying.) Winston gets down on all fours, incarnated as a "[b]ig bull," and "charg[es]" repeatedly at Juana's cape (156–57); John closes the novel by miming this animal farce as tragedy when, having already become bull-like by regaining his vocal *toro*, he sings a song that fingers Juana for the Mexican authorities, then charges after her to her ultimate death in a scene that's played next door to a bullring and staged as a bullfight from the bull's perspective ("I caught a flash of red," "I could see the red of her dress" [193–94]).

"Homosexual" panic is thus here a terror at the prospect of an animalizing and homocidogenic bond (a bond, that is, that incites murder). If that bond "feminizes," if the bull-shark speaks with the voice of "old woman" and "cow," this is because the feminine is imagined here, just as in the Freudian uncanny, as the originary site of a doubled relation where subject and object mutually annihilated each other in the womb-like prehistory of time. Winston's return to the novel's present *is* the return of the repressed feminine as homocidogenic mimesis. It initiates a bond that feminizes, kills, and enforces the hypnotic emulation of that murder. The strain, meanwhile, between the hypnotic and devouring versions of this bond should teach us that neither model is adequate; it's ultimately *smell* and smell alone that wraps me in the madness of an eroto-mimetic embrace, and it does so in a fashion that ruins the possibility of a nonviolent relation to the object of love.

For Juana, you see, has this ear—a bull's ear, to be precise, given to her by a bullfighter. It's "good and rank," with "pieces of gristle hanging out of it," and it "st[inks] so you [can] smell it five feet away" (30). At the climactic party that will end in Winston's death, a scene staged explicitly in terms of the "homosexual" threat, she emerges with this relic, carrying as well a sword and a bullfighter's cape:

> *They had got a little sick of bullfighting, but when they saw the ear they began to yell again. They passed it around . . . and smelled it, and say [sic] "Peyooh!" Winston took it, held it up to his head and wobbled it, and they laughed and clapped. He*

got down on the floor again and bellowed. Juana laughed. "Yes, now you are no more jackass. Big bull."

. . . I grabbed for the ear. Winston dodged. She laughed and wouldn't look at me. Something hit me in the belly. When I looked around I saw that one of the fags in woman's clothes had poked me with a broomstick. "Out of my way! I'm a picador! I'm a picador on his old white horse!"

Two or three more of them ran back and got broomsticks, or mop handles, or whatever was there, to be picadors, and began galloping around Winston, poking at him. Every time they touched him he'd bellow. . . . [He] began charging [the cape], on one hand and his knees, still holding the ear with his other hand and wobbling it. Pudinsky began to [play] the bullring music from Carmen. (156–57)

This passage is in a sense the "essence" of the novel, its primally fragrant scene. Raising the specter of a devolutionary mimesis, it says that the threat of the homosexual bond is the danger of animalization, and it insists that John must avoid becoming *that*. It tells us as well, in the very same breath, that this mimesis is an eroto-genesis: the mime assigns its players their erotically murderous parts; it binds "fags" together in a libidinal contagion that, by compelling them both to act out the impulses of others ("Two or three more of them ran back and got broomsticks") and to play in blindness their operatic roles ("Carmen"), leads to their "poking at" the groveling Winston in an erotic and imitative fratricidal rite. We know that John will later join in this rite, acting the part of the raging bull whose passion leads to the other's murder. For the moment what's crucial is that this passage, even as it presages John's metamorphosis, saturates the scene of eroto-mimesis in the rank and malodorous atmosphere of the ear. It's the ear that sets this drama in motion, inducing the entire identificatory debauch and reducing the cast to somnambulistic animals. No sooner does Juana reenter the party, no sooner do the characters smell the fetid organ, than the murderous "homosexual" mime begins: Winston descends to his animal mire, the "fags" snatch up their broomsticks, and everyone becomes uncannily possessed to act out the homicidal passion play that they don't even know they're performing. Under the spell of this primal smell, they believe that they're entering freely into a socio-theatrical pact—believe they know that they're "only playing"—whereas in fact *they really are participating* in a bullfight that ends with Winston pinned to the sofa, "blood . . . foaming out of [his] mouth," while Juana stands "over him, talking to him, laughing at him, telling him [he's going] down to hell" (157).

If Juana alone remains immune to this contagion (she knows all along that she's going to kill Winston), this is merely to signify that, as "Mother" (147), she's the fantasized origin of all that the others mime: she "is" the rank identificatory animal men try to deny that they are. Both human and animal, bullfighter and bull (the ear is after all hers), Juana represents the doubled mass that a civilized masculinity ought to have surmounted and that it must now locate elsewhere. It's "she" (and not me) who kills Winston, she who "emits" the smell that orchestrates the return of a delirious and somnambulistic sociality. It's she who forces men to share this smell in a bond of unfreedom that "births" them into a murderous being-(in)-objects. And it's she who therefore allows us to see what the novel insists that we *do* see: that in the beginning is the smell, the odor—an overmastering and blinding aroma that binds even as it enslaves, enforcing an erotic connection to others only in the mode of a mimetic violence that the text at once requires men avow and projects as an abhorred femininity.

But that isn't all. If the "homo" in the "homosexual"—the threat of his likeness, the danger of the double—leads to the indistinction of a vaginal mimesis, the "sexual" in that figure takes us somewhere close, but also someplace different. It takes us, in short, to the anus. We shouldn't be surprised to find ourselves there, since anal eroticism is almost always in the air where dominant representations of homosexuality are concerned. When Winston takes up the ear from Juana and sinks down to his hands and knees, his explicit coding as a gay man evokes that form of eroticism, refiguring the smell of the ear as the smell of his own uplifted rear. Given, furthermore, that the scene imagines the gay man as both animalized and animalizing, this figuration gestures toward a Freudian myth of human prehistory, in which men were only bound together in asocial "bonds" of an essentially olfactory and finally anal kind.

Long, long ago—this fable says—in the animal womb of time, individual "humans" came together only briefly, frenziedly, to experience the most intense sexual pleasure "man" has ever known. Sex at that time was a smelly business; both anally and genitally pungent, it "convulse[d] our physical being" in a way it has not done since.[27] But sex at that time was not yet human sex; it was animal sex, archi-narcissistic, in that it did not seek as good sex should to bring about ever larger social units, but tended rather to foster an uncivilized and violent separation. It was not a sex guided by the civilizing hand of love, but a sex in the grip of the death drive. Civilization proper, as Freud says, is Erotic through and through; it "is a process in the service of Eros, whose purpose is to combine single . . . individuals, and after that families, then races, peoples and nations, into one great unity, the unity of mankind" (122). The sex of our beastly ancestors couldn't perform this combinatory function because it was prompted by the periodic smell of the menstrual process, and it consequently brought humans together only occasionally, momentarily, impermanently. It was only when that sex became harnessed to the Erotic function that it could properly be called "civilized" at all, and this of course happened, according to this myth, when the human animal stood up.

For at that point, the role of the smelling apparatus "was taken over by visual excitations, which, in contrast to the intermittent olfactory stimuli, were able to maintain a permanent effect" (99). Love ceased to be blind and became thereby a constant factor in the life of human beings. Since, moreover, "the founding of families" (and thus of society: civilization for Freud is familial-social) results from the fact that "the need for genital satisfaction [now] took up its quarters as a permanent lodger" (99), we can begin to decipher one of those series of equivalence so common in Freud's work, and so telling: human society is a regime of permanence, a regime of vision, a regime of love. What binds us together is an Erotic impulse whose work is facilitated by the permanence of visual stimuli, insofar as what gets "seen" is first and foremost the others' genitals.[28] There are thus, on this reading, either (permanent) social bonds of an essentially Erotico-visual nature, or there are no bonds, no relations, whatsoever. Either I smell the other and remain completely self-enclosed, a roaming and sniffling Narcissus whose very sexual union with the other is curiously non-Erotic and non-bonding; or I see the other and join with him lovingly, in a sociable manner that bonds us without annihilating our autonomy and difference.

The problem with this sociogenic myth, of course, is that in the regime of smell there was also a libidinal "bond," a relation to the "other." But this bond was impermanent, violent in its sexual imperiousness, ruled by a blind and olfactory convulsiveness that bonded me periodically only to "myself" in the mode of a loveless other. For who can this other be but myself, as soon as we grant that it's *his* smell that compels me to act out my own instinctual nature? Drawn and bound to the animal other by the irresistible pungency of his odor, I'm pierced by that odor, forced to share in the smell of the other and to take him breathlessly in. I frantically inhale his fatal emanations, and this inhalation infiltrates and convulses me *from within*, crumbling my being down to the core and commingling me with (the smell of) the other in a quivering mass of panting prehumanity. "Before" the regime of visual love, the smell of love thus bound "men" in a heap of animal-human being. Bound them, yes—but not civilly, not pacifically. This aromatic sexuality ruins the equation of love with sociality by destroying subject and object in the very gesture of bonding them. Far from fostering the unrelated self-enclosedness that Freud imagines he fears, it succors instead what we must insist is an excessive and passionate relation of nonrelation: a narcissistic (un)bondedness in which "I" am "me" only to the extent that I mime myself by obeying an olfactory instinctual injunction that comes implacably from the other. Man here "socializes" with his fellow in a sightless and erotic mimetic compulsion that prevents him from freely socializing at all. And if, finally, we take seriously Freud's contention that "civilization is a special process, comparable to the normal maturation of the individual" (97–98), we must grant as well that his fable imagines a contemporary reliving of this (non)relation in the development of the individual psyche. Each one of us, on this reading, must pass through something like an olfactory primacy—a "nasal" phase—that predates both the oral phase and the pacific communality of visual object love.

But where are we to locate this primal phase? Let us listen once more to the myth: it is, Freud tells us, "anal erotism" that "succumbs in the first instance to the 'organic repression'" of smell (100). When man stood up, he lost all (conscious) interest in the smell of the other's anus. But he also, unfortunately, lost a good deal of "interest" in sex itself, since

it was not only his anal erotism which threatened to fall a victim to organic repression, but the whole of his sexuality; so that since this, the sexual function has been accompanied by a repugnance . . . which prevents its complete satisfaction. . . . All neurotics, and many others besides, take exception to the fact that "inter urinas et faeces nascimur *[we are born between urine and faeces].*" *The genitals, too, give rise to strong sensations of smell which many people cannot tolerate and which spoil sexual intercourse for them. Thus we should find that the deepest root of the sexual repression which advances along with civilization is the organic defence of the new form of life achieved with man's erect gait against his earlier animal existence. (106)*

It is perhaps necessary to translate these speculations, in order to say what Freud at once acknowledges and obscures. What the passage surreptitiously "argues" is that, in the blindness of our olfactory beginnings, *we did not differentiate between the anus and the genitals*. Organic repression targets both genital and anal sexuality because it doesn't matter to the regime of olfaction *where* the smell comes from, but merely that it binds in erotic coercion. Despite Freud's emphasis on the centrality of the menstrual cycle—despite his insistence on the periodic and genital nature of the animal's libidinal relations—the introduction of anal eroticism raises the twin specter of a fundamental genital irrelevance and a permanently unbonding bond. The anus never ceases to put out its beckoning smell; its appeal is ongoing, continual, everlasting, and there was therefore nothing to prevent the human animal from more or less constantly obeying the wild and olfactory mimetic order of the other-himself. The frenzy of rutting, the incontestable aromatic rewards to be reaped from the genitals, sexual intercourse itself, and even sexual reproduction—all of this no doubt took place, but only as the strictly incidental benefits of a sexuality motivated by the constant and reproductively useless conjunction of nose and anus. The very movement, indeed, from olfaction to visuality could speculatively be thought of as man's ambulatory erection into a register that can finally "distinguish" the genitals. Where the nose fails, the eye succeeds; where smell amasses, vision maintains a respectful distance that lets things show up as they "truly" are: other as other, genitals as genitals, anus as anus. Without the installed supremacy of such an organ, we could never overcome a primal confusion, where all is in all and each in the other; where I am the other, the other is me, and anus and genitals are the interchangeable occasions for a savage and onanistic olfactory paroxysm.[29]

The "new form of life" *must*, therefore, repress the olfactory centrality of the lower life form, even at the extraordinary risk of "the whole of [man's] sexuality." If it fails to do so, the genitals may never show up clearly enough for the reproductive sexuality at the root of the first bond to take place with requisite regularity. The human animal thus stakes his sexuality in a repressive gambit that makes sex sociable by seeking to separate the genitals from the anus. It should come as no surprise, then, that, in the gesture of that repression, the womb retains an olfactory significance, but only inasmuch as it remains fantasmatically conflated with the rectum. If "[m]any" people "take exception to the fact that . . . we are born between urine and faeces," if "the genitals . . . give rise to strong sensations of smell which . . . spoil sexual intercourse," this is because the socialized psyche performs a yoking of genitality and anality, in which the womb both figures and displaces an olfactory phase that must be called *nas(an)al*. It's precisely in response to this phase that the other visually abrupts in Cain, banishing "gay bonds" into novelistic prehistory. The gay man's conflation of genitality with anality signals the threat of a prehistoric sociality: an animal (a)sociality that stands to civilization as the death drive stands to Eros, narcissizing all bonds by organizing them around an olfactory destructiveness that doesn't even care to know what (reproductive) genitality is. The failure of this repression, then—the gay man's emergence in the present of *Serenade*—marks perhaps this book's greatest strength. It seeks to trick us with a return of the organically repressed, to bemire us in a smell that it makes us know is no more the mother's or the gay man's than it is the straight male self's. It insists that there is no "birth" here but stillbirth, no object love that doesn't stagnate from the start in death, mimesis, olfaction. There's no victory of vision over smell that doesn't remain contaminated by the nasal, no genitality that isn't also anal, no (homo)sociality that's not somehow "vaginal." There's no human being who isn't also the rankest and most bellicose animal, no "man" who's not decomposed in the smell of the "feminine" others that disgust him.

No bond, then, but unbondedness. No love except the unloving animal passion of a deadly and olfactory mimesis.

Love Stinks

And yet the novel at least attempts to cure this state of affairs. The direction of its proposed treatment can be charted in Freudian terms: "Love for [another] oneself knows only one barrier—love for [true] others, love for objects."[30] What's required, then, is the introduction of an object whose difference from the subject will make the love-bond less identificatory, more libidinal. The Cainian novel thus begins in the fashion I've described: by banishing the mimetic bond to its prehistory and seeking to establish an object relation—this time, with a woman. Since women are somehow not so like men, not so "homo," the bond with them could presumably be a "hetero"-bond with an actual "other." It would be a bond more fully "objectal," which preserved the distinction between self and other and opened the possibility of a true social pact between (free, singular, unique) subjects. Given, moreover, that the homosexual's belligerence is imagined to take place through the medium of smell, what must be effected through the love potion is a complete and pacifying *anosmia*: an olfactory forgetfulness or deodorization, a fumigatory elevation into visual object love and peaceful relations with others.[31]

This much should by now be clear. What's less clear, however, and what needs now to be articulated, is the other side of the bind I've been describing. Why, in Cain's work, does the love-treatment fail? By what extraordinarily luckless catastrophe do the options turn out to be narcissism or—narcissism? The answers are at once simpler and more troublesome than they might at first appear. They have to do both with the fantasized maternal origin of the mimetic "bond" itself, and with the complexity of the novel's attempt to produce a therapeutic *narrative*: to narrationalize the transition from (homosexual) narcissism to pacific object relations.

We need only ponder this movement for a moment to see the kind of problem it poses. For as it turns out, the aromatico-mimetic "bond" does not simply *precede* civil relations. It's also an *effect* of civilization, since the gay man who figures it is, as we've seen, the product of an "overculturalization." The love-cure must consequently entail both a civilizing progression *and* a regression to a less civilized, more primal, condition. Moving triumphantly "forward," I must also, paradoxically, crawl "back"; but slinking backwards I inevitably find myself narcissized once more, so that the closer I come to being cured by love the further I also recede from that cure.

Love may be, then, as the lovers in *Double Indemnity* imagine it, a trolley car that takes its passengers "straight down the line" toward an inescapable conclusion (19). But the "straightness" of that line must be imagined more on the model of a Möbius strip than of a two-dimensional rail or track. Whatever the streetcar's velocity, however strenuously it might seek to propel both passengers and readers beyond a fixed point of animal-narcissistic origin, it carries them exactly nowhere, but merely returns with fatal vengeance to an original condition that it thereby doubles. The gay man who represents such an origin in *Serenade* will therefore fail to die. Sharp can still wonder, near the book's end, if the baseball player he's watching in Guatemala is "doing things to [him] that [have] nothing to do with baseball" (184), because the streetcar that the novel names "desire" can't free the hero from the threat of gay bonds without also trapping him in them. The "[n]ever again" with which the book closes marks the definitive failure of these efforts, and it locates that failure in the compulsion to repeat an originary and deadly mime: Sharp returns to Mexico, renouncing the voice that the book set out to give him ("You sing . . . Señor Sharp?" "No. . . . Never again" [195]); he consequently both resumes the condition with which the novel opens (voiceless in Mexico) and assumes as his own the narcissized, feminine, and animal bellicosity that the novel has by now attributed to that voicelessly amassed state.

But the bind that thwarts therapeutic progress doesn't just operate at an abstract level. It's also inscribed in the body of the love object that the novel begins by introducing. For Juana, of course, is both woman and Mexican Indian. If the woman in her is meant to address the "primitive" aspect of the mimetic bond, and to offer a forward progression out of it, her racial character is equally necessary as a regressive remedy for that bond's excessively civilized dimension:

Everything about her said Indian. . . . But she wasn't any of the colors that Indians come in. She was almost white, with just the least dip of café *con leche. Her shape was Indian, but not ugly. . . . She had plenty [of breast-works], but her hips were round, and her legs had a soft line to them. She was slim, but there was something voluptuous about her, like in three or four years she would get fat. All that, though, I only half saw. What I noticed was her face. It was flat, like an Indian's but the nose broke high . . . and the eyes weren't dumb, with that shiny, shoe-button look. They were pretty big, and black, but they leveled out straight, and had a kind of sleepy, impudent look to them. Her lips were thick, but pretty. (3)*

The impossible temporality of the love-cure is figured here, on the novel's first page, by an almost hysterically apologetic multiplication of the conjunction "but." Juana is Mexican, but she's also "white"; she's "Indian, but not ugly"; thick-lipped "but pretty"; black-eyed but not, as this apparently suggests, "dumb." The conjunctive hysteria works at once to condense and confound a racist discourse, since the "but" both installs a hierarchical opposition between whites and Indians by declaring the temporal priority of whites, *and* demolishes that opposition by locating both sets of "racial" attributes in one unthinkably present body. "*Everything* about her said Indian," the passage begins, and "[a]n Indian [is] about eight thousand years behind the rest of us" (14). Juana thus ought to stand at the fantasmatic beginning of an evolutionary narrative, and to instantiate the "stupidity" and "ugliness" that the conjunctive structure attributes, by a kind of negative assertion, to the primitive.[32] But that very structure requires the passage to describe an "Indian" who *isn't* ugly, primitive, or stupid, but is in fact beautiful, civilized, and bright—"almost," as Sharp puts it, "white." To say that Juana is "Indian, but not ugly" is therefore both to propose that (all) Indians are ugly and to embody that proposition in an Indian whose manifest beauty undermines the statement the example ought to demonstrate. The "but" becomes a kind of "and," the negative affirmation an affirmative negation. Juana is Indian *and* beautiful, Indian *and* smart, Indian *and* civilized. The very gesture that plots racial difference as temporal progression tends simultaneously to ruin that story by freezing or "circularizing" the narrative temporality that would keep such difference in place.

On one hand, of course, this narrative circularity issues from and redoubles the logic by which the racist seeks to justify his desire for the hated other. The hysterical conjunction represents, in this sense, the novel's desire to coerce its hero into love—out of "homosexuality"—and the passage can accordingly be translated in terms that go something like this: "I loved her even though she was Mexican, because to fail to love her would be to continue to love Winston, and we all know where that leads." But on the other hand, the terms that *Serenade* sets for itself force us to state the case in an exactly opposite formulation. It's not just that Sharp can love Juana only because, despite being Mexican (by which the text means "ugly"), she's also beautiful (by which it means "white"). Alongside this way of putting it, we must also concede that Sharp can only love her *because* of her racial makeup—because, that is, despite being beautiful (white), she's also Mexican Indian, with all that this here implies: ugliness, stupidity, and above all, a beneficent "primitiveness." In order for our hero to move out of eroto-mimesis he needs to be introduced to an object that's neither a man nor a "civilized" creature at all. But then again, as all the evidence goes on to demonstrate, it's precisely in coming into contact with such an object that he's ensnared in a therapeutic bind that makes it impossible to "move" at all.

Thus there is, in a first piece of evidence, the catastrophe looming in the love object's name. "John" begins by loving "Juana." The nominal replication serves to predict a prolongation of narcissistic belligerence, since it tells us that, however much everything might happen "as if" under the sign of object-libido, the "other" that John discovers to love is finally none other than himself. Oates's conception of a world that "extends no farther than the radius of one's desire" (111) now takes on a quite different set of contours. Far from meaning that a preexistent object-world emerges only to the extent that an ego invests itself in it, it now means instead that the ego *invents a world by cathecting itself "objectally."* The world turns out to issue or "radiate" from the ego itself; it's never anything more or less than that ego's delirious and identificatory repetition. The name of the "object" that John would love can in this sense only be something like Juana. For the Cainian novel, like the Freudian dream, must be characterized as "completely egoistical," in the strictest and most curious sense of that term. "Dreams are completely egoistical," writes Freud:

Whenever my own ego does not appear in the content of the dream . . . I may safely assume that [it] lies concealed, by identification, behind [another] person. . . . On other occasions, when my own ego does appear in the dream, the situation in which it occurs may teach me that some other person lies concealed, by identification, behind my ego. In that case the dream should warn me to transfer on to myself . . . the concealed common element attached to this other person.[33]

The dream, in short, is a regressive recapitulation and psychic presentation of that unrepresentable condition in which I *am* the object, and the object is me. In it, the ego reigns everywhere, colossal and supreme, but only on condition that it never be quite "itself," that it fail to escape the mime by which it can alone be subjectively incarnated. The story Sharp tells may, in this sense, be fruitfully compared to a dream—a point that several of Cain's critics have made.[34] But to say this is to indicate that there can be no question of his supplanting narcissism with object love, no question of overcoming a bellicose, feminine, and animal mimesis to institute the masculine subject-of-love. If we can call Sharp's narrative a dream at all, it's because it seeks to represent and diegeticize the prehistoric "homosexual" unbondedness which the novel begins by banishing, and which is in the strictest sense *un*conscious, *un*representable, non-narratable, except inasmuch as it erupts into consciousness as the distorted dream of a subject succeeding in really being itself.[35]

Here, then, lies the psychoanalytic explanation for the novel's impossible temporality: it follows from the fact that the narrative expresses symptomatically—that is, in distorted form—the scenario it simultaneously represses. The cure-by-love can't but be fixated, can't but stall in a perpetual simulation of progressive-regressive motion, since the narrative attempt to represent that cure is the manifest expression of an unconscious scene that is in essence prehistoric—and that has, accordingly, no proper temporal structure at all. Eroto-mimesis abolishes time in its relentless abrogation of distance; there is no "story" to being-(in)-objects, no "before" and "after" in the identificatory mime, just as there is, within that mime's grip, no spatial distance to delimit the self from the other whom it lives—immediately. If the story Sharp tells is thus the expression of the unrepresentable bond it represses, its temporal form is bound to be deformed by the timelessness of that prior bond. It is, finally, this deformation that accounts for the opening's conjunctive hysteria, and that lets us now link that hysterical beginning to the melodramatics of Cain's aesthetic mode.

For Paul Skenazy is surely right to describe Cain's stories as "extravagant melodramas of violence and passion."[36] They operate in what Peter Brooks has called, in his book on melodrama, "the mode of excess,"[37] and this is in fact just another way of stating what Cain's critics find so objectionable in him: that his writing reeks of its own worst excesses; his stylistic tricks are overdone; and his stories exhibit an excessive brutality, an excessive senti-mentality, an excessive sexuality—even an excessive banality—and certainly a grandiose sense of the melodramatic gesture. The relevance of hysteria to such effects is perhaps evident enough from common usage: we know that the hysteric, like the melodramatist, always "overdoes it"; she forever creates a sensational scene by displaying too much affect too extravagantly, or by proclaiming loudly and all too morbidly the overexcitability of her "nerves." Even a more professional formulation acknowledges a distinctive hysterical hyperbole, since hysteria is clinically that form of illness in which the body "knows too much." It's a debility that may indeed be defined as the excessive insistence in the somatic present of the psyche's traumatic and irrecoverable past. And this insistence gives it, as several recent critics have argued, a repet-itive temporality that links it closely to the melodramatic mode I'm describ-ing. "Much melodrama gives the impression of a ceaseless returning to a prior state," writes Tania Modleski, because the melodramatic text, like "[t]he hysteric . . . in Freud's famous formulation, suffers [mainly] from reminis-cences."[38] Melodramatic time *is* hysterical time, the "converted" expression of a memorial malady. It's a time so haunted, so macerated by a past it can neither remember nor fully forget, that it acts out that past as hysterical re-turn, contorting the text in a spasmodic circularity that seeks perplexedly to recover and express what must otherwise remain inexpressible.

Such considerations lead me to suggest that the dream Sharp dreams isn't merely "egoistical"; it's also melodramatic and—therefore—hysterical. His narrative, too, "suffers [mainly] from reminiscences," in that not just the ending but nearly all of its main events can be read as repetitions of earlier ones. In the story he tells he *re*gains his voice, rather than simply "gaining" it; he *re*meets Winston and so loses his voice *again*; he *re*turns to Mexico, *re*encounters Juana, and competes once more with Triesca the bullfighter for the undivided prophylaxis of her attention. It remains only to note, in com-pleting the analysis, that the topic of this story also encodes it as a hysterico-melodramatic one. The drama of voice(lessness) that *Serenade* stages is one shared by melodrama and hysteria alike, as both the frequency of aphonia in hysterical symptomatology and the centrality of the mute in the history of melodrama make clear.[39] Since we know, moreover, that hysteria is conventionally a "feminine" complaint, let us at least hold open the possibility that what Sharp's dream forever circles back upon, what perpetually speaks in it without managing to speak, is the repressed monstrosity of its "feminine" voice: animal and putrid, bellicose and mass—the voice, in this case, of a no-one-in-particular, which can make its way into representation only as textual symptom, or as the failed operatic ejaculation of a singular masculine self.

And love? Have we not now strayed some distance from the topic at hand—from, that is, the cure-by-love and the object meant to effect it? Not at all, and we need only return to that object's body in order to be sure of it. For if the dream of love is a hysterical reproduction of the subject's identificatory pre-nativity, the object thus dreamt must surely bear the mark of this hysteria. That mark, I want to suggest, is once again the mark of race, the "primitive" inscription of the object. This inscription turns out to signal a form of somatic excess, in that it isn't a term in addition to "masculine" and "feminine," but merely the hysterical repetition of a "femininity" that Sharp must repress yet resurrect:

[My feeling about Juana] was mainly what any man feels toward a woman, but partly what he feels toward a child. There was something about the way she talked, the way she held her head, the way she did everything, that got me in the throat, so I couldn't breathe right. It wasn't child, of course. It was Indian. But it did things to me just the same, maybe worse on account of it being Indian, because that meant she was always going to be like that. (Serenade, 21)

The passage moves from an insistence on the subsidiary role of race in the phenomenology of love to an admission of its centrality. It mutates, that is, from a claim that it's "mainly" the woman in Juana that gets to John, and only "partly" the Indian-child, to the proposition that it's the eternally childish and Indian "way she [does] everything" that "[gets him] in the throat, so [he can't] breathe right." The dream of love can in this sense be said to rewrite race as the most feminine aspect of the object. Since the primary point of dreaming up Juana is to enable a movement into heterosexual love, her racial character can only be meant to render that object more heterosexually lovable. It does so by bloating the object with otherness, insisting hysterically on its double difference from the masculine subject-of-love. Race thus turns out to figure at once the prolongation of prehistoric primitiveness and the repetition of a contemporary difference that should let the subject distinguish himself in a loving cessation of mimicry.

But the very hyperbole of the strategy employed suggests a certain nervousness. It's almost as though Juana's body can never in fact be different "enough" from John's; it must have heaped upon it the accumulated signs of its difference—must bear the burden of a hyperbolic "femininity"—because that body is from the start *identified with* the one from which it's meant to be distinguished. The manic accretion of difference made lovable defends against an unthinkable similarity. The initial duplication at the level of the name can thus be interrogated for its deeper significance. "Juana" may, in a provisional sense, be thought of as a doubling of "John"; but "John" is also derived from "Juana," since the novel gives to the latter a referent that betokens an ontological priority:

> We climbed down and stood looking at [the lizards], when all of a sudden [Juana] began to scream. "Iguana! Iguana! Look, look, big iguana!"
>
> I looked, and couldn't see anything. Then, still as the rock it was lying on . . . I saw the evilest-looking thing I had ever laid eyes on. It looked like some prehistoric monster you see in the encyclopedia, [with] a look in its eye like something in a nightmare. She had grabbed up a little tree that had washed out by the roots, and was closing in on him. (51–52)

From iguana to Juana, and from Juana to John: the phonic resemblance suggests that the series begins with an animal whose name precedes the others, progressing from there to the woman named after it and ending with the masculine subject-of-love. If the person Sharp dreams up to love is thus in part a projection of "self," the sequence tells us that the person in question must also be said to *precede* and *predict* the emergence of that self. The object projected is an object repeated by a subject who is himself a repetition of that object. The self who "projects" must accordingly be said regressively to "return" as well. And what he returns to can be seen, in the oneiric hysteria of *Serenade*'s present tense, as an animal condition, a bellicose activity: a decompositional somatic amassment that dissolves the man and the Mexican woman in the mutual mire of a reptilian body that is the site of their originary union.

For clearly, this body is where they first "meet." To say that these names originate in "iguana" is also to imply that the characters who bear them are somehow like their titular progenitor. And if we ask what that progenitor is "like," we can hardly be surprised by now to discover the central terms of our argument: feminine and racial, violent and malodorous. It's *feminine*, then: let's make no mistake. The iguana is Juana—a Juana-iguana—since the intimate proximity of their names betokens an initial doubling, where Juana is the animal and the animal is her, and their mutual confrontation in the visual field can only inspire an implacable violence ("Look, look, big iguana!" gives way instantaneously to "Quick, bring machete!" [51–52]; the pre-specular union is immediately succeeded by the uncanny fury of a specular duel). It's *racial*, also, because this "evilest-looking thing [Sharp has] ever laid eyes on" is labeled "prehistoric"—like something "you see in the encyclopedia" (52)—and we already know that the novel associates such "primitiveness" with the racial character of Mexican-Indians ("An Indian [is] about eight thousand years behind the rest of us" [14]). And it's *violent* as well: not just because the sight of herself in the guise of the "monster" (52) excites in Juana an impulse to murder; what's still more crucial is that the ensuing duel turns out to embrace John also, mingling the humans by the blood of their wounds and fusing them in the internecine field of a deadly reptilian corporeality. "She was bleeding up to her elbows *and now it was my turn*"; "When I cut the string and grabbed, *I got teeth*" (52, 53; my emphases). The subject-of-love becomes here his object in a mutual bloodletting that binds them together in the body—the mouth—of the lizard that bites them. Sharing that mouth, commingling within it, Juana and John are reduced to the bile of a primitive and racialized reptile; they're dribbled together—mimetically mired—by the incorporative action of a rancorous beast that refuses to let them be themselves.

The novel's distinction between cure and disease has by this time completely collapsed. Love can now only (re)institute violence—it *is*, in short, eroto-mimesis—since John has become the uncanny object of his own hysterico-melodramatic dream. *He* is the one that he dreams up to love as something distinguishable from himself; it's he that is the monster he must not be, he that is this bellicose mass, in which race and femininity have been conflated in a way that makes their hysterical resurrection an impossible mode of cure. Dying to love—loving to death—the subject is aborted so that *It* might be born: a monster whom John can only render "as dead as a reptile ever gets" (53), and who therefore crawls out of the book's last sentence, with Juana in her grave and John fairly ruined, in order to mock the white male pretension of a lovingly pacific and self-respecting bond. The "nightmare" that Sharp sees in the reptile's eye (52) is in this sense the replicative reflection of the dream he's busy telling: a dream where love is the distorted repetition—the hysterico-somnambulistic return—of an insurmountable war.

But the novel can hardly leave bad enough alone. In the interest of an insatiable consistency, it also has to tell us how the monster "stunk" (52). It must cloud again the narrative air with the olfactory dimension to this dream, and it asks us, even, to dream along with it, in order to partake with John and Juana in a totemic feast of the odoriferous beast. That feast should close out the reptilian nightmare; immediately upon its completion, having smeared Juana's nipples with iguana and eaten it, John speaks his name for the first time, sings in a voice that doesn't "sound like a priest anymore," and likens this return of male prowess to the movement from blindness to a sight regained (55–57).

A masculine subject would thus seem to have been born; John now appears to have newly emerged, distinguishing himself from a breast-feeding object and slaying—devouring—the olfactory beast "within." Here it is,

then, at long last: the death of the creature that we must not be; let us indulge in the fantasy of consuming it, since in doing so it's "us" we devour:

> *Never mind how [the iguana] stunk. It was enough to turn your stomach. . . .*
> *[But] I held on and socked him in the pot. . . . For three seconds it was like I had*
> *dropped an electric fan in there, but then it stopped. I took the top off and fished him*
> *out. . . . Then I found out why it was that something had told me to put him in the*
> *pot alive, and not cook him dead, with his head cut off. . . . When he hit that scald-*
> *ing water he let go. He purged, and that meant he was clean inside as a whistle.*
> *(52–53)*

"Clean as a whistle," ready to be devoured, in order that a subject might
odorlessly emerge. Perhaps—but we have reason to doubt it. The text will assert in a moment as well that "Mexicans are the cleanest people on earth,"
that they decidedly "don't stink" (73), even though we know already that
Juana, at least, does smell, and that the conflation of race with femininity
makes the issue of where the odor comes from an undecidable affair.[40] The
monster must in this context simply be *decreed* no longer to reek; otherwise
one risks, in consuming it, repeating the olfactory belligerence that the oral
relation is meant here to cure. And despite its effort at deodorization, repeating this belligerence is exactly what the passage ends up doing. Immediately after calling attention to the lizard's anal evacuation, Sharp casually but
boastfully mentions that the therapeutic feast he's busy preparing puts off a
"smell" that's also "a stink" but that nonetheless "smell[s] right, like I knew
it" would (53). The purging at the anus has thus failed to perform the requisite purification. It seems, instead, to have put the smell "out," to have spread
it around as a cloud or shroud, in a manner so thorough that the therapeutic love-scene is defiled by it, the nas(an)al relation superimposed on the oral,
and the subject reborn from an anus that's here the only available organ of
expulsion. The literally unthinkable nature of the scenario is very precisely
its point: first I'm aborted from the animal's anus, and I then cook and devour that animal, calling it "breast," in order to try and deliver myself properly by way of an oral-nurturing bond. How can we be surprised at the results

of such a calamitous sequence? How can we be astonished if John, with Winston just killed and the cure apparently complete, "stumble[s] back to a bathroom" and retches (158–59), pouring out the subjective substance that the cure required him to take in, in much the same way that, in *The Postman*, the smell of Cora mingles with dinner to inspire in Frank an urge to vomit (6–7)? It's hard to imagine a more thoroughgoing conversion of oral nurturance into olfactory disaster.

That nurturance may, then, at least for a while, give John back his voice with "some touch of sweetness . . . that [it] had always lacked" (56); but it also begins by splitting that voice in a way that predicts a renewed vocal failure and the present repetition of unending self-rivalry. John first discovers his voice regained when he hears his "echo" come back to him from the arroyo (56). Later, while working in Hollywood, he turns a "B picture" into a feature film by adding a soundtrack in multiple harmony, composed of "five voices . . . all me" (101). And still later, the jubilant omnipotence of vocal recognition turns murderous when, after fleeing with Juana from the States to Guatemala, John hears himself singing over the radio but believes he's listening to someone else who's copied his vocal tricks (180–81). Far from guaranteeing a masculine singularity, voice here becomes the mark of division, alienation, death. John sounds "like" himself rather than merely being himself, enters into vocal rivalry with himself ("Well, he's heard me sing it" [181], he says of himself on the radio) rather than pacifically bonding with true, individuated others. Voice in this sense merely repeats the olfactory belligerence of the prehistoric relation; it spews out the identificatory stench of a suicidal-murderous and delirious compact. Need we recall, then, at this late date, that it's John's voice at the end of the book that leads to Juana's murder, just as in the novel's olfactory prehistory the rivalry between him and Winston is imagined also as a vocal affair?

We needn't, I think, except to reiterate: the end is the beginning, and the beginning is the end, and each is the site of an orificial conflation that renders time a hysterical collapse. John kills Juana with the voice that she gives him because that voice is secretly indistinguishable from the bellicose utterance that Winston bestows on him, even before the novel begins. Such an utterance, as we now know, is thoroughly and nas(an)ally soiled; it's "feminine" and malodorous, mimetically massed, and it belongs as much to Juana as to Winston. For to say that John "is" in some sense both of them is also to propose that *Juana is Winston*. The logic contracts upon us, one last time—implacable, hysterical, double. Sharp tries to help us dream our way out of it, but Cain keeps awakening us to the nightmare that there is, in truth, no way out, because the love object is indistinguishable from the loveless non-object of identification.

Cain tells us, for example, that there's a *"terror"* in Juana, and that terror is inseparable from "[t]rue beauty." He links that beauty to a scary collapse of spatiotemporal markers—and thus to the novel's narrative circularity—by arguing that "[t]he eternities and the infinities are in it, and [that] they strike at the soul, like death." And he recounts, lastly, how this terrible beauty lurks predatorily "below the surface," so that Juana is figured now not by the iguana but by the homocidogenic shark:

[A] black fin lifted out of the water. . . . It was at least thirty inches high, and it didn't zigzag, or cut a V in the water. . . . It just came up and stayed a few seconds. Then there was the swash of a big tail and it went down.

"Did you see it, lad?" [asked Conners, the sea-captain].

"God, it was an awful-looking thing. . . ."

"It cleared up for me what I've been trying to say to you. Sit here, now, and look. The water, the surf, the colors on the shore. You think they make the beauty of the tropical sea, aye, lad? They do not. 'Tis the knowledge of what lurks below the surface of it, that awful-looking thing . . . that carries death with every move that it makes. So it is, so it is with all beauty. So it is with Mexico. I hope you never forget it." (79)

So it is, and so be it. There's nothing to say about this, except perhaps to remember that the shark is already Winston, and that to conflate it with the Juana-iguana is to blur again the novel's attempted gestures of individuation. The original non-object of "homosexual" rivalry is now the object of heterosexual love. Winston is Juana—"Papa" (133, 134) is "Mother"

(147)—and this means that John's suicidal matricide is also and ever a patricidal suicide. From Winston in *Serenade* to Nirdlinger in *Double Indemnity* to Nick Papadakis in *The Postman Always Rings Twice*: the "father" in Cain must forever be killed, since the oedipal structure that his books erect is always in the state of imminent collapse, always a hysterical, anti-oedipal repetition of the bellicose and amorphous mass. Cain invokes the oedipal triangle only in order to wreck it.[41] There's never a thought of "exiting" that structure—never even the remotest possibility that Winston and Sharp might bury the hatchet and Sharp submit to peace and the Law—because Cain knows that the oedipal injunction requires one *to identify (peaceably) with the very person—the father—with whom one is prohibited from (rivalrously) identifying*. Identify without identifying, murder without killing: this is what the oedipal resolution demands.[42]

The Cainian corpus knows too well the deadly seriousness of such an impasse. It knows, for one thing, that what's meant to transform a homosexual-rivalrous paternal identification into a pacifically oedipalizing one is love itself—love of the father, fear of loss of love.[43] It knows that to posit the existence of such love is merely to repeat, within the oedipal structure, the eroto-mimetic unbondedness that the structure is meant to overcome. Cain therefore refuses, again and again, to offer a loving resolution to Oedipus, to propose as solution to the identificatory problem an Erotic impulse that is from the start confounded and bloodied with identification. "[I]n the blindness of love," Freud finally concedes, "remorselessness is carried to the pitch of crime."[44] *Serenade* would have us add the refrain: that love is me, and it is you, for it's the blinding olfactory mime that binds us in ties of mutual murder. There is here no pacifying or lovemaking "triangle," no oedipal-socializing structure at all, if by that we mean one that pretends to separation along the twin axes of love and identification. As the entire novel has by now made clear, Sharp cannot just "desire" Juana and "identify (peaceably) with" Winston, but must identify with and desire both—which means, of course, at least in this context, that he loves them to death and dies into love, from an enveloped-enveloping internality that fails to distinguish between its "objects," as well as to separate them out from the subject. Winston is the shark is Juana is John. The father is the mother is the daughter is the son. Sharp, in short, is merely (an) "It"—gendered-ungendered, pre-(pre)oedipal—since despite the novel's official pronouncements, the primal non-bond of olfactory love knows not even a sexual differentiation, but only an unending affective ambivalence: a group amassment or narcissistic throng, with no voice and no vision, no self or other, which abolishes all of its members in the olfactory rage of an indistinct mire that only the man will then try to call "feminine."

3   The Apocalypse of Male Vision

Vomit in William Faulkner's *Sanctuary*

"A power that disrupts the most well-ordered entrails"

To read William Faulkner's *Sanctuary* (1931) is to risk going crazy: this, at least, is what we must surmise from the testimony of the novel's early reviewers. Henry Seidel Canby insists that the novel leads to "the end of all sanity in fiction."[1] *Sanctuary*, says another reviewer, threatens because it gives "flesh" "to . . . creatures almost too sick or too depraved to be called human" at all.[2] Granville Hicks calls Faulkner's characters "twisted shapes in the . . . wreckage of a mad world," and goes on to suggest that the demented content of his novels has as its corollary a deranged form that prevents them from achieving tragic status.[3] And A. C. Ward condemns the book for going, in essence, "too far," claiming that "there must be limits of sanity beyond which literary experimentation can . . . produce only pathological documents with no significance as works of art."[4]

There is however a strange division within this apparent unanimity. On one hand, these critics suggest that the danger of *Sanctuary* lies in the author's veering away from subjective expression toward a dementedly ocular objectivity. Hicks, for example, locates the threat in Faulkner's peculiarly visual "detachment"—the "strangely focused powers of observation" which we are forced to share (124). And Canby compares Faulkner's method to both cinematic vision and portraiture, while speaking derisively of "the dry light of complete objectivity" in which the author "weighs his subjects" (108).[5] On the other hand, however, and despite the critical antagonism that this visual detachment evokes, it's also the case that the objects of *Sanctuary* are not for these critics objective enough. The world of the novel displays nothing more than "the exacerbated sensibilities of the author";[6] it remains the excessively subjective expression of a "mind" that's been confidently labeled "disordered,"[7] even as it appears to give us all "object" and no "mind" at all. *Sanctuary*'s apparent visual disinterest is thus for these critics a peculiar form of interest. Faulkner "is cruel with a cool and interested cruelty," as Canby goes on to put it; "he hates his Mississippi and his Memphis and all their works . . . with a hatred that is neither passionate nor the result of thwarting, but calm, reasoned, and complete" (108). A hatred simultaneously dispassionate and total, a cruelty that's cool yet still absolute: Faulkner doesn't manage to repudiate his objects except insofar as he's invested himself in them, and this suggests that his optical dispassion is meant to keep him on the outskirts of a world in which he will turn out to be.

Or perhaps we should say that the world is in *him*. I want, at any rate, to argue here that this is what the critics intuit in their collective uncertainty about the location of the novel's derangement. If Faulkner seems too much "in" and "out" of a world that he treats with ocular detestation—if the novel's madness appears to reside both in an excessively visual objectivity and in a surfeit of subjectivity—this is perhaps because *Sanctuary* is concerned to produce this confusion. My claim is that it does so, moreover, by staging a drama of failed differentiation by which the visible world originates in an act of expulsion that founds a self by rejecting the "thing" that the self will call "object." Such a hypothesis needs of course to be elaborated textually. I shall elaborate it, in what follows, by paying attention to the novel's effort formally to enact this failed differentiation, and to the consequences of that failure for questions of gender and sexuality. One of my basic contentions is that these formal gestures are a central part of what makes *Sanctuary* Faulkner's "crime novel." They entail an apparently detached objectivity that has abandoned the modernist marks of subjective exploration (stream-of-consciousness, internal monologue, the syntactical complexities of a Faulknerian style), while nonetheless smearing the objective "eye" with an unlocalizable subjectivity. Such a strategy links *Sanctuary* to Cain's *Serenade* and Hammett's *The Glass Key*, in that it endows the novel with a formal "simplicity" that is at once complexly expressive and the very substance of thematic meditation.[8]

But before developing this reading in detail, I want to clarify my large hypothesis by turning once more to Freud. His late essay "Negation" (1925) offers a striking theoretical description of the drama that *Sanctuary* textually enacts. It does so most fully in a passage that begins by ruminating on the faculty of judgment—a passage which suggests that the judging "function . . . affirms or disaffirms the possession by a thing of a particular attribute," and then continues as follows:

> *The attribute to be decided about may originally have been good or bad, useful or harmful. Expressed in the language of the oldest—the oral—instinctual impulses, the judgement is: "I should like to eat this," or "I should like to spit it out." . . . That is to say: "It [the object] shall be inside me" or "it shall be outside me." As I have shown elsewhere, the original pleasure-ego wants to introject into itself everything that is good and to eject from itself everything that is bad. What is bad, what is alien to the ego and what is external are, to begin with, identical.*[9]

"What is bad," "what is external," "what is alien": the world, on this model, emerges from the start as nothing less than an inedibly bad object. Precisely inasmuch as the object *exists*, it has been primordially rejected as bad; exactly insofar as there's something "out there," I have ejected an indigestible portion that becomes for me, by the fact of its ejection, an external object of primordial distaste. Freud is therefore not merely describing the confrontation of a pre-formed ego with an object-world that precedes it. Rather, this is a description of the process by which a subject and its world *are created in an act of oral destructiveness*. The world *begins*—it begins by being in me—and it ends up by spilling out onto the floor; it can be "made up" in regurgitative fantasy only because it's already "inside," can be repudiated only on condition that I once chewed it up in the form of a thing that becomes at once "not-me" and "not-good" from the moment I open my mouth to spit it out. "Bad" is accordingly a word I apply to the object of an alien and repulsed internality. That object is bad *because* it was (in) me. It's bad because its prehensile viscosity figures my muculent presence in an object I create by spitting both out and up—and because, moreover, it continues to do so even after the world thus invented has hardened to a state of apparent objectal solidity.

But let us be perfectly clear about this. If the object is bad for having once been "inside," it's nonetheless true that, even when in me, that object had never quite managed to *be* me. The vomited thing begins by adhering to the gullet of a primally anonymous devouring. It starts by sticking in the throat of a no one (not-yet-a-subject). It deprives that no one of a uniform amassment by refusing resolutely to go all the way down, and this means that there is in me, from before the beginning, something I cannot and must not call "self": something that's in fact much *more* than myself, and that by the excess of its unintegrated tenacity signifies the paradox of an originary loss. The primal expulsion that founds "me" and "it" takes place in the orifice of a prior deprivation. Before there's an object or a subject to lose it, there's something within that robs me of being; before I've even egoically emerged, "I" have already been lost to myself by virtue of the (no)thing that begins by being in me and causes me literally to throw "myself" up, in order to heal a primordial breach in the proto-narcissistic and pre-egoic unit.

Of course, Freud does not—and cannot—say this. For him there can be no loss without a subject, nothing to lose except an object that's known by a subject already to *be* an object. For him the way to secure a real world that's more than a vomitory projection of "self" is to forget the oral origin of that world and decree it always already to have been there in order that a subject might lose and then find it. When he goes on to suggest, therefore, that "a precondition for . . . reality-testing is that objects shall have been lost which once brought real satisfaction" (216), we must use the passage on orality against him to say that the drama of dissatisfied desire is itself here a kind of reaction formation in which a bad object is happily vomited, feared, and even lost, in order that there might at least be an object rather than the threat of a nameless nothing that the objectless object is when it's in me. Vomit spews forth—the object is born bad—in an effort to fill out the deprivation that I am. The subject must found itself in oral expulsion if it's to be saved from the faceless cavity that threatens quite literally to gnaw out its insides. To lose or fear the thrown-up thing—to spit up an object *so that* I might lose it—is at least to pretend that there's something out there that is separate enough to be found or mastered.[10] I therefore meet the negation that's in me with the counter-negation of a primal repudiation: a gustatory hate that be-tokens the subject's first affective relation to the "object";[11] a regurgitative loathing that hallucinates a world whose objectal solidity is forever disrupted by my bespattered presence in it, and whose very condition is a certain self-loss that cannot be mourned, cannot be taken in, without introducing this black hole in being back into the very guts of a subject and opening me to be swallowed once more by an omnidirectional and internalized mouth.[12]

And Faulkner? What of *Sanctuary*'s "shrewdly plotting mad[man],"[13] the author with the frankly disordered mind? How does the oral origin of the object pertain to a book that would drive us insane by having us *look* too hard at a world that it also appears to despise? Let us defer again to the judgment or taste of an early reviewer. The author of *Sanctuary* "writes . . . with a power *that disrupts the most well-ordered entrails*," says R. E. Sherwood.[14] Why? Not because of what the book makes us see so much as because it won't let us quite see it. Despite its apparently ocular objectivity, despite what we'll discover is an unusually intense thematic interest in questions of vision, voyeurism, and narcissistic gazing, I want to argue that what looks here like "looking" turns out to be "eating," and that what gets eaten is precisely the (no)thing that can't be assimilated without reintrojecting the negated negation that will come now completely to devour me. Faulkner confronts us with this vomit-in-the-world by literally spitting it up in our eyes. He pretends to maintain a distance from the object that would keep it both solid and visibly apprehensible. But he then exposes the precariousness of that distance by disintegrating the object, decomposing it, rendering it again the barfed out blob that's the infirm "ground" of all objectality—and asking us nonetheless to eat it with our eyes in a way that disrupts the most well-ordered entrails and causes us to throw it right up again.

Sanctuary's remarkably persistent concern with intermediate states of being (mud, phlegm, blood); its focus on bodies that tend to a certain decompositional viscosity; its interest in a sluggishness of human intentions that dissolves the will, and consciousness itself, into the torpor of semiliquidity; and its desire to instigate projects of visual mastery only to dramatize a breakdown of vision so severe that it doesn't even show us the corn-cob rape that is the book's central "event"[15]—these are all strategies, as we shall see, for making visible the unrepresentable and invisible stain that *is* our overpresence in the things we try to see and master. Vision in this way becomes a catastrophe, the apocalyptic encounter with an oral expulsiveness. Faulkner turns it into a sense for imbibing that part of the self which *Sanctuary* shows to be optically inassimilable.

It remains now only to note, before turning to the novel itself, that this problematic of vision and orality is bound inextricably to gender and sexuality—to questions, indeed, of a "maternal relation." What, after all, is this (no)thing I spit up if not the fantasy of maleficent motherhood? Isn't the mother one's very first "object," the thing the infant believes it creates in an effort to externalize the badness within? The mother "is" the unmournable object, the one who cannot be taken back in; with the help of a culture that perpetuates the ego's originally accidental confusion between badness and a maternal maleficence, she becomes the primal and perhaps permanent representative of a deprivation that—should I assimilate it—would then be (in) me, and from there will consume me in an objectless despair. The entire point of throwing "her" up is in fact to attach that devouring propensity to a discernibly external object: "real," masterable, and *visible*. For no sooner does Freud repress the implications of an originary and oral destructiveness than the representational-visual vocabulary of psychoanalysis gets dramatically mobilized: "It is now . . . a question . . . of whether something which is in the ego *as a presentation* [i.e., a mental image] can be rediscovered in perception"; "all *presentations* originate from perceptions and are repetitions of them"; "[t]he antithesis between subjective and objective [arises from the mind's capacity to reproduce a perceived thing] *as a presentation*" (237; my emphases). And so on: if an object can now be lost and then found, it's because it has become objectal enough to be seen, psychically represented, recognized and grasped in the visual field.

Freud insists that the goal of this search is to recover a good (maternal) object of edible and assimilable—of *lovable*—proportions. Not only does he fail to tell us, however, how an object born bad can ever turn good, but by bringing this process into view through vision—by tying the search for the good and the real to a sense that requires a distance from its object—he makes our visual movement toward the world a perfected repetition of an oral hatred that seeks in vain to establish a space between the self and the mother it throws up. The repression of vomit is the triumph of vision in the name of a matricidal misogyny. As long as the fantasy of vomit persists, the distance from the object required for me to hate *it* (rather, say, than "us") remains in a state of imminent collapse. The vomited thing always threatens to turn on me, to become once more the (no)thing that was (in) me and that still bears the masticated marks of that encounter. It's only with the supremacy of vision installed that hatred can become *dispassionate*, gaining for itself a separable object in which we remain unimplicated, and rendering sight its instrument of preference for mastering a world that threatens to invade us with the (no)thing that our culture conflates with the mother on whom we have first expelled it.[16]

If, then—as I will suggest—the world of *Sanctuary* is a maternal "object" that's thrown up from the breach of primal deprivation, Faulkner's evident hatred of that world is on one hand inseparable from a virulent misogyny. The ocular cruelty that the reviewers identify repeats and perfects an oral repudiation that founds the world in matricidal hatred, and hence the novel's extraordinary lack of sympathy for a character such as Temple. At the same time, however, by confronting vision with the regurgitated thing that is our subjective overpresence in the world, *Sanctuary* prevents us from achieving the distance required for a properly passionless hatred of the object it wants to call "mother." When one reviewer suggests that the novel threatens not only madness but "sterility" and a dephallicizing "atrophy";[17] when the reviewers as a group can't even decide if the book sadistically encourages us to rape or identifies us masochistically with the rape victim,[18] we need to take seriously these insights and confusions by insisting that vomit is the ruin of masculinity that collapses a reader it imagines as male into the maternal object-to-be-mastered. The "I" cannot rape here without being raped—can hate no "object" without hating itself—since "I" is the streaming "extensive identity"[19] of a vomitory and "maternal" being-in-the-world. Nothing can happen in the space of this world that doesn't precisely implicate "me." No vistas open, no objects emerge, except in a mucilaginous yawning that gobbles me up in the stickiness of a passion that spits me disgustedly out again. The novel in this way seeks to disperse us in the visually unmasterable viscosity of an object that is none other than "ourselves," but that the book will demand we consume in a ruinously masculine and ocular ingestion.

A final hypothesis, then, before our disgorgement: *Sanctuary* drives male readers to distraction by making them envision the vomitory "mother" that it also forces them to eat—to like—and therefore, to be.

Spitting Up the Spaces Between

I shall return in the following section to *Sanctuary*'s treatment of gender and sexuality. In order to do so most fruitfully, however, it's important to start by offering an account of the narrative mode I've been describing. This mode is both objectively realist and non-realist in its operation. Its spatiotemporal unfolding, to begin with, may give the illusion of realistic integrity, but it tends at the same time toward forms of collapse that enact the logic of oral expulsion and thereby produce the apocalypse of vision to which I have alluded.

Take for example the novel's opening passage:

From beyond the screen of bushes which surrounded the spring, Popeye watched the man drinking. A faint path led from the road to the spring. Popeye watched the man . . . emerge from the path and kneel to drink from the spring.

The spring . . . was surrounded by a thick growth of cane and brier, of cypress and gum in which broken sunlight lay sourceless. Somewhere, hidden and secret yet nearby, a bird sang three notes and ceased.

In the spring the drinking man leaned his face to the broken and myriad reflection of his own drinking. When he rose up he saw among them the shattered reflection of Popeye's straw hat, though he had heard no sound. . . .

Behind him the bird sang again, three bars in monotonous repetition: a sound meaningless and profound out of a suspirant and peaceful following silence which seemed to isolate the spot.[20]

The passage could be said to condense the features of *Sanctuary*'s narrative method, and we shall return to it more than once in the analysis that follows. For now what's crucial is to note the *blurriness* of the image it offers. No sooner are we given access to the book's world than it seems to thicken and break down; no sooner does the action come into focus than its precise location, in both space and time, becomes a matter of such radical uncertainty that it's almost impossible to apprehend it. *When* does this opening "begin," for example? Is its first moment the one described in an initial sentence that has Popeye "watching" as "the man" (Horace) drinks from the spring? Or is it rather the instant to which the third sentence leads us—an instant that by the logic of chronology must clearly be *prior* to the "initial" point, since in it Horace "emerge[s] from the path and kneel[s]" *in preparation* to drink? Such questions insist—they clamor for answer—only to resist all gesture of reply. It cannot suffice to choose one moment and grant it a definitive chronological priority. For the first effect of this inversion is to hold the past "within"

the present in a manner expressive of a time so distressed as to wreck the ordered heterogeneity of flow while also conserving its traces. Horace emerges
from the path to drink water *while he is already drinking from the spring*. The
instant with which the novel begins is very precisely a doubly exposed one,[21]
which spreads out the present in one profuse image that captures the actions
belonging to two. The novel in this way implicates sight in a present simultaneously captured and missed. It catches our ocular movement up in a time
that's on one hand compressed, accelerated in the virtual concurrency of its
images, and on the other, distended, protracted, elongated into a practically
undifferentiated and eternally monotonous "now."

Such a procedure has implications for the treatment of space as well. An
object that's liquidated by the time I'm describing can neither quite remain
"right there" nor disappear into nowhere, as it carries with it the traces of its
past locations as much as its past points of time. It can't, therefore, be dis-
closed where it "is" without bleeding back to the places it's been and dissolving the logic of fixed place in time. Horace is both at the edge of the
spring and out on the path that approaches it. He is in the one spot as much
as the other—is "at the same time" in two different places—as the narrative
prevents him from being in either by stretching him rather between those
points. Space—like time—is both doubled and abolished. Distance collapses
as places proliferate in the oxymoronic expanse of an "image" that is "in itself" the conflation of two. The visual object becomes here the casualty of a
method that seeks to register and destroy it, as the novel both captures the
visualized thing in images of tantalizing objective clarity and handles those
images, spatiotemporally, in a way that empties the visible into the spaceless
space and timeless time in between the points actually seen.

There results an intensely disquieting experience in which the promise
of escaping such vision by attributing it to a (deranged) character oscillates
with the panic of aporia to short-circuit even the most basic forms of sense-
making. We might, for example, be tempted to ascribe this first perception to
Popeye; he's after all the one who "watches" in the scene at hand, and he is
perhaps disturbed enough to perceive the world in this way. But the novel

systematically prevents us from making this attribution with certainty. Most significantly, in the opening scene, this move is thwarted by the textual registration of the bird's song, which repeats auditorily the spatiotemporal distortion of the novel's first image. The notes of that song proceed in a "monotonous repetition," appearing to be sequentially distinct while threatening the very principle of sequence. They issue from a place at once "nearby" and "hidden": a place, in other words, that's marked and effaced by the resonance of a sound that collapses location by occluding the specific site of its issue while expanding to fill all available space. If we're to limit the lunacy to Popeye, then, we must attribute this perception to him—and nothing in the passage allows us to do so. He's nowhere shown to be listening to the song and isn't, anyway, the type to hear it in terms like "meaningless and profound." If the sound belongs to any character—and not to the narrative's "objective" perspective—that figure would surely have to be Horace, who does meditate on profundities and is shown to be listening.[22] But this confronts us with a shared derangement that solves exactly nothing. We're forced now to superimpose two options if we're to entertain either, to locate distortion both(-and-neither) in Popeye's perspective and(-nor) in that of Horace. The interpretive act of choosing between options collapses into the very same process of "seeing" the unseeable space-in-between that it's meant to escape by explaining. And what that space both is and contains—what it in fact envelops by being—turns out to be the vomitory (no)thing that must be expelled from the perceiving subject and then fended off in the object if a self and its world are ever to meet in the visual field at all.

Here is a first piece of evidence for this claim:

Popeye . . . squatted in his tight black suit . . . twisting and pinching cigarettes in his little, doll-like hands, spitting into the spring. His skin had a dead, dark pallor. His nose was faintly aquiline, and he had no chin at all. His face just went away, like the face of a wax doll set too near a hot fire and forgotten. (5; my emphasis)

The spit with which Popeye here spoils the spring is, I suggest, the substance of disturbance, the stuff that disintegrates vision and object and makes it impossible to distinguish between them. It signals the enactment, within this first scene, of a drama that repeats and textually amplifies the modal derangement I've been describing. And it does so by permeating the novel's "content" with the formal effects of an optical besmirchment that *Sanctuary* now explicitly links to a confrontation with oral expulsiveness.

For let us make no mistake: the spring that Popeye here salivates into is the same one from which we have seen Horace drink. It's also—and more crucially—the spit-stained *mirror* upon whose surface the latter *sees and fails to see* himself reflected. In "lean[ing]" to drink he first discovers "the broken and myriad reflection of his . . . drinking," only to find upon rising up that this splintered and alien image of "self" has itself been replaced by the "shattered reflection of Popeye's straw hat" (4). Vision is thus here a self-encounter that fails at the same time to find the self. *Sanctuary* starts with a specular scene—begins with a moment of narcissistic gazing—that wrecks the objectivizing function of vision by putting the "subject" in the externally visible place where the object should be. It proceeds to expose a self-alienation at the heart of psychic identity, supplanting the reflected "ego" with an other (Popeye) in order to show that selfhood is grounded in visual identifications that can't but take me away from myself. But beyond both of these—and this is what's central—the novel insists that this specular drama cannot even enable the subject to find a coherence-in-self-alienation. For when the alien image "is" Horace it's already torn into bits and pieces ("broken reflection"). And what comes then to take its place is less a human figure at all than an anti-figural dispersion of matter ("hat") that's triply incapable of reflecting back to him even the most fleeting sense of self-sufficiency.

The "self" that one sees when one looks at the world, then—it's *not*-self, *not*-human—above all, *not-whole*. "I" can discover it only in pieces—only in liquid shards of refraction—and only in order to lose it once more in the slivered ruins of a fluid objectality. The subject who sees "is" the thing that it sees, but just inasmuch as the optical process is caught in the static turbulence of a mirror that blends and renders not subject and object but rather a kind of liminal stuff, dispersed and suspended in a liquid that joins as it tears them—together—apart.[23]

But the point here is not just that Popeye's expulsion causes this ocular ruin. It's also that he *embodies* such spit, that he *is* vomit, and that he is it in and as the self's own anti-reflection. His face is "like the face of a wax doll set too near a hot fire and forgotten" (5). "He smells . . . like that black stuff that ran out of Bovary's mouth and down . . . her bridal veil" (7). He is, in short, *before* he spits up, a kind of expulsion-in-disintegration,[24] which the novel insists is no less than "Horace" by capturing it in the latter's liquid and broken self-reflections. Emma Bovary's oral ejection; the face that melts into a featureless mass; the mirror reflection of splintering not-me, of self as dispersed and liquid non-matter: these are expressions, though different in kind, of subjectivity as alien matter, whose ultimate logic is to break wholly down and reveal itself as the hole-in-being that the subject projects in defense against the threat of internal consumption. What Popeye makes Horace see in this sense is both the muculescence that he "is" and the nothing that such stuff only stands in for. He makes him confront the spaces *between* these liquidly shattered pieces of "me," and thus requires him optically to assimilate the tear or interior rent in being, whose originally nameless recognition prompts a first projection of vomit as world.

It's therefore useless to talk anymore of a narrative mode that's distinct from its content. The book is about an ocular ruin that's simultaneously performed by its mode, in a way that mixes us up in its world no less than it does Horace. Placed, for example, in Popeye's mad mind by the opening I've described, we're forced to look quite helplessly on as that place becomes a reflection of "self" as shattered expectoration; asked then to identify optically with Horace, we not only have to confront that spit as an incoherent self-image, but are also haunted by the memory of a moment when Horace was himself no more than the blurry blot of an "object" lost in the space-in-between that he is.

There is indeed here *no one* to "see" through who doesn't turn into a vomitory object, no chance (conversely) of seeing through eyes that don't encounter the world vomitorily. Temple's face is said to be "putty" (59) and thereby equated with the (no)thing of Popeye's. Snopes's face looks "like a pie took out of the oven too soon" (210). The face of the woman who lets Ruby board with her is described as no less than a kind of "collapse" (201), and Ruby is identified by way of her name with the stains of pink and dripping shrimp that Horace insensibly feels himself to die into and become (17). The "negro murderer's" hand is a "blob" (134). Temple's "insides move in small trickling clots" (90), which then become linked to her outward appearance as her hair is called "clots" and "a curled spill of red" (56, 136, 36). Miss Reba's body is a "billowy" amorphousness (143); the faces of travelers are smeared into "stain" (168); and Ruby's child is a slimy little mass, "slick with faint moisture, its hair a damp whisper," and its liquid eyes the color of "weak milk" (116, 160).

Examples like these cannot—again—be made to say quite the same thing. What links them is their dementing insistence on making us see the human being, not in its hard or well-sculpted outline, but as a kind of incontinence of matter, which effaces its form in the act of devolving from solid into imperfect states, and which far from staying visually "in place," seeps out from under every attempt optically—imagistically—to fix it. Vomit becomes here a general condition that is the aberrant agony of matter. The human figure is haunted by its material and a-figural dissipation, so that to see through any such figure is also to regard oneself—to see the site from which one sees—transformed into one stage or other of matter collapsing into (no)thing. At the extreme, and just as with Popeye, such matter resolves itself into a breach or anti-material *hole*. Red's dead head has "a small blue hole" in it (249). Temple's eyes are "empty as two holes," "with the blank rigidity of a statue's eyes" (69, 238). Her mouth opens "round . . . like a small empty cave" and is "gaped and ugly like that of a dying fish" (138, 238). The woman whom the "negro murderer" kills is visually reduced to the hole in her throat that spurts a "bloody regurgitation" (114). Sleeping travelers are "sprawled . . . open-mouthed, their throats turned . . . upward as though waiting the stroke of knives" (168). Miss Reba's mouth is a yawning cavity that gapes and chokes at every mention (157), and even her dogs are said to have mouths that "gape . . . pinkly upon needle-like teeth" (146). It's pointless to extend the catalogue further. The list already tells us that, "beneath" the vomitory stuff in which we're forced to find ourselves, there opens a hole or space-between being that the novel repeatedly thinks of as mouth, as if to insist that the thing within is a gnawing deprivation which is fantasized orally, and which the self projects as object in order at least to be spared self-consumption.

The vomitory object is at bottom this exteriorization of an internal orifice. It appears here equally as regurgitating wound and in the form of devouring hole, because it bears the trace of a state in which I am both wounded and wounding—both the faceless interior cavity and the object of oral consumption—and in which to consume is therefore to cause a kind of internal bleeding or drain that spits my lifeblood out into the limitless void that opens within. The point of throwing up such a "thing" is to render objectal and practically assailable a devouring propensity that otherwise remains so bound up with "self" as to make it unmasterable. The fullest measure of *Sanctuary*'s power resides perhaps just here: it requires us to see this (no)thing, not as an alien hostility out there, but as the self-consuming passion by which "I" *am* the unlovable "object," forcing on us a being-as-nothing that makes us again the agentless agent of an unlocalized and bewildering violence.[25]

We already know that this is not what vision is meant to achieve. It should surmount the condition in question by sustaining a requisite distance between "myself" and the thing I spit up. It's meant to *perfect* an oral hatred that fails to keep me out of the object, and so to let me master a world that continues to threaten to impinge upon consciousness but now can appear to do so from without. We might even say that the "badness" of the world is the psychic rationale for the subject's drive toward that world's affectless visual mastery. If the object seeks to invade and devour me, do I not need, then, to repel and subdue it? If the world is "bad" by virtue of being the externalization of my internal mouth, must I not sublimate a failed oral hatred into a kind of optical triumph that lets me deny my own implication in the destructiveness of an object I can then keep at bay?

Sanctuary insists on this project's failure by linking the eye to a mouth that it merely repeats in deranged reciprocity:

Often in the night [Temple] would wake to smell tobacco and to see the single ruby eye where Popeye's mouth would be. *(225)*

She leaned beside the door . . . then . . . came to the woman, her face small and pale, her eyes like holes burned with a cigar. *(92)*

[Temple's] head was tousled, her face puffed, two spots of rouge on her cheekbones and her mouth painted into a savage cupid's bow. *(214; all emphases mine)*

The mouth becomes here a burning "eye" that returns to sear an oral hole in the place where the visual organ should be. It turns—equally—into a lethal weapon that requires the precision and distance of sight ("bow") but is both wielded from the site of blindness and takes for its target the ocular orbs ("cupid" is blind, and shoots out the eyes). Such a debasement by way of equation is exactly the terrifying point of these moments. *Sanctuary* doesn't want merely to say that the mouth "destroys" or "spoils" the eyes, but also that it *is* an eye—that it's an agent of (blinded) vision—and that it is this only in the name of ruining sight by shooting or burning the eyes into oral-ocular holes. Vision fails to surmount the oral because it finds itself in the world, in and as a mouth that "sees" in order to wreck the eye that it is. Far from being an organ of distance that would let me stay out of the object and master it, the eye becomes lost in an oral proximity of which it is both subject and object.[26]

Popeye's eyes of "soft black rubber" (4) represent an alternate image for this process. If they look like "knobs" that would "give to the touch and then recover with the whorled smudge of the thumb on them" (6), this is because the identity of the seer is here "in" the object as much as in the eye, and the mark of the other has always already imprinted itself on an ocular organ that's thereby degraded to a vomitory consistency somewhere between a liq-

THE APOCALYPSE OF MALE VISION

uid and solid. Nothing—finally—is more striking in this regard, and nothing more frightening either, than the blinded figure of the aged man that the novel labels "Pap." His eyes are simultaneously holes and filled with a vomitory stuff that makes them look like "clots of phlegm"; his name refers to a food that gives the impression of prior mastication, and so suggests that he is himself an expression of this ocular vomit; and the novel has him—irresistibly, inexorably—*consume the very stuff that he is and that's already spit into his eyes*, since it makes him a creature "whom the world can reach only through [the oral] sense," even as it suggests he can't eat unless the disparate things on his plate are chopped and mixed and drenched with sorghum in a way that makes what he takes in a vomitory mush or pap (12).

Eye as pap, then, "Pap" as person—and "person" itself as nothing more than an oral orifice that blindly ingests the eye-mouth-pap that it already is. This is the nightmare that *Sanctuary* enacts as much in the mode of its representation as in its thematic content. Pap is in fact a perfect figure for the novel's implied or ideal reader, whose "eye" the narrative mode solicits only in order to spit up into it, and whom it lets neither in nor out except in oral-ocular consumption of self in the mode of (no)thing. Words like "spluttered" (55), "whorled" (3, 6), "clotted" (56, 316), "guttering" (55), and "smutty" (121); the "viscid smears" of heaven-tree blooms that lie on the sidewalk outside the jail (135); the inexplicable "smudge" that Popeye leaves, as a child, in a wastepaper basket (304); and the "loblollies" that Horace and Narcissa make in the "canal of [mud]" of their childhood (122)—these, too, are no more "motifs" than narrational attempts to render visible a visually obscene opacity of matter, which is the optical-oral black hole of a book that deploys a self-canceling mode in order to make us consume that breach.

Let us sum up by counting the ways in which *Sanctuary* does this: the narrative eye is subjective-objective; the world that it sees is real-but-unreal; every moment is both now and then, and place is always here-over-there; the object is stickily present-but-absent, me-not-me, being-nothing; the novel's content takes place in a mode that ruins the visual access to content; and derangement—lastly—is everywhere-nowhere, a generalization of disturbed particularity that's indistinguishable from a narrative vision which at least pretends to objective apprehension.[27] What could a reader possibly "take away" from such an implosive encounter? How can anything like a meaning survive a mode that requires each element to reabsorb its determinate negation, failing even to respect the distinction between seer and seen, subject and object, reader and the object of readerly attention?

It cannot, of course—and does not—survive. Meaning is, like everything else here, sucked back swirling into the field of its internal self-consumption. It's made at every specific moment to include an opposite term that destroys it, and then force-fed to the reader in the form of a significatory (no)thing, "meaningless *and* profound" (4), which "roar[s] silently out of a peaceful void" that it thereby opens up in our insides (296). Any attempt at a reading that's more thematically oriented than the one so far offered will have to confront this tendency toward oxymoronical (anti-)significance. It will have to confront the novel's tendency to say things that it also does not say, to equate thematic elements that it also poses in opposition. It will have to confront a book in which there is no sense but (non)sense, and in which all moral pronouncements or judgments are swallowed up by this meaningless meaning in order to keep us from claiming a goodness that escapes implication in a bad devouring. And this reading will have to confront the effects of these meaningful-moral collapses on the novel's treatment of gender and sexuality. The female other or object-to-be-mastered will turn out ceaselessly to flow back into the masculine subject-to-be-loved, as any effort to spit out the bad is blocked by an introjection of self in the mode of the thing it expels.

I want in a moment to develop such a thematic reading of *Sanctuary*. For now it's enough to indicate that, if Pap is a figure for the ideal reader implied by such a process, the bird whose singing punctuates the opening stands perhaps for the only muse that this (anti-)aesthetics of self-consumption can manage to invoke: a vomitory muse, for a vomitory novel, spitting the meaningless profundity that we are up into our ears—our eyes—our mouths.[28]

"Nature is 'she' and Progress is 'he'"

And yet the novel at least attempts to contain the threat it invokes—attempts, that is, to displace it through a thematics of gender and sexuality. There are two components to this containment. On one hand, the novel tries to project the (no)thing outward and label it feminine. On the other hand, this movement requires that vision turn out to work and to be masculine; though what it finds in the world may be (no)thing, at least that thing is not for the moment a reflection of the male self, but is instead a feminine object that can in theory be mastered. I argue later that *Sanctuary* ultimately subverts the misogyny of these gestures. For the moment what's crucial is that we grasp that the defenses I've described are first performed (for us) by Horace, who retains a centrality at the level of theme that the novel modally denies to all characters.[29]

For the (no)thing that Popeye makes Horace take in is almost immediately disavowed in the name of a certain image of woman. Horace sits in the very next scene with the men at the bootlegger's house, speaking of his wife and his reasons for leaving her in terms that both repeat and refigure the terms we've already encountered. "[I]t wasn't Little Belle that set me off. . . . It was a rag with rouge on it," he says. "[T]here it was, stuffed behind the mirror: a handkerchief where [Belle] had wiped off the surplus paint when she dressed" (15). Or again, in a passage to which I've already alluded:

[I left my wife because] she ate shrimp. . . . And I still don't like to smell shrimp. But I wouldn't mind the carrying it home so much. I could stand that. It's because the package drips. All the way home it drips and drips, until after a while I follow myself to the station and stand aside and watch Horace Benbow take that box off the train and start home with it . . . thinking Here lies Horace Benbow in a fading series of small stinking spots on a Mississippi sidewalk. (17)

The incontinence of matter that the mode renders general is here thematically constrained, as it were, by a gesture that re-presents the stain as an exterior threat to man. The rag stained red by his wife's "surplus paint," the stinking series of small pink spots that portend and consummate masculine death: both quite clearly figure for Horace the threat of an explicitly sexualized femininity. They rewrite vomit as a substance whose color makes it the trigger of male revulsion, precisely inasmuch as that color alludes to the menstrual fluid expelled by the woman as legible mark of her sexual maturity. Vomit is in this way displaced to an orifice belonging only to the other. Horace "knows" he isn't the stain—knows he is not the (no)thing that Popeye first reflected back to him—because he has already learned that this stain refers to a female emission. It's in the name of exactly this "knowledge" that he flees from his wife in the first place. The fact that he *does* flee indicates, however, the fragility of his defenses. Knowledge of woman risks always becoming an epistemologico-sexual calamity, in ways made clear by another account of the crisis that makes Horace leave his wife.

Here is the account I have in mind:

From my window I could see the grape arbor, and in the winter I could see the hammock too. But in the winter it was just the hammock. That's why we know nature is a she; because of that conspiracy between female flesh and female season. So each spring I could watch the reaffirmation of the old ferment hiding the hammock; the green-snared promise of unease. What blossoms grapes have, that is. It's not much: a wild and waxlike bleeding less of bloom than leaf, hiding and hiding the hammock, until along in late May [Little Belle's] voice would be like the murmur of the wild grape itself. (13)

This "waxlike bleeding less of bloom than leaf" returns us to the wax face of Popeye that Horace encounters as "self," and so makes visible the defensive transformation of vomit into feminine fluid. More crucial for our present purpose is the character of this female "nature," however. The "conspiracy" between femininity and season turns out to be linked to the cosmetic artifice that's contained in the reference to rouge we've examined, since the "feminine" bleeding this passage calls nature is a kind of rampant and fecund unfolding that produces a native space of deception—of overtly feminine dissimulation—at the very core of the natural world. Nature is "she" because nature *conceals*, "hiding and hiding the hammock" from view; it conspires with the woman by abetting her purportedly inborn propensity for furtiveness, repeating and expressing the tendency of the female to wrap herself up in exfoliating and self-occluding self-extensions.

Such self-extensions are no more natural than they are in any simple sense artificial. Cosmetic artifice is the *nature* of woman—the truth or principle of feminine being—and it follows that, exactly inasmuch as nature is "she," the natural world itself takes on the character of its own self-perversion into artifice. The feminine bleeding that is nature's "ferment" becomes synonymous with an oxymoronic process of natural subterfuge. And since this generative artifice-nature hides the hammock *from view*, the female principle with which it's equated must too be seen to be anti-visual. Femininity is, on this account, the oxymoronic seeping smear that opens up (by closing off) an invisible space in the field of the visible, becoming thereby both substance and origin of an anti-ocular hole-in-being that's imagined as stubbornly exterior to man.

I'm suggesting that there is here a troubling of male vision which serves nonetheless to secure the distinction and psychic singularity of the masculine self. Horace *sees* the (no)thing "out there," as optico-representational ruin, and this sight confirms his egoic integrity by showing him that the oxymoronic object is not after all "in here." Vision now breaks from the narcissistic circuit to find a properly external object. The prior confusion between inside and outside—which threatens the subject with self-consumption at the hands of a bad object outside-within—is stabilized by an optics that no longer finds a "self" in the object at all, but projects the threat of psychic self-canceling onto a feminine externality. Sight thus becomes the psychico-cultural support for Horace's disavowals and projections. It mutates mysteriously, but not too surprisingly, into the sign and psychic mechanism for a culturally sanctioned displacement of (no)thing from mouth to vaginal opening. It transforms into the sense that knows the difference between the inside and outside, turning a genderless interior vomit into external female blood. And it performs this weird mutation in order to help secure a gendered opposition whose banal familiarity hardly mitigates its significance or cultural force. Horace has said that "nature is 'she'" in the mode of self-perversion into artifice; but he also believes that "Progress is 'he'" (15), in and as the masculine triumph of "law, justice, civilization" (132). Woman takes on the burden of (no)thing as anti-ocular and seeping non-being, in order that man might always already appear to have progressed beyond it.

When, accordingly, in looking at a photograph of Little Belle, Horace finds the image suddenly troubled "like something familiar seen beneath disturbed . . . water" (167), the visual disturbance is rapidly righted and the image restored to its tender musings because the troubling is contained in advance by its association with a feminine exteriority over which male vision in principle triumphs. Nothing perhaps speaks louder of this triumph, of both its assurance and its ultimate fragility, than the transformation of the mirror itself from a narcissistic implement into an instrument of objective vision and knowledge. "There was a mirror behind [Little Belle] and another behind me," says Horace. "[S]he was watching herself in the one behind me, forgetting about the other one in which I could see her face, see her watching the back of my head with pure dissimulation. That's why nature is 'she' and Progress is 'he'; nature made the grape arbor, but Progress invented the mirror" (15). The disasters of narcissism are here rewritten as a kind of natural female deceit where the woman successfully perverts the mirror in bleeding and "green-snared" self-multiplication, while man makes proper use of its surface for the progressive purpose of discovering and repudiating a coagulated female dissimulation "out there."[30]

This opposition between "he" and "she" is not, moreover, restricted to Horace, but is one that *Sanctuary* in part endorses. The primary site of this endorsement is Temple; its mechanism parallels one with which we are by now familiar. Just as Horace displaces the (no)thing from Popeye-himself onto woman, so too the novel will humanize Popeye-the-corn-cob-rapist by exposing the cruelties he has suffered in childhood and letting us hear the vulnerable "whinny" of his anguished and impotent sexual desire (258),[31] while at the same time dehumanizing Temple by making her nymphomanic grotesqueries the final sign that she got what she deserved because she wanted it all along. More than Gowan's drunken irresponsibility in leaving her alone at the Old Frenchman place; more than the Jefferson District Attorney whose incendiary remarks, in prosecuting Goodwin, incite the lynching of an innocent man; more than the Southern patriarchy that made her, or even the gangster who kidnaps and rapes her, it's Temple's "grimace of taut, toothed coquetry" (48) that the novel holds responsible for the terrible events of which she is one victim.[32]

The terms in which *Sanctuary* couches this censure bear a striking resemblance to those of Horace's cultural fantasy of woman. Unable not to play the coquette, Temple manifestly acts out a "nature" whose purpose is to flaunt through artifice a sexualized body that it never intends to give up. Her *"clotted* curls" and "curled spill of *red"* (56, 36; my emphases) are now the involuntary outer expressions of an inner menstrual-sexual "ferment." And this exterior coagulation attributes to the woman an (in)visibility (the "clot" resists clear objectivization), in much the same way that the young girl herself is repeatedly shown to frustrate male vision in "running," "speeding," and "vanishing" "silhouette" while at the same time provoking vision with a "squatting swirl of knickers or whatnot," "a fleet revelation of flank and thigh" (28, 30). Temple becomes the novel's main figure for the natural artifice of a sexual "bleeding" that reveals by concealing the object from view. The protraction of her bloody emission on the journey following her assault (137) merely makes disturbingly clear the extent to which the novel rethinks the ontic hemorrhage at the heart of being in terms of an explicitly feminine draining which it—the book—has linked already to a natural-unnatural destruction of vision and of the male culture that vision secures.

But there are problems with the terms of this complex opposition. Not only is the link between mirror and Progress an inherently unstable connection—so that, far from enabling the discovery of a feminine "dissimulation" out there, reflecting surfaces become "stagnant pool[s]" (155) that remind us of the spring in which Horace is shattered, or even take on the characteristics of an "orifice," swallowing up "all reluctant light" and withholding any properly legible image from the field of vision (151, 150). Nor is the difficulty simply that the "hole" of femininity continually risks sliding back to an ungendered state: Temple's wound is predicted by, and rewritten as, the "bold" "scarlet" of her "protruding" mouth (36, 238), and the "flank" of nature becomes less feminine than a generalized orifice that's repeatedly said to be "choked" with weeds (42, 46, 90, 200). These problems are serious enough, and I shall return to them later. For now what's crucial is that they are symptoms of a larger incapacity to tell a coherent story of origins about vomit, nature, and law, the relations between masculinity and femininity, and their hierarchical distribution.

Here is a first attempt to tell such a story:

The worst [girl at Temple's school] said boys thought all girls were ugly except when they were dressed. She said the Snake had been seeing Eve for several days and never noticed her until Adam made her put on a fig leaf. How do you know? they said, and she said because the Snake was there before Adam, because he was the first one thrown out of heaven. . . . But that wasn't what they meant and they said, How do you know . . . How do you know? until she told them and held up her hand and swore she had. That was when the youngest one turned and ran out of the room. She locked herself in the bath and they could hear her being sick. (151–52)

The first thing to note about this passage is that it fuses a parable of origins with a story concerning male desire and its relation to sexual difference. Encountering Eve for the very "first" time, seeing her suddenly as sexual being, the Snake is led by the yearnings unleashed to try to win her to the devil's party. The story therefore seeks to suggest that the sexual visibility of the woman stands at the origin of paradise lost—and of the human condition itself. Such visibility is, however, once more bound up with (in)visibility. Precisely and only when she covers herself does Eve come into the Snake's field of view to set the catastrophe in motion. Only after she puts on the fig leaf does she become properly "visible" at all, and this must mean—given that the parable is framed by a discussion among several girls about how to make boys want them—that the Fall is caused by *the woman's deceptive concealment of self as erotic unveiling.* The natural and Edenic artifice of a Mother who reveals by hiding herself from view is now what stands at the very beginning, the historico-mythical genesis of woe. Woman is naturalized as original bad object—rendered the eternal (because primal) foul blot—precisely inasmuch as femininity is here derived from a principle of self-negation, which troubles the field of masculine vision and incites in man, from the very first moment, an epistemologico-sexual hunger.

It shouldn't in this light surprise us that the scene repeats and "feminizes" the temporal confusion of the book's first image. The woman's self-revealing concealment precipitates the tragedy from which it results; her donning the fig leaf marks the assumption of sin's token before any sin,[33] just as the (in)visibility it produces mars in advance all Edenic fulfillment with a more or less metaphysical desire that requires the inaccessibility of its objects. Nothing besides the badness of woman is explained by such a story. Its moments cannot be brought into focus except in (a)chronological haze. The corruption and sin that should be its issue can no longer be derived from it, since the superimposition of pre-/post-lapsarian blurs the significant chronology of genesis with the anti-temporal and anti-significatory logic of both-and-neither. If that logic is now called "feminine" because of its figuration in Eve, this is merely in order to suggest that the postulate of a primal Mother obviates the need for any genetic account of the human condition at all. Corruption and mortality are already there, confounded with innocence and immortality, because the Mother of us all was always already a woman—and womanhood is characterized by its tendency to efface the boundaries supporting all cultural distinctions.

It is exactly here, however, that the attempt to externalize the feminine principle confronts its first major difficulty. For how can male culture *ever* get established if this is really how it all begins? How did there ever come to be anything besides an a-civil and (un)natural (no)thing, which blots in advance all singular distinctions, if in the beginning is nothing other than the "femininity" this passage describes? Eve is after all the mother of all humans, not just the primal paradigm for Woman. The gesture that's meant to eternalize her badness is thus compelled by the story it tells to suggest that humanity can't but embody the state it also expels. *All* of Eve's progeny will inherit the tendency toward (anti-)visual indistinction. All of her offspring—whether male or female—will repeat and incarnate the first object's badness, because that object is from the start internal to masculine culture itself.

We should not, accordingly, be surprised if this scene takes place in the vicinity of an orifice that can only through force be limited to the female. The Snake tempts Eve precisely to *eat* the fruit from the Tree of Knowledge. The result of this eating, as Faulkner well knows, is nothing less than *expulsion* from Eden—the throwing up of perishable beings into the transience of a world at large—as though the calamitous fall into history were a kind of ontological vomit in which humanity is the ejected product of the Mother's disastrous ingestion. If such a formulation retains the woman as fount of a misfortune that it calls human, the very return of the discourse of vomit troubles the gendered implications of that move by literally rewriting the birth of mankind as the spilling out of human being in a fluid that breaks past the boundaries of sexes.

The results of this are not far to find in the scene's ambivalent negotiations. For even before the Mother "throws up" to "found" a condition that she also instantiates, there reigns a masculine disgust at woman that makes her erotically invisible-hateful. The question that therefore needs to be faced is how man will ever come to install her, within the domain of vision and culture, as an object either worthy of love or capable, at least, of inspiring desire. Culture can neither emerge nor survive without such an installation. The institutions of "justice" and "law" depend upon a sexual propagation which they seek also to regulate. It therefore becomes imperative that man libidinally override his disgust, in the name of the values that the novel would have him representatively institutionalize. Placing Adam before the beginning is, on one hand, an attempt to secure this transformation: to oppose a principle of at least proto-culture to the feminine (anti-)principle, in order to establish a civilized origin that's independent from the woman. Adam can now *command* Eve to be the thing his desire requires. He can—precisely—clothe her in order to awaken desire as a kind of curiosity which puts to sleep the disgust that precedes it and opens the path to sexual union. But he can do this only in a highly paradoxical or oxymoronical manner: by calling a lovable other into view in the form of its self-concealment, and making that other exist in and as the space in between male love and hate. This gesture makes her "be" for man only in the mode of a cultural negation whose logic is that of expulsive projection. For before the vomitory genesis of man, Eve *is not* (visible, lovable)—there is only Adam and his "command." Where then can she possibly come from if not from somewhere "inside" of that man, as though this story combined the myth of the Fall with that of Creation, as though Eve were in fact created by a command that expelled her from Adam's (in)side and made her be what Adam refuses to be? Adam spits Eve up with his words in order not to have to remain her. The object of male disgust begins as an interiority to a masculine culture that has not yet established itself, and the passage could thus be thought to return us to the Freudian story with which we began, in order to say that the subject of culture requires the eternal prolongation of vomit.

The woman's apparent "dissimulation," in this light, results from the ambivalence that men foist upon her. It's a masculine rewriting of the feminine double-object (object of fear, object of love) as an attempt on the woman's part to make herself more lovable than she "in fact" is. If that rewriting entails in *Sanctuary* the refiguration of vomit as blood, a second story of origins—which Faulkner mostly cut in revision—helps explain this transformation's mechanism and its ultimate failure:

> *[Horace] dreamed that he was a boy again and waked himself crying in a paroxysm of homesickness like that of a child . . . alone in a strange room. It seemed to him that . . . the last thirty-five years had been a dream, and he waked himself calling his mother's name in a paroxysm of terror and grief.*
>
> *. . . Sitting there in the bed in the dark, he believed that he had irrevocably lost something, but he believed that if he turned on the light, he would lose even the sense, the knowledge of his loss. So he sat there, hugging his knees. . . .*

After a while he could not tell whether he were awake or not. He could still sense a faint motion of curtains . . . but he was talking to his mother too, who had been dead thirty years. She . . . seemed to emanate that abounding serenity as of earth which his sister had done since her marriage and the birth of her child, and she sat on the side of the bed, talking to him. With her hands, her touch, because he realised that she had not opened her mouth. Then he saw that she wore a shapeless garment of faded calico and that Belle's rich, full mouth burned sullenly out of the halflight, and he knew that she was about to open her mouth and he tried to . . . clap his hand to her mouth. But it was too late. He saw her mouth open; a thick, black liquid . . . splayed out upon her fading chin and the sun was shining on his face and he was thinking He smells black. He smells like that black stuff that ran out of Bovary's mouth. (SO, 60)

Perhaps the most telling and strangest point here is that the terrified flight from woman turns out to be a running toward her. Despite Horace's insistent protest that, in leaving his wife, "[i]t wasn't [his sister] Narcissa [he] was running to"—despite his claim that he hasn't "quit one woman to run to the skirts of another" (107)—he now "dream[s] he [is] a boy again and wake[s] himself calling his mother's name in a paroxysm of terror and grief." He awakens "crying in a paroxysm of homesickness like that of a child . . . alone in a strange room," then sits tight in the fetal position, afraid even to turn on the light, because the novel wants now to pose a regressively "uterine" relation to the woman as an idyllic recovery of "home." The woman who must be sustained in ambivalence is now imagined once to have been a non-ambivalent object of attachment. She's imagined almost as a part of the self that has been "irrevocably lost" through maturity, as though in the necessary quandary of vomit man must split off the good from the bad and imagine an originary non-ambivalence from which he has sprung and to which he can return. The name our culture gives to this woman is, as we know, "mother." We should not be surprised, however, if this name slides not just into that of "sister," but also into the names of those women for whom Horace's adult ambivalence is both quite desperate and profound.

For just as, in the previous passage, the human condition resulting from the Fall turns out to inhabit a moment before it, so the original object here is tainted by those which come to replace it and through which Horace seeks to find it. The mother is fused in this "dream" with Ruby by being clothed in the "faded calico" the latter is repeatedly said to wear (8). She's blended as well with Horace's wife (Belle), whose "rich, full mouth" he finds on her face. She's combined implicitly with Narcissa since for Horace the sister and wife are "interchangeable" (*SO*, 27). And she's confused—even—with Temple and Little Belle, both of whom are repeatedly linked to Belle by way of the "savage" lips that all three women share. If, on one hand, this collapse contaminates the mother by peopling her with objects of ambivalence, this is because it also, on the other, says that all objects of male desire substitute for a maternality that men can idealize as non-ambivalent only by first losing it. Faced with the dangers of woman as object of vision and sexual desire, male culture imagines a primal object of unequivocal fusion, which it "prohibits" both in order to institute distance from the mother as a condition of masculine "Progress," and to explain man's unending failure to find a thing that he couldn't stand to recover at all.

The mother, in other words, is on this reading an object man *invents as lost*. She is an object that *must* not be found, because to find her is to discover the logic that masculine culture requires of its women. To find her is to "lose even the sense, the knowledge of . . . loss," and so to confront the necessity of losing her if man is to be able nostalgically to imagine a "good" form of primal fusion. For what it means to lose this loss is to recover fusion as terror, annihilation. It's to discover the mother as origin of the "stuff" that Horace equates with Popeye—to find that the gangster spews out of her "open" "mouth" as a "thick, black liquid." But it's also to discover that the mother is herself indistinguishable from Popeye (she's endowed with the "fading chin" that the novel elsewhere gives to him [5]), and therefore that she's Horace himself, in the form of that shattered yet viscous reflection that Popeye forces Horace to encounter. The object of non-ambivalent attachment thus becomes—once actually encountered—the oral-expulsive/consumptive object that the masculine subject can't stand to be, and that he therefore re-figures in horror as the monster who threw him up to begin with.

In light of all this, it's perhaps unsurprising that Horace's literal attempt to go home is less than fully successful. When he begins, on the very next page, to move into the house of his youth, that house is immediately coded maternal by the "old and thick" oak in "the center of the lawn." The tree is "circled by a crude wooden bench, onto the planks of which the bole, like breasts of that pneumatic constancy so remote from lungs as to be untroubled by breath, had croached and overbosomed until supporting trestles were no longer necessary" (SO, 64). Horace wants precisely to envelop himself in these pneumatic breasts. "He [sits] on the bench, smoking, his back against the tree," recalling "the peaceful twilight-colored rain" (SO, 64) of a youth "irrevocably lost." The perfectly peaceful bosom of the tree becomes the suggestive medium through which he attempts to recover a restful plenitude that he thinks inheres in maternal relations. The problem, however, in the wake of his dream, is that the mother will threaten to turn to an indistinct and devouring "thing" that reveals itself as "self." The mother shows up here not just in the arboreal breasts where Horace seeks to find himself cradled. She's also figured by the overgrowth of nature that surrounds and threatens to engulf the house, by the "gutters . . . choked with molded vegetation" that "stain . . . the [house's] bricks with dark streaks" (SO, 61), and by the nails in the boards on the windows, from each of which "depend[s] a small rusty stain, like a dried tear or a drop of blood" (SO, 62). Maternal sanctuary is here transformed to a strangled and terrifying coagulation-hole; it reveals itself once more as a substance that's both devouring and optically unmasterable, a substance that Horace can scarcely any longer externalize or keep out.

The acuteness of the danger thus posed is stressed by the house's connection to the Old Frenchman place. Horace's home is surrounded by "cedars [that] need . . . pruning . . . their dark tips a jagged mass like a black wave breaking without foam" (SO, 61; my emphases). The place of Temple's desecration is a "house [that lifts] its . . . bulk" "above a black, jagged mass of trees," "a gutted ruin rising gaunt and stark out of a grove of unpruned cedar trees" (7,

8; my emphases). Such a descriptive conjoining suggests that Horace's return to the home-as-mother leads inexorably to a psychic bind that implicates him in rape and murder. The encounter with Temple will repeat for him a maternal proximity that contaminates the mother and reveals the maternal sanctuary itself as a kind of devouring repetition of self. But his attempt to respond to this crisis by embracing male "justice" and "civilization" will pose the risk of an identification with Popeye as obscene figure of law—a figure who embodies that law in the form of a lawless fury.

For Popeye is the man through whom the book exposes the toxic character of masculine attempts to manage the bad object. He is the man who "knows" he is Temple—and knows he also must not be her, if he's to be a "man" at all. He is her because, as we've seen already, he is (like her) the materially incontinent and (in)visible "reflection" of the masculine subject as (no)thing. He is her because the novel insists that he, like she, is characterologically oxymoronic, inhabiting a liminal space to begin with between adulthood and childhood. Temple is described as "a small childish figure no longer quite a child, not yet quite a woman" (89), "her very attitude an outrage to muscle and tissue of more than seventeen and more compatible with eight or ten" (69); Popeye's hands are "little" and "doll-like" (5), his arm is "frail, no larger than a child's" (231), he "lurk[s] about . . . like a sullen and sick child" (109), and his doctor in childhood says that "he will never be a man, properly speaking," "never be any older than he is now" (308).[34] The relation of doubling that these moments suggest could hardly be much clearer—except, perhaps, in the way in which Popeye is said to couple the natural with the fake, just as the novel says that Temple does. He is, in the opening, opposed to and defiling of a natural setting that the book seems at this point to think of in terms of Horace's mother-idyll. He wears an incongruous and tight-fitting suit (4, 7), resembles a "lampstand" and looks like "stamped tin" (7, 4), expectorates into the feminine waters, and abrupts upon "the sunny silence" (4) as if to blot the natural landscape with the specter of a culturally coded threat. But he also "claw[s] . . . and hiss[es] . . . like a cat" (7) in a manner that makes his ominousness "natural" no less than

115

it renders nature cultural by infusing it with a "vicious" (4, 7) intent that here belongs to the urban menace. Add to all this that nature gradually becomes a "jungle" or "lake of ink" whose "blackness" is the color attributed to Popeye (7); that the bird whose song punctuates this opening seems to be "worked" mechanically, "by a clock" (5); and that Popeye repeats nature's peaceful "silence" in the form of a voyeuristic stealth that ends in rape and murder—add these difficulties to those just mentioned and it becomes clear that the novel effects a radical twinning of the artificial/cultural and the natural, of the masculine and the feminine, in order to say that the culmination of masculine "Progress" is a repetition of what culture imagines as nature's tendency to efface the distinctions on which culture rests. Culture is bad since it stains a pure nature that's bad because savagely threatening to culture. Nature stands as beneficent idyll whose instinct is the source for a violence that civilization wreaks on the natural.[35]

It's precisely within this context that Temple's rape can best be grasped. That rape is, perhaps above all, an attempt to make the object bleed, in order to bring to the visual field the invisible and unnatural (no)thing that man must not be—but that he is—and that he will try to escape by seeing. Popeye's assault reveals the futility of masculine projects of visual mastery except as eroticized violation. The woman can only be repudiated through a denial of the narcissistic component to masculine sexual love, a denial that *decrees* the distinction in question, *makes* the object be "not-me," and frees man to treat that feminine object with the violence he would like to wreak on the (no)thing that opens him up from within. The sexual character of this violation is meant to abet the disavowal. It asserts a potency and erotic mastery that are of course quite radically in question—Popeye, let us recall, is impotent—so that the man might be convinced that *he* is not the thing being mastered, and can maintain his distance from the wound that he makes bleed.

It's clear from Popeye's name, moreover, that this erotico-scopic violence belongs to the masculine law that prohibits it as much as does the (no)thing that the act of rape repudiates. "Pop" = father; "eye" = vision. Popeye is both a "Daddy" to Temple (236) and a creature of visual predilections, who begins the novel as a nameless pair of eyes, takes his sexual pleasure in watching (258), and is evoked throughout the book as a will-to-visual-mastery. It is from here a very short distance to see that the fathers whom justice serves, and who dispense that justice also, are disguised repetitions of an impotent voyeur who rapes a girl to deny that he is her. A member of the mob that lynches Goodwin says when he sees Horace: "Do to the lawyer what we did to [Goodwin]. What he did to her. Only we never used a cob. We made him wish we had used a cob" (296). Justice literally repeats here the act that it seeks at the same time to punish. "We got to protect our girls," says another man, because we "[m]ight need them ourselves" (298). The ominous implication is of a paternal rape of "our girls" in the name of their ambivalent incorporation.

Temple is, in this regard, exactly like the dogs at the whorehouse who hide from the drunken violence of their mistress: "savage, petulant, spoiled, the flatulent monotony of their sheltered lives snatched up without warning by an incomprehensible moment of terror and fear of bodily annihilation at the very hands which symbolized by ordinary the licensed tranquillity of their lives" (155). She too is violated by the (paternal) hand that symbolizes the licensed tranquillity of her existence. Popeye's hand *is* her father's hand, since if Popeye is "Daddy," Judge Drake is Popeye, both in the mode of inassimilable "object" and its sexually violent denial.

When the Judge comes to take Temple from the courthouse after she has doomed Goodwin to the bonfire, the language is so explicitly sexualized as to suggest that the father repeats the act that he's meant here to avenge (he walks "erect" "down the aisle" beside her; she "cringe[s] back, her body arching slowly" in a "shrinking and rapt abasement" [289]). When the Judge sits, in the book's final scene, with "his hands crossed on the head of his stick" (317), the novel reveals his implication in what "justice" seeks to disavow. The detail links him to the patriarch Pap, whom we know is a figure for the self as (no)thing, and who also sits "in a splint-bottom chair [with] his hands crossed on the head of a . . . stick" (42–43). It's not by chance then that Temple invokes and accuses the "old man with . . . clots for eyes" at the moment of her rape. "'Something is happening to me!'" she says, "scream[ing] at [the old man]. . . . 'I told you it was! . . . I told you all the time!'" (102). Pap is the internal truth of a Judge who is at the same time Popeye, and the scream is thus both a plea to be saved and a charge that's leveled at a masculine law that enacts by proxy the rape it deplores.

The act of rape can thus be seen to expose both the violence toward which "law" tends and its ruinously regurgitative basis. It reveals, indeed, in the realm of sex, the (no)thing that law pretends lies elsewhere, a fact that's emphasized by the "few scattered corn-cobs gnawed bone-clean" that Temple discovers in the barn before her assault (93). Popeye will rape her with just such a cob, tool of his ocular-sexual mastery. The fact that the cobs have been orally ravaged suggests, however, that if man is impotently incapable of the mastery that rape attempts to secure, this is not just because the phallus is prosthetic. It's also because even this prosthesis is haunted by a prior encounter with the oral from which it cannot escape. The instrument of man's phallic mastery bears the marks of the internal mouth that the act of rape is meant to disavow. To try to label this orifice feminine will not, of course, work either, since what presumably gnaws the cobs is the rat that Temple encounters in the barn. That rat—like Popeye—assaults her. It has, like him, "glowing" electric eyes. And it stands "erect . . . its forepaws curled against its chest, . . . squeak[ing] at [Temple] in tiny plaintive gasps" (93), in a manner that's meant proleptically to connect it to Popeye's sexual "whinny." The thing that has eaten the substitute phallus is thus none other than the rapist himself. Pop-eyed violence and the vulnerable anguish of an oral-ocular and impotent despair are here inextricably intertwined, since both derive from and differently express the vomit(orality) that structures all being and that the law both rejects and includes.

The disturbing depth of Horace's crisis can in this light be grasped with precision. It results from the fact that he can neither save himself from being the "object" by projecting its stain onto Temple, nor escape his implication in the violence with which men respond to this failure. He can't do the first of these, as we have seen, because the ambivalent coding of woman leads to a flight and recoil from her, which takes the shape of a return to the mother who turns out to be "oneself" after all. And he can't do the second because the sanctuary of law is shown to be bound up with its inevitable violation. It's not too surprising, given this quandary, that Horace smokes a corn-cob pipe,[36] whose unlighted bowl he "slowly finger[s]" when he finds Temple Drake's "pencilled name" "scrawled on the foul, stained wall" of a bathroom (172). The fingering of the bowl enacts the rape that the cob of the pipe signifies, and enacts it in response to Horace's discovery of Temple as sexual blot. Nor is it surprising that Horace is himself by profession a lawyer: the fact contributes to the conflation of law with the violence of the man whom the lawyer doubles (Popeye), and it implicates Horace still more deeply in the perpetration of that violence.

Finally though, that implication becomes most evident in the rape scene itself. The structural amnesia within that scene, whereby the narrative mode elides the book's horrific central event, couples the reader with Horace by way of their mutual incapacity to stand outside of Temple's brutal desecration. *Sanctuary* seeks here to spill us into a rape that its mode (un)depicts. Refusing to give us the act itself as a simple object of knowledge—ceaselessly circling around the event, representing it in displaced form and leading us up to it only to blot it—the book no more lets us decline to envision the rape than it allows us to see it. It forces us, indeed, to visualize it, *but only from the position of a radical internality*. It makes us want to see the assault while refusing ever to represent it. It gives us an external vantage point on it only in the "phlegm-clots" that Faulkner has watch over it (102), and that—as we know—aren't "external" at all. And it thus makes us regard the event as the blot of a narrative space-in-between, requiring us to place ourselves "in" it in order to see what it doesn't quite show, and so to engage in an ocular consumption that spatters us out across the act's surface and swallows us into the "objects" we "see." To try to know the event objectively would be to be essentially Popeye, who also strives for an affectless mastery of an object that he insists is not him. To be smeared, on the other hand, by the novel, into its vomitory textures, is to be forced to see oneself instead as Popeye-Temple: victim and victimizer, subject and object, eye and mouth, culture and nature—and of course, perhaps most importantly, masculine-feminine, (wo)man.

Horace is himself seeped into this muculently extensive identity when Temple tells him the story of her rape in a way that elides it as much as the narrative does, focusing exclusively on "the night which she had spent in comparative inviolation" (215). For within the impossibility of knowing and mastering an event that's never "given," he's forced (if he's to know it at all) to collaborate in the attack by psychically placing himself in it.[37] He's forced—*we're* forced—to circulate in the space of Popeye-Temple. We're made not only to be Popeye at the moment of the latter's most toxic self-assertion, but also to confront the ruin of the distinctions that this assertion attempts to establish. We're made to participate in a rape in which the male "tool" has been orally savaged, and in which—conversely—the female victim says that she "thought about being a man, and as soon as [she] thought it, it happened. It made a kind of plopping sound, like blowing a . . . rubber tube wrong-side outward," and "[i]t felt cold, like the inside of your mouth when you hold it open" (220). We're forced to inhabit this penile cavity as we spill into the narrative lacuna. We're asked to become at once a woman who invents for herself a phallic instrument while hollowing it into an oral hole ("like the inside of your mouth"), and a man who has no such tool except in the form of a phallic prosthesis that has been "gnawed bone-clean." And we're forced—accordingly—to rape and be raped, to be the excessively "civilized" violator and the (un)natural object of violation, and so to circulate in a textuality that spreads us out as the spaces between the distinctions that culture both sanctions and requires.

It seems almost inevitable that Horace should find himself barfing within pages from here. He attempts perhaps, as he thinks elsewhere, to "vomit . . . himself out of [the world]" by spitting into it the "evil" he cannot abide in himself (255). This is a final purification, a last apocalyptic attempt to expel from the self an unwanted object. To immerse ourselves in such a gesture is to partake in the novel's final collapse of distinctions that let men see from a distance the (no)thing they don't want to know that they are:

> *[Horace] thought of [Temple], Popeye, the woman, the child, Goodwin, all put into a single chamber, bare, lethal, immediate and profound: a single blotting instant between the indignation and the surprise. . . . And I, too . . . ; thinking of a gentle dark wind blowing in the long corridors of sleep; of lying beneath a low cozy roof under the long sound of the rain: the evil, the injustice, the tears. In an alley-mouth two figures stood. . . . [Horace thought] of the expression he had once seen in the eyes of a dead child, and of other dead: the cooling indignation, the shocked despair fading, leaving two empty globes in which the motionless world lurked profoundly in miniature.*
>
> *. . . He had a cup of coffee and . . . it lay in a hot ball on his stomach. Three hours later, when he got off [the train] at Jefferson, it was still there, unassimilated. . . .*
>
> *He walked quietly up the drive. . . . The house was dark, still, as though it were marooned in space by the ebb of all time. The insects had fallen to a low monotonous pitch . . . as though the sound were the chemical agony of a world left stark and dying above the tide-edge of the fluid in which it lived and breathed. . . . He opened the door and felt his way into the room. . . . The voice of the night had followed him into the house; he knew suddenly that it was the friction of the earth on its axis, approaching that moment when it must decide to turn on or to remain forever still: a motionless ball in cooling space, across which a thick smell of honeysuckle writhed like cold smoke.*
>
> *He found the light and turned it on. The photograph [of Little Belle] . . . appeared to breathe . . . beneath the slow, smoke-like tongues of invisible honeysuckle. . . .*
>
> *Then he knew what that sensation in his stomach meant. He put the photograph down hurriedly and went to the bathroom. He opened the door running and fumbled for the light. But he had not time to find it and he gave over and plunged forward and struck the lavatory and leaned upon his braced arms while the shucks set up a terrific uproar beneath her thighs. Lying with her head lifted slightly . . . she watched something black and furious go roaring out of her pale body. She was bound*

naked on her back on a flat car moving at speed through a black tunnel, the blackness streaming in rigid threads overhead. . . . The car shot bodily from the tunnel in a long upward slant, the darkness overhead now shredded with parallel attenuations of living fire, toward a crescendo like . . . an interval in which she would swing faintly and lazily in nothingness. (221–23)

Horace's initiation into evil is practically speaking over at this point. Nothing worse will happen to him—nothing, that is, save devastation and retreat. The bonfire that, some seventy-five pages later, consumes Goodwin in "a voice of fury" (296) merely answers this apocalyptic terror with a second and socially sanctioned one, which seeks to keep the town from knowing what Horace is already unable to forget. The passage at hand could indeed be thought to chronicle Horace's failure to unknow the "thing" he has discovered within. It moves, accordingly, from what we might call a defensively gendered and manichean despair to a furiously oral unraveling of the terms in which that despair is couched.

For the passage begins by purifying negativity, cordoning it off as force of pure death, in order to save it from implication in the life of masculine culture. Death itself now takes on the character of anti-ocular (no)thing. Death becomes "a single blotting instant *between* the indignation and the surprise," ruining the vision of eyes that—being "*globes* in which the . . . world lurk[s] . . . in miniature"—are both the moribund world itself and the place where the death of that world is reflected. The effect is decidedly, if ambiguously, metaphysical. (No)thing becomes confounded with "nothing" by way of this deathly apotheosis. A negativity that inhabits the structure is figured as external force, rather than as a "thing" bound to being and marshaled hierarchically in the name of the law. Horace's fantasy of existential "cauterization"—in which the story's principal figures are wiped out with one gesture—signals less an acceptance of negativity than a wearily anguished embrace of a death whose apocalyptic figuration hides its embroilment in the life that it seems to oppose.[38] If that death is yet imagined *as* (no)thing, this is merely because, to begin with, even this opposition must be gendered. Death becomes a submission to the fantasized feminine that men cannot master. Either one is killed by a "chamber, bare, lethal, immediate and profound," whose maternal-uterine implications are amplified by the "corridors of sleep" that enclose one under "a low cozy roof" through which "rain" can be heard. Or one is subject, within this fantasy, to the fatal desiccation of maternal abandonment: "marooned in space by the ebb of all time," strangled by "the chemical agony of a world left stark and dying above the tide-edge of [its] fluid"—to the point, indeed, where the earth is drained of its vital lubrication and groans with an excessive "friction" that will stop it from turning on its axis. Death is itself here a woman who envelops or discharges man into oblivion. She is the fantasmic representation of a blot to masculine knowledge, which ought to be internal to man—internal to life itself—but which is here imagined as the absolute other of what can be known.

This is, however, only half the story. The fantasy at hand takes place once more in a proximity to the oral, a proximity that makes it impossible for that fantasy to work properly. Not only does Horace encounter, for example, two lovers whispering in an "alley-*mouth*," as though to suggest that an ungendered orifice is already starting to yawn and gape in the space of a death that he tries to call feminine. Nor is it just that the picture of Little Belle begins to breathe when wrapped in "*tongues* of honeysuckle"—a process suggesting, in the light of my argument, that death as uterine envelopment-abandonment is also an incestuous-narcissistic mouth (breathing, licking) that could just as well be the man's own. Both of these details portend an undoing that's scary enough in itself. But there is something perhaps still scarier, something yet more internally devastating. There is, indeed, from the very start, an alternate image of Death itself in the blinded orbs of the child's death-mask. Those orbs are the "globe" they reflect, and they thus predict and repeat in advance the "hot ball" in Horace's upset stomach, precisely inasmuch as *the world is itself here shown to be such a "ball"* ("a motionless ball in cooling space"). Death can thus not only be seen already to be "in" the eye that it blots; it *is*, still more, an eye or orb, in the form of a brute inassimilable lump that Horace throws up and calls the world in order not to have to be it. Since, moreover, the world is elsewhere "a disc suspended in nothing-ness," which is in its turn an "*orifice*" swallowing "all reluctant light" (151, 150), the full extent of the current danger can now perhaps come clear. Death is an eye which is also a mouth which is also the internal ball as "world." It can no longer be reduced to a feminine threat that blots from out-side and may, in despair, be claimed or genocidally dispensed. Rather, it in-habits the world by *being* it, swallows the globe that it has also become, since the earth is itself the blind eye and inner mouth that the initial fantasy sought to project as outer limit of being.

This "feminine" death turns out therefore to inhabit the masculine sub-ject himself. Horace vomits it only to find himself spattered and dispersed in the world he throws up, becoming once more the woman "he" rapes through a pronominal shift in the final paragraph: "*he* had not time to find [the light] and he gave over and plunged forward and struck the lavatory . . . while the shucks set up a terrific uproar beneath *her* thighs." This "her" (whom he is) is on one hand Temple, who spends her night of "comparative inviolation" on a mattress filled with corn shucks. The figure condenses as well the step-daughter whose photograph "he" has just been regarding. It contains a trace of the oneiric mother in the "black" stuff that goes "roaring out of her . . . body." And it refers us, finally, to Popeye himself, who is this blackened vom-iting-vomit that then becomes disseminated in the "blackness streaming . . . overhead." All of these figures have been condensed in that "hot, hard lump" that is the world inside of Horace's stomach. All of them now come shooting out of him—and him, of course, streaming out of them, bound to that "car shot bodily from [a] tunnel in a long upward slant . . . toward a crescendo like . . . an interval." All of them are this penile projectile, which is now sim-ply a regurgitative hole expelled from the cavity it tries to invade. And all of them are, as should now be clear, an apocalypse that *must be lived*, in the form of a (no)thing that's ocular-oral, identificatorily extensive, internally and mutually devouring. If that hole seems to be vaginal in that it belongs to the woman's "pale body," the collapses I have been describing ought to prevent such an easy designation. The correlation of the woman's spewing with the vomiting in which Horace engages makes it impossible to pin down the gender of the hole in the thing he has within him. That cavity is, to be precise, ungendered because universal: an oral-ocular blot to being that's figured here as global—that is, as universe—and that can only by way of force be attached to a given gender. *Sanctuary* might finally be thought of as a textual repetition of this globe: a non-sanctuarial and monstrous "object," which devours by making us see ourselves in an orally (anti-)ocular hole within what we like to call our "selves."

4　The Killer in Me Is the Killer in You

Violent Voice in Jim Thompson's *Pop. 1280*

"The laughter of nothingness"

Jim Thompson is, as he himself might have put it, one scary son of a gun—scary enough to frighten even those critics most fully committed to the consoling character of crime fiction. Robert Polito is typical in his assessment of the genre and of Thompson's place within it. "Crime fiction," he writes, "ordinarily . . . constitutes a comforting and conservative genre"; it follows the "trajectory [of] classical comedy," in that "a demonic impulse . . . and a calamitous action . . . hurl a personality . . . to the rim of annihilation before the crime is solved . . . the personality reintegrated, and the society allowed to resume its harmonious mission." Thompson's writing is in this sense distinctive because it "inverts . . . the consolations of genre." His "novels begin with the appearance of integration and order, then chart a descent into madness and extinction. The demonic impulses . . . are unleashed rather than quelled at the conclusions of his books, with the result that . . . Thompson's hero . . . achieve[s] not a new life but a terrifying nothingness."[1]

　　With minor variations, this is essentially the story that all of Thompson's best critics tell.[2] And though I remain unpersuaded by claims for the general conservatism of crime fiction, I do share the sense that Thompson's work is especially disquieting. This feeling is for me bound up with two particular aspects of his writing. There is, to begin with, the centrality of first-person voice to the effect of his best work.[3] That work is dominated by narrators who are enormously compelling and solicitous of our sympathy, and yet quite often literally psychotic, willfully deceitful or else dissociative, and possessed of a voice whose enthralling character seems inseparable from an introspective intensity that moves toward the abolition of its world—and even finally of itself. Geoffrey O'Brien's account of this process is especially compelling. He speaks of how the "voice [in Thompson's novels] turns out to [belong to] someone who doesn't know who he is, who's no longer sure which story he's telling, who may have been lying to [us] all along."[4] The "books describe a space defined entirely by that . . . voice," which "eat[s] away at" the "reality" that it begins by "carefully construct[ing]." "Being itself erodes" in this way, right before our eyes. "The voice starts out talking about the things surrounding it, but in the end only the voice remains" (152).

This omnipresent yet devouring voice leads to the second issue that interests me. Barry Gifford has written that Thompson gives his protagonists "what can only be described as the most bizarre senses of humor in the annals of crime fiction."[5] And indeed, this comic dimension to his work is pronounced in virtually all accounts of it. O'Brien writes of Thompson's "blend of outrageous humor, disturbing violence, and simmering identity crisis" (152). Polito describes how the "witticisms that in Hammett or Chandler flaunt the . . . hero's [mastery] become for Thompson's characters evidence of mental imbalance" (8). And R. V. Cassill argues that Lou Ford's humor (Ford is the narrator of *The Killer Inside Me*) is the "'crack in the china cup that leads on to the land of the dead'" (234).[6] It's part of a tendency to "put people on" that is here inseparable from "the dramatized revelation that Ford puts himself on in a somewhat different sense—that is, he wears himself as a disguise, his other self tragically invisible." Ford on this reading "is echoing the joke that lies at the still center of the turning world. . . . [His] is the laughter of nothingness[, t]he ridiculousness of the spaces between the stars, given tongue by the criminal human" (234, 236).

Finally, Tony Hilfer describes "the anarchic comic energy of Id" that animates the narrator of *Pop. 1280*. He suggests in particular that Nick Corey stands as a kind of "Superego running wild," which has "appropriated" the id's vitality for its own excoriating and comic purposes, and which represents "a Presbyterian conscience that . . . turns to irony as an instrument of discord" in the face of existential despair (150). Hilfer's argument is especially suggestive in the context of the issues raised so far. Indeed, I shall be claiming that what links the questions the critics bring together—humor and a disintegrating first-person voice—is precisely that psychic agency that Freud in his second topography called the superego. I want to develop this claim, however, largely through an early text that anticipates Freud's structural theory—through, that is, his book on jokes, and especially his discussion of dirty jokes. As we shall see, this discussion opens up our concerns to questions of gender, sexuality, and the body, elaborating the scarily comic meanings of what the superego as agent of culture tells us to label "dirt."[7]

The material that interests me in *Jokes and Their Relation to the Unconscious* (1905) hinges upon a discussion of smut. Freud has been arguing that "[s]mut is . . . originally directed towards women and may be equated with attempts at seduction." *Men*, in other words, began talking dirty, and they did so because they felt "sexually excited" and wanted through speech to arouse such excitement in the women who initially caused it. "If a man in a company of men [nonetheless] enjoys telling or listening to smut," this is because "the original situation, which owing to social inhibitions cannot be realized, is at the same time imagined. A person who laughs at smut that he hears is laughing as though he were the spectator of an act of sexual aggression."[8] Such a spectatorial component to laughter is by no means incidental to smut. It corresponds to part of its original, primordial intention. For smut is from the beginning "like an exposure of the sexually different person to whom it is directed. . . . [I]t compels the person who is assailed to imagine the part of the body or the procedure in question and shows her that the assailant is himself imagining it. . . . [T]he desire to see what is sexually exposed is [thus] the original motive of smut" (98).

It's at this point that Freud proposes what one might call an oedipal theory of smut and dirty jokes:

Generally speaking, a tendentious joke calls for three people: in addition to the one who makes the joke, there must be a second who is taken as [its] object . . . and a third in whom the joke's aim of producing pleasure is fulfilled. . . . In the case of smut the three people are in the same relation. The course of events may be thus described. When the first person finds his libidinal impulse inhibited by the woman, he develops a hostile trend against that second person and calls on the originally interfering third person as his ally. Through the first person's smutty speech the woman is exposed before the third, who [is] bribed by the effortless satisfaction of his own libido. (100)

The "first person" allies himself with the "third," who begins by "interfering" with the seduction of the "second." What could be clearer than the oedipal character of the situation thus described? One need only substitute the relevant names in order to be certain: the son allies himself with the father, who begins by interfering with the son's attempted seduction of the mother. The genesis of smut in this sense repeats the history of the male child's sexual development. What starts as pre-oedipal desire for the mother is rendered oedipal by the father's prohibitive "interference" with that desire, which resolves the crisis into a normatively oedipal renunciation of incest, and a sexual hostility toward the woman that's consolidated through bonding—that is, through identification—with the father himself.[9]

If such a scenario psychically underpins the social significance of smut, the derivation of dirty jokes is not then far to seek. Those jokes arise from an *increase* in the "social inhibition" that produced the alliance between first and third persons to begin with. Smut, that is, is to peasants and "common people" what dirty jokes are to civilization, to "society of a more refined education" (100). Only people in this latter group make use of the complex linguistic techniques required to turn ordinary smut into that more refined form of utterance we call the dirty joke. Since, moreover, the "higher education" of these people goes hand in hand with their greater "repression" (101), and since repression is itself the product of oedipal prohibitions, the greater refinement of dirty jokes could be said to result from an ever more stringent enforcement of oedipal Law—and here we arrive at the significance in this narrative of the superego that, at this point in time, Freud was not yet able to name.

For it is, of course, what Freud will come to designate the superego that he calls here the "third person."[10] Or rather, the social process he describes in *Jokes* through the derivation of smut is one that he will recapitulate and complicate with the concept of the superego, which mediates between the "first person" and his society by representing that society intrapsychically. The superego in this sense names the internalization of the "third person" by the "first." It allows the "first person" to emerge as such—to become a "person" in the social sense—by installing within him a paternal representative that at once prohibits incestuous satisfaction, encourages identificatory emulation, and promises social recognition. The condition of an alliance between men is thus an internal division of the male self. The boy can come to be symbolically affirmed, in a process that the dirty joke mirrors in miniature, only by way of a "third person" whose internalized image he's asked to "be like" and instructed never to succeed in being. For this "third person" says at once: "'You *ought to be* like this (like your father)'" and "'You *may not be* like this (like your father)—that is, you may not do all that he does; some things are his prerogative.'"[11] It stands as both a regulative ideal and a prohibition against attaining that ideal. The result is a variant of the bind I touched upon in chapter 2, a bind in which the "first person" is defined by a structurally insurmountable rift, since the closer it comes to being "itself" in the mode of the ideal, the greater the violence inflicted upon it by the superego as prohibitive function.

It's important at this point to note the peculiarly linguistic terms of the discussion so far—its framing by way of distinctions between "first," "second," and "third" persons. The discursive character of such distinctions is reinforced by the fact that, as Freud tells us, the superego originates in a verbal prohibition that the "third person" speaks to the "first." He writes: "For what prompted the subject to form an ego ideal [was] the critical influence of his parents (conveyed to him by the medium of the voice)."[12] Or again, in *The Ego and the Id*: "it is . . . impossible for the super-ego . . . to disclaim its origin from things heard," from "auditory perceptions (instruction or reading)" (54). The "first person" is thus a "person" by virtue of his having internalized the father's voice—or at any rate, a voice that represents and stands in for paternal authority. And that "first person" equally seeks recognition through the medium of *his* voice. The original intention of smut—to arouse the other through speech—is transformed into a masculine alliance that is at root linguistic, and in which the "first person" "bribes" the "third" with a speech designed to provoke laughter. "Everything in jokes that is aimed at gaining pleasure is calculated with an eye to the third person," Freud writes (155). The "first person" speaks, within this context, in order to evoke the signs of such pleasure. This evocation confers upon him the status of "successful" first person. The laughter emitted by the "third person" gives the speaker the external recognition that compensates for his instinctual renunciation by constituting him as a subject who is possessed of his own voice.

But at the same time, this giving of pleasure signals the impossible bind of this process and the divided character of the self's voice. For if the other can only be made an ally to the self through pleasure, this means at the psychic level that the superego has its roots in the id, that the ego must do battle with it by constantly trying to please it—and that, accordingly, the conflicting demands of ideal and prohibition are intensified by the superego's endowment with the infantile rage and appetite that its installation is meant to repress. The relation between ego and superego becomes in this sense one of moral masochism;[13] the former takes pleasure in giving the latter the ceaseless satisfaction of punishing it, in a way that transforms the third person's laughter into the superego's ridicule and scorn. In the context of the discussion so far, this means that the "first person" is one whose voice has always already split apart. It's a person in dialogue with an internal alterity with which it cannot reach accord. It's a person who speaks in order to be recognized by an other whose speech negates it, who forever excoriates the self for not speaking with the voice in which it forbids it to speak. And it's a person whose voice colludes in the violence in which its inner other takes pleasure, in a way that leads, at the extreme, to a form of paranoid dissociation in which the "first person" hears itself addressed by the superego as a "third."[14]

Perhaps we can now start to see what is so scary in Thompson's work. That work documents, I will be suggesting, the inescapable pathology of the superego that we have examined in Freud. His narratives enact an attempt to gain recognition through the medium of a first-person voice. They seek to do so in part through humor—through jokes that often themselves approach the character of smut, that construe the reader as a "third person" (that is, as father/superego), and even often ask him to bond over the spectacle of the woman exposed.[15] In this sense, the novels could be said to consolidate the oedipal process itself; if they seek through humor to induce in us the pleasurable discharge attendant upon the socially circumscribed undoing of repression, they also recapitulate the process by which the oedipal crisis is resolved through the narrator's identificatory alliance with the reader/father—and his internalization of the superego.

But at the same time, these books are disturbing because they chart the regressive way in which the superego itself is endowed with the transgressive force of unoedipalized impulse. The fusion of these two components—oedipal father, pre-oedipal son—is especially marked in the tendency toward scatology in Thompson's work. For as we shall see, shit is perhaps the deepest sign of the superego's source in the id. It's the substance that initiates the chain of events that culminates in the castration complex and the formation of the superego, since the anal phase is where we first[16] experience a prohibition that at once produces the self by marking its limit and creates a crisis in self-definition by indicating the inner character of what must now be reviled as not-self.

The superego, as heir to this process, is meant to mark its completion; it's meant to consolidate a self that knows the borders between inner and outer, between civilized individuation and a pre-civil pleasure in bodily waste that's felt as part of the self. The sullying of the superego's voice with excrement thus marks the subversion of oedipalization. It signals the regression from superegoic interdiction to rampant appetitive fury—while nonetheless turning the Thompsonian narrator into a superego/father who cannot escape his roots in a kind of excremental ambivalence, even as he punishes those who indulge in the dirt in which he remains mired. The comically schizoid tendencies of voice derive precisely from this miring. They derive from the fact that the narrative voice is at once that of the son demanding recognition from the father and that of the father ridiculing the son for (not) being what he is forbidden to be: the father. They derive, in other words, from the fact that this is the voice of a kind of hypermorality infused with the voice of shit. As we shall see, this splitting and soiling of narrative voice entails an undoing of the bond that's constituted through an aggressive visual exposure of the woman—and the turning back of that aggressive ocularity onto the masculine self.

Being Nothing

I want in what follows to develop this argument by focusing on Thompson's last major novel, *Pop. 1280* (1964). This book is especially fertile terrain for the kinds of issues I've raised, not least because its narrator is a sheriff who clearly stands as a distorted refraction of Thompson's own sheriff father. But in Nick Corey, Thompson in fact refashions his father in startling ways, turning him into a morally tortured and yet homicidal buffoon. Nick, in short, kills in response to the intensity of his moral fervor. The novel will ultimately make a connection between this hypermoral violence and the humor of his buffoonery—a connection to which I return later. For now, I want to turn to *Pop. 1280*'s attempt to explain the familial genesis of Nick's monstrosity. Thompson describes this genesis in a passage that critics have downplayed as reductive,[17] but that I find complex enough to demand our close attention:

I dreamed that I was a kid again, only it didn't seem like a dream. I was a kid, living in the old rundown plantation house with my daddy. Trying to keep out of his way. . . . Getting beat half to death every time he could grab me. . . .

I dreamed—I lived—showing him the reading prize I'd won in school. Because I was sure that would please him. . . . And I dreamed—lived—picking myself up off the floor with my nose bloodied from the little silver cup. And he was yelling at me, shouting that I was through with school because I'd just proved I was a cheat along with everything else.

The fact was, I guess, that he just couldn't stand for me to be any good. If I was any good, then I couldn't be the low-down monster that had killed my own mother getting born. And I had to be that. He had to have someone to blame.[18]

The passage traces a psychic sequence that comprises several stages. There is, to begin with, the mother's death and Nick's role in it—or rather, the *story* of her death and Nick's *imagined* role in it. For clearly the father here invests the event with a range of meanings, which he conveys to his son in a way that makes them part of the son's own story about who he is and how he came to be it. Nick's pathologies are in this sense bequeathed him by his father. More precisely, they result from the transmission of a specific familial story, in which Nick is compelled to play the murderous role his father assigns him— and through which the father cements his self-conception at the cost of Nick's psychic unity.

The story through which this cementing takes place is, moreover, implicitly oedipal. It's a story that imagines the son's relation to the mother as one comprised of guilt, a story whose most concrete result is the son's internalization of that guilt. This internalization has two main components. First and most obviously, it results from the son's acquired sense of having been dangerous to the mother—of literally having killed her. Second and, to my mind, more tellingly, the fact that her death takes place through childbirth suggests a conflation of this violence with the son's incestuous desire. Thompson deliberately evokes an image of Nick's passage through the vaginal canal (he killed his mother "being born"), as a way of indicating that his guilt concerns not only his aggressive wishes but his sexual ones as well. And since this story of culpability is one he inherits from his father, we might begin to suspect that it works to deny the father's own sense of responsibility for his wife's death—to deny, that is, that it was his sexuality that got her pregnant, and that this entails a degree of self-blame that is then deflected onto the son as a fantasy of filial violence that retains its sexual significance. Oedipal guilt is in this sense imagined as a paternal projection. Or, to put this the other way around, the father continues to experience sex as incestuous violation, in ways that he can't but pass on to his son and that suggest a pathological kernel at the heart of the Oedipus complex itself.[19]

It's at this point that the next two stages in the psychic sequence arise. For if Nick is forced to take on the guilt of the father in this story, this leads (1) to a withdrawal of love on the father's part, and indeed, to its transformation into hatred; and (2) to an unfulfillable desire for paternal recognition on the part of the son. The passage dramatizes this latter point with particular poignancy and effectiveness. It imagines every childhood act as an effort to secure the father's love, to expiate a filial guilt through acts by which the son becomes what he thinks his father wants him to be. Such acts reveal a split between Nick's sense of self and an internalized ideal—a split that can only be healed by Nick's becoming that ideal, by his being able to "please" the father by being, in essence, *like* him: non-murderous, non-incestuous, affiliate rather than transgressor of law. To attain that ideal would mean to be what Nick here labels "good" ("he just couldn't stand for me to be any good"). And yet this "being good" conflicts with another sense of goodness—namely, being "good enough" to fill the role of son in the father's story. This latter entails, paradoxically enough, becoming "the low-down monster that . . . killed [his] mother getting born." It entails agreeing to conform to the father's explicit expectations: failing at anything life-affirming because to succeed is to shatter the narrative of filial guilt and worthlessness on which the father feeds, and so to make paternal recognition literally impossible. Each act of "goodness" is designed in this sense to provoke the very violence it fears; punishment is for Nick the idiom of paternal recognition. Oedipalization becomes, in the process, inseparable from vengeance and spite. Nick internalizes as "the good" a sense of self as incestuous and violent. He's made to feel recognizable only if he embraces this transgressive identity, and only if he accepts an equation between recognition and self-punishment. To the extent, then, that Nick becomes a man by way of this process, he does so by incorporating a moral rage that is in essence insatiable, and that's bound up with an oedipal guilt whose inexpiable character results from the way it originates in the life of the father.

Such an account has extraordinarily wide ramifications within the novel. It speaks not only to Nick's inner world and the familial dynamics that formed it, but to his adult relationship with the town he serves as sheriff. That relationship extends the one between Nick and his father; it entails him being "a nothing doing nothing," as he himself at one point puts it (11)—his choosing a profession in which he can continue to be the excrescence required by his father's narrative, while also stifling the subjective agency (i.e., doing nothing) that his father has taught him to experience as dangerous and productive of guilt. This choice of profession helps us see that Thompson is weighing the oedipal pathology for its social effects:

> Always before, [in campaigning for sheriff,] I'd let the word get around that I was against . . . things like cockfighting and gambling and whiskey and so on. So my opposition would figure they'd better come out against 'em, too, only twice as strong as I did. And I went right ahead and let 'em. . . .
>
> Well, anyway, by the time it got ready to vote, it looked like . . . all a fella would be able to do, without getting arrested, was to drink sody-pop and maybe kiss his wife. . . .
>
> So, all and all, I began to look pretty good to folks. It was a case of nothing looking better than something. . . . And when the votes were counted, I was still sheriff.
>
> I'm not saying there weren't a lot of folks who really liked me. There was a lot of 'em. . . . But it seemed . . . I didn't have as many friends as I'd used to. Even the very folks I'd favored, them most of all . . . weren't as friendly as they had been. They

seemed to kind of hold it against me because I hadn't *cracked down on 'em. And I didn't know quite what to do about it, since I'd never really got the habit of doing anything. (58–59)*

"It was a case of nothing looking better than something": the phrase signals a return of the ambivalence upon which the passage quoted earlier turns. For to say that nothing looks better than something is to say that the townspeople *want* Nick to do nothing; they want him to resist "crack[ing] down on 'em," want him *not* to exert the authority that would define them as lawful citizens. The reason they want this, clearly enough, is because the lack of adequate enforcement enables them to enjoy themselves. Laws are concerned here with prohibitions, with curbing sexual and aggressive appetites, and the enforcement of them in this case risks outlawing all but the most innocent pleasures. Since, moreover, the sheriff is the person who would engage in that enforcement, he could be said to stand in a roughly analogous position to one of the things that we psychically mean by "father": the father as prohibitive function, denying pleasure to a populace that would otherwise indulge itself ceaselessly, and insisting thereby on the socialization of the town-as-son.

But it's easy to see that things are more complicated in this case. This is so, to begin with, because Nick starts by *agreeing* to be the "nothing doing nothing" that the town wants him to be. He declines to enforce the law in almost any way at all, allowing instead the indulgence for which he says the people elected him (64, 66). The fact that he does so—coupled with the fact that he risks being voted out of his job—indicates that the town in its turn exerts a certain authority over its sheriff, that the "father" in this scenario is at the mercy of powers greater than himself—namely, the authority of the "sons." This ascription of authority threatens the distinction between agent of prohibition and the embodiment of lawless desires. For not only does it tell us that the father's authority is, precisely, invested in him by those who embody the impulses he must control, but also that those who are most indulged by Nick are *those who are most moral.*

The people with whom he's most permissive are those who "hold it against [him] because [he hasn't] cracked down on 'em,'" who feel most morally outraged by his lack of moral assertiveness.

The results of this are several and far-reaching. It means, first of all, that the town is indeed like Nick-as-son, in that it conflates recognition with punishment, identity with being guilty. Nick's reluctance to "crack down" on the townspeople represents his failure to affirm them in guilt, and so to confer upon them a sense of being something, not nothing: a sense of being socially recognized, rather than swaddled in the individualized darkness of their private and incommunicable sins. Second, the moral outrage of those who indulge suggests that filial vice is itself the origin of moral self-righteousness. The law's prohibitive strictures gain their energy and authority from the violent impulses against which they do battle, in a way that raises the disturbing specter of a socially deconstituting *moral violence*. And third, Nick is caught in a bind that results from his having internalized this specter—and having done so in the form of the father as regulatory-prohibitive ideal. Precisely inasmuch as he's a father to the town, he's also forced to be its son; the more he obeys the inhabitants' injunction to be and to do nothing, the greater their (superegoic) anger and their desire to replace him with someone else. To be the father is thus to be faced with an insurmountable bind. It's to confront a son who wants in part to be recognized by being punished. But it's also to confront that son *in and as a father*, who turns you into a son and then declines to recognize you except by punishing you with all the instinctual violence of the son—and punishing you precisely for being the thing (the nothing) that this father/son requires you to be.

I'm suggesting that Nick and his town represent complex reflections of each other, and that this reflection signals the contamination of law with lawless desire, oedipalized father with pre-oedipal son—and of course, the other way round. This contamination is nowhere more evident than in the practical universality of guilt among the people of Pottsville. The most obvious example of this is Nick: sheriff and homicidal maniac, violator of law and—as he himself comes to see it—moral killer, scourge of God. I pursue this case in detail later. For now, it's important merely to note that almost every person we meet replicates on a smaller scale the obscenity of a social uprightness fused with social transgressiveness.[20]

When Nick gets himself in a fix with the town's most respected citizens, for example, he finds his way out by speaking cryptically of sexual transgressions and of criminal activity on the part of young people, in a way that has the men terrified and angry, certain that Nick has discovered their crimes and those of their wayward sons (153, 154). Or again, there's the case of Robert Lee Jefferson, the lawyer who's shown to be basically good—to feel, for example, the injustices of southern society and its racism. Jefferson at one point punches a man in the mouth for calling him by his first name. That man is, to be sure, a scoundrel; but the novel asks us to contemplate the inadequacy of this as a justification for violence:

I said I guessed Henry Clay didn't really know a lot about law, after all. "If he did, he'd know that calling you by your first name would be laying a predicate for justifiable assault."

"What? . . . I'm not sure I understood you."

"Nothin'" I said. "You sure gave him a punch, Robert Lee. . . . Maybe you'd better be kind of careful for a while. . . . Henry Clay might try to get back at you."

Robert Lee snorted. "He doesn't have the nerve, but I wish he did. That's one man I'd enjoy killing. Imagine him calling me by my first name!"

"Yeah," I said, "just imagine that!" (129)

The irony here is in many respects characteristic of Thompson's protagonists. It resides in the distance between Nick's revealed intelligence and the image he habitually projects of a buffoon. He doesn't, for the most part, come off like a man who would know words like "laying a predicate for justifiable assault," and Robert Lee is momentarily confused and disarmed by the fact that he does indeed know them. More important, however, is the barb embedded in the reply itself. For clearly Nick is trying to say that calling Jefferson by his first name does *not* lay a predicate for justifiable assault. He drives this point home by himself addressing the man by his first name: "You sure gave him a punch, Robert Lee."[21] And the irony is itself increased by the fact that Jefferson is forever urging Nick to go out and arrest people, but clearly *expects* Nick not to arrest him in the case at hand. As Nick himself puts it in a later scene: "Practically every fella that breaks the law has a danged good reason, to his own way of thinking, which makes every case exceptional. . . . Take you, for example. A lot of fellas might think you was guilty of assault and battery when you punched Henry Clay Fanning" (155). The argument here is not just that Robert Lee is wrong to have punched Fanning; it's also that the universality of law is a mark of its deepest limits, a sign that it must essentially ignore the variety of human particularity—and consequently, that the law is at once necessary and impossible, at once an instrument to protect one from violence and one that includes within itself the need for its own violation. Finally, there's the way in which this relatively trivial act of violence shades over into murderousness. When Jefferson, who besides Nick comes perhaps closest among the male characters to inhabiting a moral high ground in the book, starts fantasizing about how much he'd like to kill the man he's just knocked down ("That's one man I'd enjoy killing"), the distance between morality and transgression—pacific sociality and murderous violence—becomes very short indeed.

There is, moreover, a turn of the oedipal screw within this process. For if, as I suggested earlier, the townspeople want to revel in a violence directed against the vices they indulge, those vices will themselves turn out to be of an oedipal character. Take for example Henry Clay Fanning, the man whom Robert Lee punches. Fanning is "what we call a cotton-patch lawyer," a man who "[knows] all the [legal] privileges he [is] entitled to . . . but [doesn't] have much sense of his obligations." When he discovers the bodies of Uncle John and Tom Hauk, he believes himself entitled by law to some kind of reward: "County pays a ree-ward for corpses pulled out of the river. . . . So why don't I get a bounty for . . . these?" The trouble is that Fanning's idea of law is libertarian to the point of lawlessness:

None of his fourteen kids had ever been to school, because making kids go to school was interferin' with a man's constitutional rights. Four of his seven girls . . . were pregnant. And he wouldn't allow no one to ask 'em how they'd got that way, because . . . it was a father's job to care for his children's morals, and he didn't have to tolerate any interference.

Of course, everyone had a pretty good idea who'd gotten those girls pregnant. But . . . there wasn't any way of proving it, and with Henry Clay being kind of mean-tempered no one talked much about it. (128)

The horror here resides not merely in the fact of incest itself. It lies in an encoding of incest within the statutes of law, in an insistence that, lawfully speaking, the law has no right to legislate against incest, to prevent it or even to "talk much about it." Fanning defends this proposition with the thesis that the father himself ought to stand as absolute legislator: "[it's] a father's job to care for his children's morals, and he [doesn't] have to tolerate any interference." Self-serving as such a justification may be, it also marks the perverse character of the law that Fanning here flouts. For as we have seen, the novel itself imagines law to be founded on the authority of the father; its version of law is an oedipal version, in which the man who enforces it stands as a kind of social superego to the town's irrepressible urges. Fanning's appeal to the father's authority is thus in keeping with the community's rules and its own self-understanding. The father *is* an absolute legislator. But just as, in the passage discussed earlier, this legislation is complicated by the mutual contamination of impulse and repressive agent, so the commission of incest is here justified by an appeal to the father whose social embodiment prohibits it. Oedipal transgression is thus in one gesture outlawed and installed within the law. The father is both he who prohibits incest and he who (lawfully) commits it. The townspeople's tacit collusion with Fanning's acts further suggests the extent to which his incestuous transgressions are, paradoxically, social/anti-social.

But the most revealing instance of this guilt concerns the man who runs against Nick for sheriff. This man is, by all accounts, a morally righteous citizen. And yet Nick chooses to campaign against him not by encouraging him to come out against the town's transgressions, but rather by encouraging the town itself to come out against his opponent's transgressions. He does this by planting small seeds of doubt about Sam Gaddis's moral credentials. That is, he indicates to Robert Lee that there are "dirty, filthy stories . . . going around about [Sam]"—stories that he (Nick) won't stoop to repeat, since he knows they're untrue (67). The brilliance of this strategy resides in how little it requires Nick to do. He can in essence continue to be a "nothing doing nothing," leaving Robert Lee and others to fill in the blanks he has left unfilled. Better still, he can in good conscience go on insisting upon Sam's probity, can continue to say that he doesn't believe in the stories he hasn't bothered to make up, since he really can't give credence to tales that he knows no one is telling.

The result is that the townspeople do indeed begin to tell those tales, and to do so with an alacrity that's at once alarming and funny. Within pages Nick is hearing from Rose (one of his mistresses) about all the terrible things Sam has done—things that Rose heard from Nick's wife, Myra, who heard them from Mrs. Robert Lee Jefferson, who heard them from Robert Lee himself. "[A]nd you know," says Rose, "Robert Lee . . . wouldn't lie" (76). The communal character of these stories—the essential lack of origin indicated by their "she said that he said that she said" structure—points once more to the generality of the guilt that they describe. The townspeople tell the stories with gusto and a kind of imaginative fervor because those stories at once express the transgressive desires that they themselves share *and* enable them to participate in the "moral" pleasure of censure. Not surprisingly, the stories themselves are dominated by fantasies of oedipal transgression. Sam is said to have "raped a little two-year-old nigger baby"—an act that, if not literally incestuous, carries incestuous undertones, which it allies with an interracial desire that has often been metonymically linked in our culture to incestuous wishes.[22] He's also said to have "beat his own father to death with a stick of cordwood" (75). And several more of his fantasized crimes concern familial violations, and have the feel of slightly displaced expressions of oedipal transgressions.[23]

This collusion of drives with a violent morality is rendered most explicit when Nick confronts Sam at a public gathering:

"If you didn't rape any little defenseless colored babies or beat your poor ol' pappy to death or feed your sweet trusting wife . . . to the hawgs or—if you didn't do none of them dirty low-down things . . . how come so many folks say you did? . . . [H]ow come folks say that you done things that would out-stink a skunk . . . if it ain't true? Or . . . are you sayin' that you're telling the truth an' that everyone else is a dirty no-good liar?" (169)

The effectiveness of this strategy resides once more in how little Nick has to do. He need not actually accuse Sam of anything, but has only to ask him a question that, as he knows, is unanswerable. For Sam *cannot* respond to the question within the terms that Nick poses. Not to defend himself is political suicide. But to defend himself is to call the people whose votes he requires liars. Worse still, it's to indicate that those people *are themselves guilty (in fantasy)* of the crimes of which he is accused. For where else could those crimes have originated if not in the transgressively upright minds that ascribe those crimes to him? The townspeople's rage at Sam is in fact directly proportional to the pleasure they take in "creat[ing]" "stinking dirty dirt" where there isn't any "for real" (76). It is, accordingly, unsurprising that the scene ends in a moral orgy. Sam is "on maybe about his sixteenth" attempt to answer the question "when someone [flings] a prayer book. . . . And that was kind of like a signal, like the first crack of lighting in a storm. Because the air was suddenly full of prayer books and hymnals, and everyone was shouting and cussing and trying to get their hands on Sam. And all at once he disappeared like he'd been dropped through a trap door" (170). The use of prayer books and hymnals as weapons makes the scene's point disturbingly clear. The tokens of civilized morality become the instruments of a violence rooted in the transgressive wishes they pretend to oppose. Sam, in other words, is punished in essence *because* he is not guilty. His innocence is intolerable to a culture bound by a kind of pathological guilt, in which moral rectitude is fueled by an appetite whose indulgence drives it to vengeful fury. Civilization in this sense expresses the (oedipal) impulses that it's meant to repress. The town is literally constituted—but this also means *de*constituted—by an oedipal indulgence that is the very source of its moral self-righteousness, and that turns such righteousness into a violence that seems here to issue in murder (the reference to a "trap door," on this reading, being a metonym for lynching).

Talking, Looking, Laughing: Like a Man

I've been speaking so far of the socio-oedipal pathology in Thompson's novel and, in particular, of the ways in which that pathology is enacted by Pottsville's residents. My argument at this point requires that we return more explicitly to the figure of Nick. For if, as I have claimed, being a sheriff entails his being a "nothing doing nothing," and if this works to confirm a part of his paternally inherited identity, there is another part of that heritage that requires him to be a killer—to be "the low-down monster that killed his mother getting born." These two aspects are not unrelated. They have to do with the split described earlier between the superego as paternal prohibition and its function as regulatory ideal. That split is complicated in this instance by the fact that the act the father prohibits—incestuous violence—is one that his story also requires the son to have committed. In order to grasp the results of this bind, I want to examine two moments in *Pop. 1280* that echo scenes so prevalent in his books that we can think of them as instances of the Thompsonian primal scene.

I'm thinking here of scenes in which the narrator encounters a mirrored self-image, experiencing in that encounter his distance from an internalized ideal. Considerations of space prevent me from tracing this pattern in Thompson's earlier works.[24] Suffice it to say that, despite significant differences in these scenes, they share a fantasmatic core that's crucial to their power and significance. That core concerns a psychic rift that's figured externally through the trope of reflection, which in turn enables a perception of the self's inadequacies, vulnerabilities, and imminent decay. The rupture reflected in this way entails the speaker's abasement before an implicitly paternal ideal. And this detail signals a conceptual shift away from the largely pre-oedipal specularity of the books in my previous chapters, as well as from the mirror phase as Jacques Lacan has famously conceptualized it—in terms, that is, of the infant's engagement with an image that pre-dates both its entry into language and its subjection to the paternal metaphor.[25] Thompson makes use of the mirror instead to articulate a pathology *within* the paternal relation, suggesting thereby the mutual contamination of (Imaginary) pre-oedipal ambivalence and (Symbolic) oedipal law.

These issues are nowhere explored so complexly as they are in *Pop. 1280*, where the scene of self-reflection I'm describing is extended by a second key passage:

I put on my Sunday-go-to-meetin' clothes, my new sixty-dollar Stetson and my seventy-dollar Justin boots and my four-dollar Levis. I stood in front of the mirror, checking myself over real good; making sure that I didn't look like some old country boy. Because I was making a little trip to see a friend of mine. . . . And I always try to look my best when I see Ken Lacey [the sheriff of a neighboring town]. (5)

[Ken's town] was a real big place—probably four, five thousand people. The main street was paved, along with the square around the courthouse, and . . . I even seen two, three auty-mobiles. . . . I mean, it was just like being in New York or one of them other big cities I've heard about. . . .

Just for example, I passed this one vacant lot where there was the god-dangest dogfight going on that I ever did see. Kind of a battle royal between two hounds and a bulldog and a kind of spotty-assed mongrel.

Why, even if there hadn't been a fight, that mongrel would have been enough to make a fella stop and stare. . . . He had this high ass in the back, all spotted and speckled like a cow had farted bran on him. . . . And one of his eyes was blue and the other'n was yaller. A real bright yaller like a woman's hair.

I stood there gawking, wishing I had someone from Pottsville with me as a wit-
ness. . . . Then, I happened to look around, and hard as it was to tear myself away, I
turned my back on that spectacle and went on toward the courthouse.

I just about had to . . . unless I wanted people to think I was an old country boy.
Because I was the only one that had stopped to look. There was so much going on in
that city that no one would ever give a second glance to . . . that! (22–23)

The first passage starts by describing a crafting of identity within the consciousness of being seen. Nick regards himself in the mirror, examines with
care his own self-reflection, in a manner that holds him up to the light of an
image of which he appears to fall short. He feels in danger of being reflected
back as an "old country boy." The phrase itself is highly significant, in that
it links a lack of full manhood ("boy") to the absence of civilized knowledge
and manners associated with the hick ("country")—and does so within a
context suggesting that what it means to "be" a country boy is in fact to be
seen as one. Accordingly, Nick tries to fashion a mirror image that closes the
gap between himself and the ideal. He "put[s] on [his] Sunday-go-to-meetin'
clothes, [his] new sixty-dollar Stetson and [his] seventy-dollar Justin boots,"
all in order to look like something *other* than an "old country boy"—to look,
that is, at once more manly and more properly socialized. The clothes he
wears could in this sense be said to mark a projection of social refinement
that inheres in the extent of their expense, as well as a projection of impermeable manhood that resides within the mythological significance of their
Western iconography.

But things get significantly more interesting than this in the second
passage I've quoted. The emphasis on specular identity is here complicated
by the recognition that being a hick is not just a matter of visibly resem-
bling one, but also a matter of *being seen to inhabit the position of a certain*
kind of looking. Nick feels like a country boy because he's "the only one that
[has] stopped to look" at the dogfight in a vacant lot. The spectacle makes
him "stop and stare," leaves him "gawking" and wishing for a witness to
corroborate his visual experience. A hick thus turns out to be a person who

146

remains enthralled by a specific type of spectacle. And that spectacle is, very precisely, a spectacle of the pre-civil. It entails a kind of prehuman violence, a "battle royal" or fight to the death that brooks no surrender and admits no prisoners. It entails as well the saturation of visible being with excrement: the mongrel dog draws one's attention in part because of its peculiarly "high ass," and in part because that ass is itself "all spotted and speckled like a cow had farted bran on him." Such a vision fascinates because of its devoluted and excremental character; its interest resides in the way it recalls a primitive mode of asocial being, which civilized society ought to have surmounted and, indeed, to find now uninteresting. If Nick risks being exposed as a hick, then, it's precisely because he continues to find this spectacle libidinally compelling—because his wish to see it is so strong that he has to tear himself away, if he's to avoid being seen to be looking in a way that defines him as uncivil and unmanly.[26]

And yet this suggestion of Nick as hick is compromised by the way the novel also insists he is not one. This becomes clear in a passage closely connected to those I have quoted. Here Nick, having managed to turn his back on the dogfight, enters the courthouse of Ken's town, tells Ken and his deputy, Buck, about his "problems," and asks for their advice. The problems he relates have to do with two pimps who have begun to treat him disrespectfully. Ken's advice is to kick them in the balls, because "when a fella starts doin' somethin' bad to you, the proper way to pay him back is t'do something twice as bad to him" (33). In demonstration of this thesis—and after treating Nick throughout like an idiot—Ken convinces him twice to bend over and be kicked in the ass. Thompson then offers this exchange:

"Hurt your arm?" Ken said. "Whereabouts?"

"I'm not positive," I said. "It could be either the radius or the ulna."

Buck gave me a sudden sharp look out from under his hatbrim. Sort of like . . . he was seeing me for the first time. But of course Ken didn't notice anything. Ken had so much on his mind . . . helping poor stupid fellas like me, that he maybe didn't notice a lot of things. (32–33)

The central purpose of this scene is to indicate the knowledge that lies submerged beneath Nick's outward idiocy. Just as one does not expect him to know a phrase like "predicate for justifiable assault," so we're meant to be surprised by his intimacy with words like "radius" and "ulna." That intimacy grants him a level of culture that's inimical to the identity of "old country boy." It suggests not merely an educational superiority but a linguistic one as well, linking the distinctions between civilized and uncivilized once more to questions of language and voice. This addition, in its turn, is crucial to the significance of the scene. It's precisely because Nick's narrational persona encompasses the voice of the civilized expert as well as that of the "ignoramus" (92) that he's able to mean what he does not say, to "tell us" that he came to see Ken for reasons different from those he states. When Buck, accordingly, goads Ken into saying that he'd kill the pimps in question, Nick tells us, "It looked like I'd got what I came for" (34)—and he gets up to leave. It's difficult to know what his statement means at this point in the story—namely, as we soon see, that Ken has indeed solved Nick's problems by setting himself up to be framed for murder. What's clear, however, is that the phrase contains a vocal or tonal doubling that suggests a capacity for dissimulation, so that Nick cannot be *reduced* to a bumpkin who fears being caught with his eyes wide open at the spectacularly uncivilized remnants within the gates of civilization.

The vocal division that I am describing is absolutely pervasive in the novel. It extends beyond our perception of Nick to our understanding of the town at large, which must contend with the tendency of his statements to veer away from their literal meanings toward a range of tonal implications that can't be reduced to declarative sense. When Nick says, for example, that "It was a real big place—probably four, five thousand people," the second half of the statement works to negate the meaning of the first. We're meant to recognize through this conjunction that a town with several thousand inhabitants is not "really big" at all—certainly nothing like "New York or one of them other big cities." The account of Nick's seeing "two or three auty-mobiles" produces a comparable effect. For even during the 1930s in which the novel is apparently set, a "big" town would surely have to be one that had more than two or three cars in it. The fact, moreover, that the dogfight happens within the confines of the town suggests that Nick's official distinction between himself as country bumpkin and the town's cosmopolitan character is being radically undermined in the process of being described.

Finally, however, this reversal of terms is itself called into question by the instability of Nick's voice. This is in part a function of the split between a cultured language and the language of the bumpkin—between Nick's use of "radius" and "ulna" and his repeated "I wouldn't say you was wrong, but I sure wouldn't say you was right, neither" (25, 152). But it's also and more crucially a question of Thompson's *refusal adequately to mark the edges of these discourses*. Nick never tells us exactly what he knows, why he's doing what he's doing, the extent to which his actions result from conscious planning, and the extent to which they're improvised. It's thus impossible to pin down the point where his knowledge leaves off and his ignorance begins. It's impossible, for example, to tell how far he believes in the town's size and cosmopolitan character, and how far he's merely having us on—impossible, accordingly, to tell at what point civilization leaves off and hicksville begins. If the town is a hick town and Nick is at least civilized enough to know it, it's equally true that Nick *really does* talk and act like a bumpkin; he really stops to gape at the dogfight, and really gets himself kicked in the ass—twice. Such behaviors suggest that he has in some sense become the alienated image that the mirror first reflects back to him—even as the narrative voice insists upon holding those identities apart, bespeaking through the spaces between them the impossibility of their smooth integration.

It is precisely within this space that the humor of the scene arises as well. That humor follows a pattern that replicates the general structure of ironic self-consumption, by which a set of distinctions is at once erected, undermined, and affirmed through the instability of Nick's voice. We know now that the distinctions in question concern the borders between knowledge and ignorance, morality and immorality, civilization and its other—and ultimately, of course, father and son. This last distinction is in fact the master difference of the novel; it contains the terms through which the others gain their significance and coherence, precisely inasmuch as Thompson imagines civilized society and its morality to be oedipal in genesis and structure. In the context of the scene at hand, this means that Nick's jokes embroil him in an inexorable double bind. They entail, in the first place, an attempt on his part to position the reader as what Freud's joke theory designates the "third person"—the proto-superegoic father—who can affirm him by way of an alliance that makes the town the butt of its humor. The jokes in this sense work to the extent that they get us to acknowledge Nick as "first person." They work because, in giving us pleasure, they require us to recognize Nick himself as producer of that pleasure, affirming his knowledge of the town's lack of culture as well as the forms of learnedness he possesses. This process enables Nick's precipitation out of the humiliating visual transaction that defines him as "old country boy." Rather than being caught looking at the uncivil spectacle of shit-speckled dogs, he is now able, through an identificatory alliance with the visual perspective of the joke's addressee, to see himself looking from a knowing distance through which he can weigh his bumpkin self against a more civil male subjectivity, in contrast to which the town is also measured and found wanting.

But inasmuch as recognition here leads inevitably to self-punishment—inasmuch as the joke-work is oedipal, in the peculiarly anti-oedipal sense that the novel gives to that term—the humor of *Pop. 1280* will also turn against the "first person." We laugh as much at Nick in this scene as we do at Ken being duped by him. We take a genuine pleasure in his stupidity and cultural inferiority. And we do so, I'd suggest, as the delegate of something deep inside of Nick. The novel places us in the space of his internalized ideal, through which Nick excoriates himself for being the uncivilized and immoral nothing that this ideal requires him to be—and that we also require him to be, at least to the extent that our pleasure depends upon his succeeding in being it. Such a process implicates us in the novel's moral violence. It does so by asking us to identify with that aspect of Nick that's at once committed to oedipal morality and fueled by pre-oedipal impulse and rage, and here we arrive at the larger significance of excrement in the scene—and indeed, at its significance for the novel as a whole.

For excrement is, as I have said, a sign of the structurally insurmountable ambivalence at the heart of the Oedipus complex. The superego may be "heir to the Oedipus complex," but the Oedipus complex is heir to shit, in that it represents the culmination of a psychic series each of whose terms entails the recognition of loss, difference, and separation. That series begins with the anal phase;[27] it starts with the consciousness brought by shit of a prohibition that limits the self—but also with a grievous awareness that this limit marks a loss, that shit is also a part of the self that the civilized psyche must renounce if it's to be called civilized at all. Part of what Thompson's novel suggests is that one's ambivalence toward this loss haunts the final point in the sequence: the acceptance of symbolic castration as the cost of a civilized male identity that has internalized the father's law.[28] That ambivalence returns in the form of the superego's uncivilized pleasure in censuring what it requires you to enjoy. The blurring of edges between civilization and its other in this sense marks the infusion of excrement into the reign of the masculine superego. For just as the instabilities of Nick's voice make it impossible to sustain the set of distinctions that we've already examined, so that voice makes it difficult to locate the border between our laughter *at* Nick for being a hick and our identification with his pleasure in the excrement he ascribes to the spectacle. The scene in fact requires us to participate in this fascination with shit, which is inseparable from the censure by which Nick helps us turn the joke against him. It isn't just, then, that the scene turns humor back upon the "first person"; it also turns it against the "third" in and through the "first," as we ourselves become caught in the bind that makes Nick both the moral center of his universe and a cultural-moral degenerate. We catch ourselves, as we catch Nick, enjoying the spectacle of shit-speckled dogs that bespeaks the incivility at the heart of male culture. We thereby become the objects of civilized vision as much as its transcendent subject. And we thus partake of the comically moral violence attendant on this double consciousness, humiliating ourselves through an identification with Nick as father and son—an identification through which we bend over to be kicked with him, by the superego's delegates, in the royal behind.

Doing Something

But the novel also charts a further displacement of this violence: a movement away from self-punishment toward the punishment—the murder—of others. We're now in a position to account more fully for this movement. For if humor is here, as I have argued, the superegoic, post-oedipal expression of unoedipalized ambivalence, we can now see how it forms the basis of Thompson's psychosocial critique. The contours of that critique return us to the psychic genesis of Nick's monstrosity, while helping us to see how that genesis is intertwined with a social one.

For Nick is clearly pushed past the edge by the way in which the demands of Pottsville replicate the dynamic I have been describing. He cannot remain a "nothing doing nothing" because the townspeople demand he "do something." They want not just their appetites sated, but their moral outrage as well. They're therefore eager for Nick to exert the authority that they pay him not to exert—which is another way of saying that they delegate to him the role of social superego, and even of moral murderer, precisely inasmuch as they seek to exempt themselves from the knowledge of their own desires. Nick himself makes this point more than once. When Rose protests against his intention to kill Uncle John for having discovered that Nick has killed Rose's husband, he says: "I'm . . . kind of tired of doing things that everybody knows I'm doing, *things they really want and expect me to do*, and having to take all the blame for it" (118; my emphasis). This is in part self-serving, of course. As Nick tells Uncle John moments later, he feels compelled to kill because he is "willing to do anything [he has] to to go on lying and cheating and drinking whiskey and screwing women and going to church on Sunday with all the other respectable people" (119–20). And yet the structure of universal transgression fused to vindictive violence tends to corroborate Nick's first claim as well. To "do something" is, if you're sheriff of Potts County, to serve the people by enabling them to indulge their appetites by proxy, in and through a moral violence that expresses the drives it represses. If Nick can manage to do this successfully, he can presumably come to be recognized as "something" rather than "nothing," as paternal authority rather than the buffoon that the town forbids yet requires him to be.

And yet his efforts to express this rage can only thwart the recognition they solicit. This is evident, first, in the fact that Nick's socially sanctioned killings must nonetheless be covert, since the townspeople want to continue believing that their morality is separable from the lust for blood that feeds its hunger. Thus Nick is required—and this is a second point—to vent the town's rage only on the lowly. "I'm really going to start cracking down," he says to Robert Lee at one point. "Anyone that breaks a law from now on is goin' to have to deal with me. Providing, o' course, that he's either colored or some poor white trash that can't pay his poll tax" (155). Or again, from a late scene in which Nick tries to tell Rose why he's tricked her into killing his wife: "By rights, I should be rompin' on the high an' the mighty, the folks that really run this country. But I ain't allowed to touch them, so I've got to make up for it by being twice as hard on the white trash an' Negroes, and people like you that let their brains sink down to their butts" (206). True moral vengeance would on this model be aimed at the fathers themselves: at "the high an' the mighty . . . that really run this country."

The fact that this rage originates in the fathers is perfectly in keeping with the fact mentioned earlier, that those who are most upright are also those who indulge most freely, and those who indulge most freely are those who cry out loudest for punishment. Nick is also pointing, however, to a displacement within this structure. He's describing how the moral masochism of the oedipal bind is turned by the fathers into sadism, and then directed outward onto the populace at large.[29] This is the price that the oedipal fathers exact for their social privilege—a price that's repeated in Nick himself, who isn't able to "romp" on those fathers since that would kill the source of recognition, but who's forced to forgo recognition anyway by being compelled to exert his authority only covertly, and only over the socially insignificant.

The results of this are once more far-reaching. The process helps explain, to begin with, the peculiar role of sympathy and compassion within Nick's moral violence. For one of the book's most striking features is surely that Nick's goodness is neither reducible to oedipal (im)morality nor completely exempt from it. Take, for example, the following passage:

Fact is, I felt real sorry for him [Nick's brother-in-law, Lennie], but right while I was [feeling] it, I felt something else. Because that's the way I am. . . . I start feeling sorry for people . . . and the way it . . . works out is it'd be a lot better if I hadn't felt sorry for them. Better for them, I mean. . . . Because when you're sorry for someone, you want to help them, and when it sinks in on you that you can't, that there's too god-danged many of them, that everywhere you look there's someone, millions of some-ones, and you're only one man an' no one else cares an'—an'— (136–37)[30]

The passage describes how violence can issue from a sense of moral impotence—how compassion can be thwarted by a knowledge of the enormity of human suffering, and how this knowledge can turn compassion into murderous rage. The presence of authentic feeling in this sequence seems to place it outside of the general structure I'm describing; it gives to Nick a human touch that's elsewhere all but absent in the novel, endowing him with a morality that can't be reduced to moral violence. The moral sense may *issue in* violence; but the violence here is not itself moral, cannot be rationalized on moral grounds. Indeed, the justification in this case appeals less to moral necessity than to social despair. It's because the world is so full of injustice as to make it feel impossible to make a difference that compassion becomes transformed into a violence designed to eliminate suffering in a manner the initial compassion can only abhor.

But if this moral sense is partially free from toxic (im)morality, the experience of impotence itself turns out to be a function of that morality. I mean by this that Nick's feelings of helplessness result from the inexorability of the bind in which he's caught. Since the social order is founded upon a pre-oedipal ambivalence imbued with moral authority, it becomes very hard to imagine the successful realization of non-toxic morality. Any impulse in this direction will confront almost insuperable difficulties. It will have to contend with a system in which oppression is rationalized on moral grounds; in which victims can be said to be asking for it because of guilt's universality; and in which the difference between victims and victimizers is that the latter have the law on their side, and have managed to turn a thirst for punishment into socially sanctioned structures of inequity, oppression, and violence.

Such a vision is admittedly extreme, and open to charges of political quietism. It has, however, the enormous benefit of exposing the costs of oedipal morality. I'd like to begin exploring those costs by looking at some scenes in which Nick does attempt to rationalize his murders. These scenes help us see the forms of dehumanization that the oedipal pathology constructs for the victims of its violence, as well as the fragility of the psychic defenses by which the fathers seek to protect themselves from the implications of their crimes.

Let us begin with a passage in which Nick calls free will into question. This occurs at the culmination of the scene in which he kills Uncle John, and consists of the final words he speaks to the man he's about to shoot:

"I'll tell you something else," I said, "and it makes a shit-pot-ful more sense than most of the goddam scripture I've read. Better the blind man, Uncle John; better the blind man who pisses through a window than the prankster who leads him thereto. You know who the prankster is, Uncle John? Why it's goddam near everybody, every son-of-a-bitch who turns his head when the crap flies. . . . Even you, particularly you . . . ; people who go around sniffing crap with their mouth open, and acting surprised as hell when someone kicks a turd in it. Yeah, you can't help bein' what you are, jus' a pore ol' black man. . . . [But] I say screw you. I say you can't help being what you are, and I can't help being what I am, and you goddam well know what I am. . . . You goddam well know you've got no friends among the whites. You goddam well ought to know that you're not going to have any because you stink Uncle John, and you go around begging to get screwed and how the hell can anyone have a friend like that?"

I gave him both barrels of the shotgun.

It danged near cut him in two. (120)

I want to focus first on the parabolic maxim toward the beginning of this passage: "better the blind man who pisses through a window than the prankster who leads him thereto." This is clearly meant to suggest a distinction between the "doer" of a deed and the agency behind that doer. The person who commits the deed is on this reading "blind"; the deed is something he can't help doing, and something whose consequences he can neither adequately foresee nor prevent. Those consequences have in their turn to do with an abjectly organized violence.[31] They issue from an act that is here defined as one of bodily excretion—an act that eliminates from the self the waste that is both part of that self and psychosocially defined as "not-self." And this expulsion is conceptualized as a kind of comic aggression. The reason, that is, that the blind man's pissing poses a problem at all is that someone may be passing below and end up soiled by his excretions. The fact that Nick is using the parable to meditate on his own condition further highlights this significance. Killing John is, within this context, analogous to or the logical extension of pissing out of a window on him, and Nick disclaims blame for this murderous soiling by suggesting that he's been compelled by a person he calls here "the prankster."

The attempt at exculpation in this sense hinges upon the question of who excretes and who directs or administers that excretion. Part of what's disquieting about the passage is that the person who administers and directs is also the person who receives. The agent of violence is blameless, for Nick, because his victims are themselves the "pranksters" who solicit their own violation, "sniffing crap with their mouth open" and "go[ing] around begging to get screwed." Such a logic returns us to the fact that Pottsville's morality is structured in a way that figures those who pay the price for (white) male power as willing victims of that power.

It should be clear by now that Nick's own part in this process is complicated. His evident racism in the passage, for example, conflicts with his condemnations of racial inequality elsewhere in the book (25–26, 62–63). This should tell us that he's here speaking in the voice of the double bind, by which the "something" he's required to do can only indulge the moral rage on which the social order is based—and can only do so by displacing that rage onto those against whom the oedipal fathers work to define themselves. Part of this act of definition entails ascribing uncivilized characteristics to those who are not "us." Nick thus speaks in the voice of the fathers when he says that Uncle John is unlovable because, being black, he "stink[s]." But what's surely most remarkable about the passage is that it exposes the fantasmatic character of this aroma, tracing it back to the civilized psyche's own excremental ambivalence. If Pottsville has made it so that Uncle John "can't help" being what he is, (black) and Nick "can't help" being what he is (white), then the passage could be said to reveal the mechanism by which this inevitability comes to be socially installed: through a moral violence that institutes the difference between civilized and uncivilized, but whose perfect expression is a pissing that also ruins that distinction, since it locates the origin of smell in the white man who tries here to piss it out.

The result of this process is a downward spiral in which Nick's manically intensified defenses become inseparable from his messianic breakdown. In a second passage on free will, he begins to speak for the first time of how he's "Christ on the cross come . . . to Potts County" and, in almost the same breath, of the moral distinction between "the fella that craps on a doorknob [and] the one that rings the doorbell" (179). This conjunction suggests that being Christ means at once soiling other people and being free from the taint of excrement. Nick—as Christ—merely rings the doorbell, summoning the victim to dirty himself on a knob that's been shat on by a third party. The increased distance from a soiling substance marks the extent to which this fantasy functions as a defense. Being Christ means being *purer* than the man who pisses through a window; it means never having the abject matter in you in the first place, never containing the stuff with which one might do harm to others. And yet, this new construction also entails an indictment of the Father(s)—and ultimately, of Nick himself. For if Nick is Christ and Christ rings the bell, then surely he who craps on the knob would have to be God the Father. It's God who does the "pointin'," who "pick[s] out the people [on whom Nick] exercise[s] His wrath" (209). It's God who instructs Nick to "strik[e] down the pore sinners that no one gives a good god-dang about" (209). Religious mania may, then, work to protect Nick from his guilt—but it does so only by replicating the problem it's meant to solve. The mania in fact reinforces the sense that to kill is to kill in the name of the fathers, to kill indeed as a delegate of the fathers, and in order to protect through this displacement the goodness of their names.

Since, moreover, Christ himself is an aspect of the Holy Father, it becomes impossible to sustain the distinctions that the mania is meant to protect. Nick is at once the father and son, the unoedipalized agent of violence and the moral authority that sanctions that violence. He is both the one who craps on the doorknob and the one who rings the bell. Not too surprisingly, such an admission has explicitly moral consequences. If Nick is Christ and Christ is Father, it will turn out that Nick-Christ-God is also the devil himself, that there is here no difference between the principle of good and that of destruction. This insight is in part embedded within Nick's very name— "old Nick" being a common nickname for the devil.[32] More importantly, it's a truth that Nick expresses in his final conversation with Buck. Here he claims again to be Jesus, "revealin' who I was [to him]." Buck demurs and suggests that he's "got [himself] mixed up with that other fella. . . . The one with the same front initial." And Nick: "That's right Buck! . . . I'm both. . . . The fella that gets betrayed and the one that does the betrayin' all in one man!" (215).

Finally, the self-canceling nature of religious rhetoric is itself accompanied by an intensification of the book's scatological elements. This is true both of shit as that which Buck and all the other "pore sinners" are increasingly forced to eat (209, 215–15), and as the substance that emanates from the agent of religious/moral violence. Nick displays a growing tendency toward gluttony, dirtiness, and sloth (see especially 3–4, 10, 22, 206), as if the more religious he becomes the more he also comes to wallow in the sins and waste matter of the body:

I found a long hair sticking out of my nose, and I jerked it out . . . and it didn't look particularly interesting. I dropped it to the floor, wonderin' if falling hair from fella's noses was noted along with fallin' sparrows. I raised up on one cheek of my butt, and eased out one of those long rattly farts, like you never can get rid of when other folks are around. I scratched my balls, tryin' to decide at what point a fella stopped scratchin' and started playin'. Which is an age-old question, I guess, and one that ain't likely to be solved in the near future. (212)

What could be stranger than a Christ who behaves in this undeniably abject manner? Or—more pointedly—what could be funnier? For we have of course arrived once more at the comic dimension to the immorality of morality, and at how Nick's religious delusions add a further lunatic twist to his vocal expression of humor. That expression has again to do with the defiling of civilized morality with its uncivilized and immoral other. But the humor here resides not so much in the fusion of biblical cadences with anti-biblical content ("better the blind man who pisses through a window than the prankster who leads him thereto"); it lies, rather, in a grotesque literalization of Christ's "embodiment" that renders His body as brute abjection. The passage is funny precisely because of this fusion of Nick as Christ with Nick as producer of "rattly" farts. It's funny because it describes a range of socially proscribed functions, which "Christ" invites us to participate in while marking them as taboo. And it's funny because the narrative voice attains at once the heights of culture in the dazzle of its comic mastery and the religious significance to which it alludes ("sparrows falling"), and the depths of depravity in the functions it describes.

No wonder, then, that when Nick "reveals himself" as Christ to Rose, she replies: "Oh, brother! . . . What a bull artist!" (209). Or again, on the following page: "Brother! . . . Are you ever full of crap." Corey is indeed "full of crap," is indeed, and very precisely, "a bull artist." As he himself will put it later, he's "the poet laureate of Potts County," a man who "make[s] up poems about piss tinkling in pots and jaybirds with the bots and assholes tying knots" (184). And no wonder that it's precisely to Pottsville that this poet feels himself called. The name is itself a reference to shit, to sitting (as we say) "on the pot." And the town is "about as close as you can get to the asshole of creation" (209), a phrase that links creativity to feces in a way that reflects how the novel's own inventive energy resides in a voice that is at once ex-cremental and hypermoral, at once the voice of God ("creation") and the voice of shit itself—the voice, in short, as we can see, of a *creative asshole*.

"Whatever's got tail at one end has teeth at the other"

I want in conclusion to consider the role that femininity plays in these issues. My claim is that, in a process similar to the ones we have traced in Cain and Faulkner, Thompson attempts to rewrite the soiling of masculine voice as feminine—and does so in an effort to save the fathers from the indictment that the novel offers. As we shall see, this effort fails. *Pop. 1280* ends with a gesture that reestablishes with a difference the terms of the critique I've been describing—terms that rely on the powerfully speculative inventiveness of the book's excremental humor.[33]

The conflation of excrement with the feminine is already clear in a pas-sage quoted earlier: the passage describing Nick's anxiety over stopping to gawk at a dogfight. Here, the dog that so fascinates Nick with its excremen-tal elements is also said to have one yellow eye: "A real bright yaller like a woman's hair" (23). The detail suggests that our earlier analysis needs to be supplemented by an awareness of how the scene's humor depends upon the structure that Freud attributes to smut. That is, the humor here enacts a res-olution of thwarted seduction through an alliance between men, enabling the joker and listener to bond through an aggressive exposure of the woman's body. The relatively disguised character of the woman—the fact that she shows up only in an oblique reference to the dog's eye—should not surprise us. This is merely an effect of the fact that the joke-work operates, like the dream-work, primarily through the mechanisms of displacement and condensation. Nor should it initially surprise us that these mechanisms work to conflate femininity with the excremental. This conflation results from the fact that smut is a form of humor that relies for effect on the sexual, but on sexuality in that peculiar sense that psychoanalysis gives to it:

The sexual material which forms the content of smut includes . . . what is excremental. . . . This is, however, the sense covered by sexuality in childhood, an age at which there is . . . a cloaca within which what is sexual and what is excremental are barely or not at all distinguished. Throughout the . . . psychology of the neuroses, what is sexual includes what is excremental, and is understood in the old, infantile, sense.[34]

To the extent that the woman, then, psychically shows up here as an object of male desire, the movement into the excremental seems almost a natural (if regressive) function of the joke-work's effort to speak of her in displaced and condensed form.

But this explanation should not obscure the misogyny of the scene's humor—or indeed, of the oedipal process that humor recapitulates. We might even say that the damage inflicted by the oedipal pathology in part resides in the way it requires a certain debasement and devaluation of femininity, which it effects through the unconscious conflation of the feminine with the abject. Accordingly, that aspect of the novel which enacts the yearning for paternal recognition participates in this debasement. The debasement itself takes a range of forms. Toward the end of the novel, for example, Nick describes the Talkington agent who comes to question him as follows: "He smiled, his bee's-ass mouth stretching enough to show one tooth, and it was like getting a glimpse of an egg coming out of a pullet pigeon" (172). This is a truly bizarre comparison that stands out even in a book as strange as this one. What's most important is that it imagines the organ of self-expression as, at once, an ass and a birth canal. The excremental creativity from which Nick's humor flows is now reimagined as something feminine, something tied to biological reproduction rather than artistic creation. And the joke, in this case, is clearly on the man whom Nick describes in this way. The passage conflates giving birth with shitting as a way of degrading the agent at Nick's door, reducing him to the grotesquely "feminine" functions centered on the orifice in his face.

A second passage extends this degradation while directing it more explicitly at women. Nick is here describing the reaction of a group of neighbors at the moment Myra tricks him into marrying her. The neighbors do not know it's a trick:

> *Everyone was pretty surprised, including me, and they were puzzled too. . . . It looked like I'd sold my pottage for a mess of afterbirth. . . . I'd been chasing females all my life, not paying no mind to the fact that whatever's got tail at one end has teeth at the other, and now I was getting chomped on. (99)*

The misogyny here is more than casual—it is, in fact, structural and central to the passage's larger effects. Its most striking instance comes perhaps in the final sentence, where woman is in essence reduced to a sexual availability ("tail") fused with oral ferocity and vindictiveness ("teeth"). The term "tail" itself embodies a certain psychic ambiguity, referring at once to the vaginal opening and to the female anus—tending, indeed, to condense the two in much the same way as does the image of an egg emerging from a "bee's-ass."

More interesting, however, is the sentence in which Nick says he has "sold his pottage for a mess of afterbirth." The statement once more contains the equation of femininity with abjection; the "pottage" in question is the sexual satisfaction derived from catching "tail," while the "afterbirth" is the abjected condition that results from being "chomped on" by female "teeth"—that is, being tricked into marriage. But at the same time, the association of marriage with afterbirth ought to remind us of the centrality to Nick's psychic life of his mother's death in childbirth. Given the need to be an excrescence that his father then bequeaths to him, we might begin to suspect that Nick experiences *himself* as a living afterbirth, so that projecting this sense onto Myra marks a gesture of defense that has its roots in the catastrophes of oedipalization. This speculation opens the scene onto questions of loss and maternal substitution. The distaste for women that we've begun to trace is in part necessitated by the need to repudiate the mother in the name of an alliance with the father. Fused with this necessity, however, is a rage at the mother for having been lost, a rage in this case for being doubly lost—first, through her literal death in childbirth, and second through the oedipal prohibitions that rewrite the act of "killing" her as a forbidden sexual act. In this sense the novel's misogyny may reflect an always imperfect and fragile displacement of fury from father to mother. And the superego whose genesis we have traced may represent an anally fueled yet vocal violence that's (1) rooted in a fusion with the mother that pre-dates anal loss; (2) directed toward recovery of the mother through the displacements that follow that loss; and (3) aimed in the form of rage at the mother for having left the son alone with a father who makes him guilty.

Such speculations help to explain the predominance of loss and suffering in Nick's adult experience of love. Here, for example, is how he describes his "good" mistress, Amy: she's lovable because of "something that [comes] from inside, something that kind of [grabs] hold of you right around the heart, that [leaves] its mark on you like a brand, so that the feel of her and the memory of her [is] always with you no matter where you [stray]" (88). This is a truly remarkable description that thinks of love as a species of loss— and therefore, as a kind of pain. The "something" inside of Amy "grabs hold of" your "heart" and marks you as with a "brand"; it leaves an indelibly painful impression precisely because it's already lost, because Nick himself, in the act of describing his present love, can only refer to it as past, as something from which he has in fact "strayed" to be left with only its "memory." This sense of loss is shot through with an at least implicit reproach. For the wound inflicted by the woman is one that forms the self by stranding it. A "brand" is a mark that's needed only for that which one won't be around to tend, that which one intends, in fact, to leave alone to wander. It's thus at once a mark of identity and a sign that makes you the property of someone from whom it also severs you. It doesn't seem far-fetched, in this light, to say that the experience described here results from Nick's sense of natal abandonment, which leads him to displace his anger at his father onto the mother and her avatars.

But perhaps more crucial to *Pop. 1280*'s misogyny is a remarkable story that Polito recounts from Thompson's early childhood. Apparently, "[f]rom

163

the time that he was old enough to frolic alone in [the yard of his maternal grandparents], whenever [Thompson] returned to the house covered with dirt [his mother] would sweep him up in her arms and scurry to the mirror. Holding his face right by hers, she would stare into the glass and ask him, 'Will you take a look at Mama's little black child. Where did your white mother get such a black son?'" (51). This story, however playfully couched, contains a conflation of blackness with dirt that seems to me part of the same semantic series as the more unsettling figuration of Uncle John as smelling. It also contains a return of the mirror that figures so centrally in Thompson's explorations of male identity. And it contains once more an insistence upon the space between the masculine self and its reflected ideal.

What's new, however, is in this case more instructive than what's similar. For here the mirror and the question of (racial) soiling *are brought into relation with the mother*. It's as if the function of this familial story were to suggest for Thompson that, behind the splits in male identity and the exposure of dirt as internal to the self, there lies a maternal figure who can take the blame for this state of affairs. In the story I've quoted, the reproach is fairly muted; the mother herself remains pure and white, while holding her son up to see how far he falls short of this ideal. But in *Pop. 1280* this relation is at once distorted and reversed. Nick at one point tells Buck and Ken that, contrary to what they have been arguing, black people must be human because "[m]y mama died almost as soon as I was born, so I was put to suck with a colored mammy. Wouldn't be alive today except for her sucklin' me" (25). Behind the humanist rhetoric of this statement, there lurks a range of more disturbing and thematically pertinent associations: that the self's own "dirt" is coded female and black; that it's something one imbibes at a breast which, if not the mother's, is nonetheless maternal; and that badness itself perhaps results from the absence of the mother's breast, so that the mammy is here a figure for the dirt that one is forced to eat through the fate of maternal abandonment—and that will ultimately form the basis of a paternally inflected, vocally based, yet excremental morality.

Precisely inasmuch as the novel "knows" about these associations, however, its misogynist equations begin to unravel in the very process of being stated. Women can no longer be blamed for being dirt once we see that it's men themselves who produce this fantasy of woman:

The farm land [owned by Rose's husband, Tom] was . . . that rich, black silt you see in the river lowlands; so fine and sweet you could almost eat it, and so deep that you couldn't wear it out. . . . You might say that land was a lot like Rose, naturally good, deep down good, but Tom had done his best to ruin it like he had her. He hadn't done it, because they'd had too much good stuff to begin with. But both the land and her were a long sight from being what they'd been before he got ahold of 'em.

. . . What he had changed was the way she thought—mean and tough—and the way she talked. When she didn't have to be on guard, she talked practically as bad as he did. (70–71)

The passage offers a meditation on the toxic character of conventional masculinity—a masculinity hyperbolically committed to the value of the male self. Unlike in the case of *Sanctuary*, however, where this commitment leads men to try to define themselves as the site of the "good," masculinity is here the location of an ineradicable "badness." It's as if what Tom finds intolerable is the very existence of anything good—as if his entire purpose in being is to render the world bad, to debase it into an unproductive reflection of his own destructiveness. Such a description may seem to place him at odds with the fusion of good and bad entailed in oedipal morality—and it's true that the townspeople seem to regard Tom as even worse than they are. In fact, however, he represents the most perfect embodiment of the Pottsville malady. For he's a man who has redescribed the bad itself *as good*, who understands his masculine authority as the sanction for a social destructiveness that's in this novel practically indistinguishable from "the social good" itself.

This redescription has particularly interesting ramifications. One of the things it suggests is a kind of moral debasement of dirt itself. For in the beginning, *this* dirt is good; it's "that rich, black silt you see in the river lowlands; so fine and sweet you could almost eat it, and so deep that you couldn't wear it out." The description reimagines dirt as something inexhaustibly productive and fertile rather than ruinous and soiling. It thinks of soil as a substance that is almost good enough to eat, that seems less opposed than integral to the health of self and world. The moral connotations of this figuration become clear in the comparison with Rose. For she is like the dirt precisely inasmuch as she, too, is "naturally good, deep down good"—inasmuch as she's only rendered bad by the way that Tom comes to poison her. The associations in the passage about Nick's mammy are in this way exactly reversed. Rather than representing that which soils the male self by abandoning and/or suckling it, femininity is here associated with a kind of primally nourishing dirt, which only becomes "dirty" through the violence of the man's touch. And this male dirtying has a vocal dimension as well. What Tom "changes" in beating Rose down is above all "the way she talk[s]." The transformation of soil into dirt is the sullying of vocal utterance itself, the infection of feminine self-expression with a masculine "mean[ness] and tough[ness]" that makes Rose "practically as bad" as Tom.

It should by now be clear that I'm wary of stark divisions between good and bad—divisions that usually signal the triumph of a paranoid-schizoid logic, which cannot acknowledge impurities or ambivalences of any kind.[35] The figuration of a primal female goodness participates in this logic. We ought, I think, to resist accepting it, not least because of the essential reversibility of its terms: because unambivalent idealizations of this sort so easily slide into devaluations, and so repeat the misogyny that they seem in part intended to combat. The passage at hand is thus perhaps important less for its nostalgia than for the rhetorical gestures by which it subverts the terms of that nostalgia. Those gestures insist on the inescapable connection between masculinity and badness, while also demonstrating, as I have shown, that badness is here never pure, never free from its embodiment in and as the good. The corollary of this is of course that goodness is never pure either. This proposition is most fully instantiated in what we might call, in the context of the novel, the *paradox of good dirt*—the paradox by which what soils is also the condition of life itself, so that the attempt to found a self or a social order by repressing dirt can only lead to the return of the repressed as source and sanction of violence. The passage at hand is useful precisely because it lays bare this paradox. It's also useful because it shows us that women are neither free from "good dirt" nor reducible to it. Rose as good *is* Rose as dirt, but this comparison is itself revealed to have its origins in Nick—and we know that his motivations are bound by specific psychosocial constraints that shape his experience of gender.

It's in this context that I'd like to close with one of the novel's most ambitious passages. I'm thinking of a fable that Nick tells Buck in the final pages of the book (216), a fable that asks us to wallow once more in the filth of an excremental humor. The passage links that humor again to questions of narrative voice and manhood. But it also works to combat the forms of nostalgic inversion I have described, making it impossible to think of dirt as something that either leaves woman untouched or belongs to her in essence.

The passage in question imagines a "convention" that takes place "back in the beginning of time." The purpose of that convention is to establish the rules of a society that's both animal and masculine, whose members are not only "dogs" but dogs who all appear to have "balls." The world before this convention is governed by an aggression by which the dogs "bite each other in the balls." And the purpose of the convention is thus to found a properly *social* order, in which animality has been surmounted and the threat of castrating violence curbed by a sociable "code of conduct."

The myth goes on to link this founding to questions of loss and olfactory debasement. In a move that echoes the one we traced in Cain, it makes the anal and the nasal crucial to its sociogenic speculations. It suggests that the smell of the anus is repressed to enable the emergence of voice, that in order for dogs to go in and "caucus"—to let their individual voices be heard—they must first leave their assholes outside, precisely inasmuch as those holes "smell." Such a formulation suggests that this order is founded on a fantasy of plenitude that's itself inseparable from a fantasy of purity. The elimination of the hole gives rise to the sanctioned illusion of wholeness; it enables the emergence of individual subjects unmarred by loss or lack, untouched by any psychic disjunctures between ego and ideal—and therefore

able to constitute society in and as a committee of the whole. Since, moreover, this shedding of the hole also eliminates the anal, it represents the fantasy of a plenitude that has as yet no knowledge of shit, no consciousness of
the excremental as that which signifies the infant's "first" loss and thereby
produces the structural ambivalences with which we have been concerned.

This is, however, a myth that recounts the failure to establish such an
order. The society it describes is from the first both arbitrary and hierarchical, in that the dog who happens to own "a copy of Robert's Rules of Order"
immediately sets himself up as leader. The basis of his power appears to lie in
a primordial violation: he got his rule book where "Cain got his wife," and at
least in some versions of the myth, this act took place in the bosom of Cain's
family—that is, he married his twin sister. Incest is thus installed as the father's prerogative at the origin of society. The fact that the rule book that installs it exists *before* the agreement upon rules further blurs the boundary that
separates the social from the pre-social. We have, in this sense, at the beginning, the establishment of order on the basis of a book that legislates transgression itself, a book that straddles the space between the social discourse it
contains and the uncivilized conditions that should precede it—but that
nonetheless gave rise to it.

The result is that this society tends to institute rather than curb violation. While the dogs are inside, "a heck of a storm . . . blow[s] up out of
nowhere, [scattering their discarded] assholes every which way, mixin' 'em
up so bad that not a one of them dogs was ever able to find his own." The
convention thus issues in the collective assumption of foreign or alien assholes, and consequently, in a generalized desire to "get someone else's ass."
In the context of the novel as a whole, this desire refers to Buck's wish to send
Ken to the gallows for the murder for which he and Nick have framed him.
"What I'm saying is this, Buck," Nick explains after telling this story. "Hang
on to your own ass, and don't try to get Ken's" (217). The fable is thus intended in part as a kind of cautionary tale: if you, Buck, go after Ken's ass, the
price you'll pay may be your own ass, as well as the metaphysical yearning
attendant upon the desire to recover it. But the story seems to me also to de-

scribe the genesis of a universal violence, in which each and every member of society *can't but* be after someone else's ass, precisely inasmuch as it may be his own. Violence in this sense becomes the fate of a social order committed to disowning it. And since that violence is imagined in the first place as a species of castration (biting each others' balls), the society could be said to institute castration (anxiety) and even incest—while of course seeking, at least officially, to banish both to the age of dogs.

But beyond these questions of violence and incest, the passage also enacts the failure of masculine plenitude and purity. For to say that each dog is required to assume a pungent hole that isn't his own is to reinstall an inassimilable anality at the heart of self and social order—an anality that's linked, through the trope of the hole, to the rift between ideal and ego.[36] The presence of this rift at once founds and ruins the social order; it produces male subjects and their society, but structures both around a nullifying abjection that generates socio-moral violence. This rift reduces the subjects of society to an animal condition, in which they socialize with nose to anus in an effort to recoup their primal losses. And it thus gives rise to a perpetual search not for plenitude, not for wholeness, but rather for the restitution of a hole that's properly one's own—a restitution that, as we have seen, can't but entail violence, and that would enable little more than the "civilized" capacity to see "ourselves" in the gap between what oedipal morality insists that we are and what it requires yet forbids us to be.

Finally, it's important to grasp the significance of the mother in this story—or rather, the significance of her absence. Conventionally, the plenitude that precedes anal loss is figured in the form of maternal fusion, and we've seen how this enables the misogynist confusion of excrement with the feminine. What's striking about the fable in this context is that it refuses this association. Plenitude is here, very simply, the fantasy of the absence of a hole. It's a fantasy that the novel exposes by founding society on the generalized assumption of an alien absence. And it's a fantasy that, since it does not figure loss as maternal, doesn't figure recovery that way either. Loss is here both ineradicable and ungendered, a structural loss that's meant to suggest that the hole is itself primordial—that *it* is what re-sides at the beginning—so that the idyll of maternal fusion is perhaps itself a myth by which we seek to protect ourselves from the knowledge of a pri-mal negativity. The mother in this sense resides at neither end of the so-ciogenic process; she's neither the object whose loss is at once prefigured and presupposed by the mythico-historical anal phase, nor the object one seeks to recover in displaced form through the oedipal pact.

Such an erasure may, in part, be politically disturbing. It certainly must be reckoned with in any political assessment of the novel. And yet I find it worth suggesting that Thompson here effects that erasure as a way of imag-ining a social order in which the abject of civilized morality cannot be easily confused with the feminine, however much the mother's loss might in fact be central to the self's formation. In this sense, the passage's strength may lie as much in its mode of address as in any content it offers: in, for example, the "I said that, well, sir," with which the story begins. For this discursive cozying up to the reader—this folksy invitation to the comic tale—marks a return of the structure described earlier, in which we're addressed by the joker as a "third person" who turns out to be indistinguishable from the "first." The process asks us to bear witness to the failure of the oedipal process it enacts. It asks us to affirm the comic "first person," even as it subverts the paternal position from which alone we might do so. And it asks us, accord-ingly, to participate in the soiling of masculine voice with excrement, a process that repeats the (de)constituting gesture of the oedipal order itself—and one that the novel declines to overcome through the misogynist confla-tion of woman with the abject that the reign of Oedipus seeks to install.

5 The Waste of White Masculinity

Excrement in Chester Himes's *Blind Man with a Pistol*

"Does anyone . . . believe that shittt?"

Critics have recently begun to take seriously the detective fiction of Chester Himes.[1] Raymond Nelson argues, for example, that Himes's crime novels represent an advance over his earlier, more purely naturalistic fiction, in that they fuse the naturalist's attention to violence with a celebration of "the rich folk-traditions of Black American culture."[2] Himes's detective-heroes are on this reading urban incarnations of black folklore's "bad nigger" (266); his crime novels offer "warm evocations" of Harlem's subcultural "institutions" (267), seeking to "envision a particular place at a particular moment of history—its customs, speech, topography, occupations, even its food—and record it for posterity" (269). Himes "permits himself no . . . nostalgia" in this project. "The most prominent characteristics of the community that he chronicles are fear and brutality" (269), and the author therefore recurs repeatedly to images of such violence: to senseless murders and suckers conned, to the squalor and degradation of racial ghettoization, and especially to images of brutalized bodies that, having been stabbed, mutilated, or decapitated, "have lost their essential consciousness [and] humanity" but nonetheless continue to function (272). The largest significance of the detective series resides for Nelson in these latter moments: "It is as if Himes were saying that . . . black Americans . . . are forced to live with knives thrust into the sensitive areas of their bodies: if the blade is left in, it means blindness, impotence, helplessness, and above all pain; if the blade is removed, it is death" (273). The detective form thus enables for Himes both an elaboration of a black subculture in which crime figures centrally, and the grotesquely naturalistic sketching of scenes that serve to represent that culture as itself the victim of sanctioned crime: as the living corpse that results from the violence of America's racial hatred.

There is, however, a catch. Since the legal institutions in whose name the detective works are in part committed to securing white power, it becomes almost unthinkable for the violent crimes of Harlem to be traced to their social roots. The chain of evidence must lead only to a "local" resolution; the solution of the mystery, if it is to coincide with the restoration of law that the detective novel conventionally requires, must stop short of the revolutionary exposure of the forces producing "Harlem" itself as a degraded urban space. In Himes's novels, such a concession has two related results. First, the team of detectives he creates, Grave Digger Jones and Coffin Ed Johnson, are required to brutalize the very people in whose name they keep the peace and with whom they also feel solidarity: "Harlem problems are violent," writes Nelson; "they can be fought . . . only by an even more uninhibited violence. It is one of the brilliant ironies of the Harlem Domestic stories that the detective-heroes can express their genuine love for their people . . . only through the crude brutality that has become their bitter way of life" (270). Second, the attempt in the later novels to indict white culture by "extend[ing] criminal investigation . . . beyond Harlem" (274) signals the breakdown of the detective form itself. The early novels, as Nelson notes, never actually try to "say" that urban blacks live a life of oppression that is comparable to "cultural lobotomy" (273). Instead, they offer "visual analogues" (273) that, though we might interpret them as Nelson suggests, give the impression of objective observation with no overtly thematic function to impede the generic unfolding of action. As soon as the novels attempt, on the other hand, to locate the origin of guilt explicitly in white racism, they become at once something more and less than the detective stories they appear to be.

What they become depends in part on how one evaluates such generic subversion. For Michael Denning, the later books represent a kind of "postmodern . . . experimentation," in which "comic absurdity is joined to . . . social vision" and "intra-Harlem violence" is replaced by "violence between Harlem and the outside white world."[3] Nelson is more ambivalent in his assessment, less susceptible as he is to the lure of formal disunity. For him the "deliberate" "deterioration of narrative logic" (275) in *Blind Man with a Pistol* (1969)—the last book in Himes's detective series—"contradicts the faith in the ability . . . to discover truth that is a basic precondition of the detective genre. The wide range of reference, the tortuous complexity of motivation inherent in Himes's attempt to bring racist white society explicitly into his novel simply cannot be contained within the limitations of his form." The result is that "the Harlem Domestic series . . . ends on a note of decay and frustration" (276). *Blind Man with a Pistol*, though "in some ways [Himes's] most ambitious novel" and an "impressively experimental" book, "might almost be considered a literary ruin" (275, 276).

The appeal for me of this last formulation is practically irresistible. Indeed, I suggested in chapter 1 that the hardboiled detective novel is itself a ruin, though one that does not "know" it's a ruin, that continues in its conventional guises to disavow the desires that ruin it. I want in this chapter to argue that Himes has written a ruin which knows it's a ruin—or better still, which knows that it's *waste*. *Blind Man with a Pistol* is, in fact, an extraordinarily self-conscious exploration of cultural artifact as refuse. In it, Himes does indeed renounce the certitudes of narrational temporality, linking this breakdown explicitly to the effacement of boundaries between Harlem and its outside. But he does so because such narrative disruption is for him the adequate strategy for capturing the ruin of cultural identity that is his central subject. The novel sets out not merely to locate guilt and violence in the white community, but to do so as part of a larger project of exposing the powerfully efficacious fictitiousness of the line demarcating "Harlem." Harlem, here, is the very real space in which white culture deposits its psychic waste matter—deposits, that is, those aspects of itself which it cannot own without contaminating itself, without losing the very purity of "self" that's secured by racism and is its fantasmic rationale. *Blind Man with a Pistol* would have white readers own up to this (anti-)subjective impurity. It seeks to have them do so in part by constructing its readers as white, while itself becoming the formal embodiment of the waste that white culture says Harlem is. The novel in this way forces an encounter with the psychic detritus that, as we shall see, it shows within its representation to threaten even the gendered purity of conventional white masculinity.

One way to approach such matters is by looking at the novel's structure. The first five chapters of *Blind Man* provide a remarkable series of interpretive problems that the rest of the novel merely intensifies. Here is a very schematic description of those chapters and their effects: Chapter 1 introduces a very old African American man who calls himself Reverend Sam, who claims to be Mormon and is living with his "wives" in a ruin on 119th Street, and who turns out to have buried several bodies in the basement of that ruin. Given this last point, it's reasonable to expect that the detective story will center on this first piece of plot: we have some deaths, now who or what caused them? Instead, Chapter 2 moves on to a second and unrelated plot line. This plot concerns an unnamed white man (unnamed, that is, until Chapter 13!) who picks up a black male hooker with a red fez at a lunch counter at 125th Street and 7th Avenue. The very juxtaposition of this event with the first scene leads us to assume that connections will be forthcoming, that the novel will now weave together its threads. But Chapter 2 is followed, not by such a weaving, but by the first of the book's "Interludes," a celebration of African American culture represented by the intersection where the lunch counter stands.

The third chapter introduces yet another plot line whose connection to the others remains obscure. Himes describes here in some detail the history of a black man named Marcus Mackenzie, who fancies himself a race leader who can "solve the Negro Problem" through "brotherhood."[4] The novel makes no attempt to link Mackenzie to any of the characters we have seen so far. Chapter 4 then cuts back to the interracial homosexual plot, though still without forging any connection to the others: Grave Digger and Coffin Ed, introduced here for the first time, see a black man with a red fez running down the street carrying a pair of pants, then encounter a white man with a cut throat and no pants, whose dying response to their quest for information is "Jesus bastard" (33). We seem now at last to be getting somewhere: one of the plot-kernels has begun to develop—there is for the first time the picking up of a previous thread—and we might then expect some further integration, more and more meaningful subordination of events to a guiding and significant narrative logic. But Chapter 5 once more disappoints these expectations. Here we're introduced to a bewilderingly large cast of characters whom the novel treats as though we should know who they are,[5] and who all belong to a scam concerning a rejuvenation fluid that bears no discernible connection to any of the previous plots. The old man who claims to want rejuvenation is named *Mister* Sam (not Reverend); one of the characters makes reference to riots, though in terms of the novel's overt development, there aren't any riots till at least Chapter 12, and perhaps not really till the book's final chapter; and the scene culminates in an incomprehensible blood bath that ends when *a man in a red fez* shows up and stabs to death one Doctor Mubuta, purveyor of the supposed rejuvenation fluid.

One could extend this confusion indefinitely, as the novel proceeds neither to solve its crimes nor adequately to subordinate its plots to a master plot. For now, it's enough to note that the developments I've outlined pose two different but related kinds of problems: (1) a crisis or breakdown in temporal ordering that's registered first as a montage effect which declines to link up events narrationally, so that those events could just as well be occurring simultaneously as sequentially; and (2) a characterological indeterminacy that's registered primarily by the repetition of figures in contexts that invite yet question the identity between those repeated "entities." My claim is that these troubles derive from an identical narrative

THE WASTE OF WHITE MASCULINITY

principle: the various plot lines tend simultaneously to intersect *and* to re-main isolated, so that we cannot fail to make connections that the novel at the same time refuses to authorize.

This means, first, that the second time we see a man with a red fez, we naturally and plausibly assume it is the same man as the first time, even though the novel doesn't explicitly corroborate this (by giving him a name from the start, for example). This is in part because he seems to belong to the same plot as before: he stands in some apparently sexual relationship to a white man, and even though all the dots aren't connected, it's easy to think that he's picked up the man at the counter in Chapter 2 and killed him while the novel took us elsewhere. Not only, however, does the murder plot never get sufficiently resolved to confirm our suspicions; and not only does the in-vestigation itself take off from a premise that seems unsound ("Jesus bastard" could just as well be a profane and desperate expletive as a name, and in any case, the man Ed and Digger end up looking for is called Jesus *Baby*). More than this and more crucially, the third time we see what looks like the "same" man, he's *abrupted into another plot* in a way that requires us to hesitate before making the attribution. We have no reason to think that the "first" man has anything to do with Mubuta. The novel has given us no cause to link them, nor does it ever do so. It at no point stitches the "plots" together into a whole that connects these characters, but nevertheless keeps spilling elements of each plot into the other, in a way that renders the identity of the fez-man radically indeterminate.

It's partly this tendency toward leakage among plots, combined with the refusal to connect those plots in any conventionally integrative manner, that's responsible for *Blind Man*'s dizzying confusion. The dynamic accounts for the apparent but inexplicit metamorphosis of Reverend Sam into Mister Sam: they share a name, both have eyes of milky blue (10, 40), but no narra-tive connection between their plots authorizes our equating them with cer-tainty. Or again, there's the "harelipped" "cretin" of the opening chapter (9, 11), a cook for Reverend Sam who seems to reappear as Doctor Mubuta's flunky in the "Interlude" following Chapter 4 ("the black harelipped cretin [placed] a sheet-wrapped figure into the back compartment of an air-conditioned Cadillac" [37]), only to be transformed into Jesus Baby ("a short, fat, black man with a harelip" [73]), who then turns out to be General Ham, preacher of salvation at the Temple of Black Jesus. Finally, there's the striking repetition of identical language to introduce characters whom the novel refuses to tell us are identical:

A woman stuck her head out of the bath. It was the head of a young woman with a smooth brownskinned face and straightened black hair pulled aslant her forehead over her right ear. It was a beautiful face with a wide straight nose and unflared nostrils above a wide, thick, unpainted mouth with brown lips that looked soft and resilient. Brown eyes magnified by rimless spectacles gave her a sexy look. (53)

The head of a woman peered around the edge. It was the head of a young woman with a smooth brownskinned face and straightened black hair pulled tightly aslant her forehead over her right eye. It was a good-looking face with a wide, thick unpainted mouth with brown lips. Brown eyes, magnified behind rimless spectacles, became larger still at sight of the gaping spectators. (123)

The gesture here once more invites a connection it also deauthorizes. The first quote is part of the political plot and describes a woman who's paid to seduce men in order to get them to contribute funds. The second describes a woman who, apparently identical in features to the first, has a TV set delivered to her home in the middle of the hot Harlem night. Nothing besides the descriptions connects them. Nothing allows us, in the face of those descriptions, fully to forget their connection. The novel in this way calls into question the notion of identity as a discrete singularity, which both remains continuous in time and cannot be confused with another.

Furthermore, the strategy of "dosed" plot leakages results in a form of narrational crisis. The riot plot, as I've already noted, interrupts the rejuvenation plot before we even know there is a riot, just as Ed and Digger say that they're searching for the uprising's perpetrators before we've been told of its existence. Such difficulties suggest that the scene with which the novel ends (a riot) happens well "before" it's represented, but happens without our being informed of it. At the same time, since the plots aren't ever adequately linked, there's no way to be sure that these are the same riots at all. The riots in this chapter *may* be different ones, the moment in which they take place may be "now," the events may be relevant to the larger unfolding—in which case the failure to redeem them semantically is cause for a different species of alarm and makes these riots themselves a kind of narrative detritus.

One could continue to extend such examples of plot leakage, just as one could the disturbances to identity just described. I want, however, merely to point to a second place where the novel repeats a roughly identical set-piece, this time in a way that heightens and intensifies the temporal crises in question:

A man entered The Temple of Black Jesus. He was a short, fat, black man with a harelip. His face was running with sweat as though his skin was leaking. His short black hair grew so thick on his round inflated head it looked artificial, like drip-dry hair. His body looked blown up like that of a rubber man. The sky-blue silk suit he wore on this hot night glinted with a blue light. He looked inflammable. But he was cool. (73)

[Grave Digger and Coffin Ed] went inside. A man stood inside the doorway examining the people who entered. . . . He was a short, fat, black man with a harelip. Sweat ran from his face as though his skin were leaking. His short black hair grew so thick on his round inflated head it looked like nylon pile. His body looked blown up like that of a rubber man. The sky-blue suit he wore glinted like metal. (116–17)

Here, the fact that the two men are the same is relatively certain. Both scenes take place in the Temple of Black Jesus; both men are preachers, both bear the same name (Jesus Baby), and both preach an almost identical sermon ("Now we're gonna feed [whitey] the flesh of the Black Jesus until he choke" [117]). Both, in some sense, belong to the same plot. What's far less certain is *when* the two scenes take place, however. The repetition of locale, of the man's description, and of elements from his sermon produce an uncanny sense of return, as though the novel were repeating a prior moment rather than developing it narrationally. Time appears to implode upon itself through the refusal of ordered differentiation. This is especially disconcerting because, in the second scene, our vision is organized by Digger and Ed, in a way that suggests they were there the first time without our being informed of it. The temporal collapse thus bleeds into an epistemological crisis. We neither can tell if we're moving "forward" nor be sure that the narrative eye is seeing what's centrally there to be seen—nor, for that matter, be certain about whose eyes it is we're seeing through. Such dysfunctions cause obvious problems in a genre that relies on the telos of sequence for the closures by which it restores legal order—and that's meant to satisfy the desire for solution it inevitably (generically) incites.[6]

This temporal impurity is not, moreover, restricted to the novel's formal dimension; it's also something that *Blind Man* incorporates into the body of its representation. I want now to turn to two moments where it does so, as they seem to me unusually rich and especially able to enhance our understanding of what's at stake in these subversions. Both examples have to do with signs that are rendered complex by their location in time; both are humorous in ways that are crucial to the power and significance of the scenes; and both open up from narrowly temporal concerns onto historical, cultural, and political ones.

Here is the first scene I have in mind, taken from the novel's opening pages:

On 119th Street there had been a sign for years in the front window of an old dilapidated three-storey brick house, announcing: FUNERALS PERFORMED. *For five years past the house had been condemned as unsafe for human habitation. The wooden steps leading up to the cracked, scabby front door were . . . rotten . . . ; the foundation was crumbling, one side of the house had sunk more than a foot lower than the other, . . . and the constant falling of bricks from the front wall created a dangerous hazard for passing pedestrians. Most of the windowpanes had long been broken out and replaced with brown wrapping-paper, and the edges of linoleum could be seen hanging from the roof where years before it had been placed there to cover a leak. No one knew what it looked like inside, and no one cared. If any funerals had ever been performed within, it had been before the memory of any residents then on the street.*

Police cruisers had passed daily and glanced at it unconcernedly. . . . Building inspectors had looked the other way. Gas and electric meter readers never stopped, for it had no gas and electricity. But everyone on the street had seen a considerable number of short-haired, black nuns clad in solid black vestments coming and going at all hours of day and night. . . . The colored neighbors just assumed it was a convent, and that it was in such bad repair seemed perfectly reasonable in view of the fact it was obviously a jim-crowed convent. . . .

It was not until another innocuous card appeared in the window one day, requesting: "Fertile womens, lovin God, inquire within," that anyone had given it a thought. Two white cops in a cruiser . . . were proceeding past as usual when the cop beside the driver shouted, "Whoa, man! You see what I see?" (7–8)

I'll return later to the striking fact that this book, which *is* a "literary ruin," opens with a representation of ruin, as if to reflect on its own dilapidation by embodying it thematically. For now, what's central is the function of signs within this self-presentation. "FUNERALS PERFORMED" poses, to begin with, a striking referential difficulty. Appearing in the window of a condemned house that seems little more than a pile of rubble, and advertising a service that, if it was ever performed there, can no longer be recalled to have been, the sign doesn't seem to "belong" to the house so much as simply to adhere to it. It refers to no current activity in the building and tells us nothing about its "now." It therefore announces nothing so much as the failure of coincidence between itself and its referent. Funerals are precisely *not* performed here—not anymore, at least. The placard stands as an ossified remnant of some past purpose or design, and its persistence within the present pries open a space of radical indetermination. Without the confidence of its assertion, we would simply be confronted with a ruin. With that assertion we're confronted instead with a ruin that, intentionally or not, masquerades as a funeral parlor, but that may perhaps be a convent instead, given the "number of short-haired, black nuns . . . coming and going at all hours."

The "meaning" of the building becomes in the process completely in-apprehensible. The sign induces and solicits interpretation by suggesting there's more here than meets the eye, while thwarting interpretive gestures by misnaming the "more" to which it calls attention. It does this, moreover, not out of some theoretical commitment to the arbitrariness of the sign. Rather, it does it in order to say that in Harlem this arbitrariness is the prac-tical effect of a historical process ("jim crow") that renders the ghetto a waste land made up of the accumulated traces of failed and socially defeated aspi-rations. The sign here "misnames" because it's a refuse, a part of the ruin pro-duced by white racism and to which it also "refers." In the apparent absence of any attempt to make the building contemporarily significant, its meaning becomes inscribed in a placard that cannot be adequate to its referent, be-cause it too is the historical waste of an irreducibly past intention—an in-tention that refuses obliteration but is denied a properly narrative develop-ment, and that therefore haunts the meaning of the building with the mem-ory of what it once was.

Of course, the enigma posed by this scenario is to begin with the reader's alone. The building remains invisible to the characters, who—if they're black and live in the neighborhood—don't "know" or "care" "what it look[s] like inside," or—if they're city or corporate officials—either "glance at it unconcernedly" or simply "look . . . the other way." The very pervasive-ness of ruin in Harlem seems to render the sight of waste too visible to be seen. Its invisibility is signaled, indeed, by the windows of the condemned house, which are largely covered over with "brown wrapping-paper" that makes the interior inaccessible to sight.

Only with the appearance of a new sign in the window does the build-ing become for the characters in the book what it already is for the reader: si-multaneously visible and illegible, visible *by virtue of* its illegibility. "Fertile womens, lovin God, inquire within" is how that sign reads. The illegibility clearly resides here at something of a different level than before, a level that requires a revision of both the building's significance and my account of the placards' structures of signification.

For the interpretive difficulty now inheres partly within the sign it-self. "Fertile womens" and "lovin God" do not, shall we say, "go together." Himes himself puts it funniest and best when he says, "Fertile womens was for fools, not God" (8). The statement suggests that the building's indeter-minacy is less the result of a palimpsestial logic that preserves the traces of a failed past project than the contemporary product of a significatory in-tention that baffles conventional comprehension. The white cops literally "discover" the building by way of the traces of this new intention. For them, the house first comes into view through a violation at the level of the signifier, which immediately implies, to them and to us, the possibility of a criminal violence that requires investigation. The fact that the cops then lead us into the ruin from which we had been barred suggests an en-forced identification with white law (a point to which I return) and en-ables a refinement of the argument thus far. The scene in question drama-tizes, that is, the process by which Harlem comes "into view": not as a sim-ple and illegible ruin unanimated by any contemporary intentions, but rather as a ruin *that's also inhabited*, that's internally and currently (if de-gradedly) vibrant, and that becomes meaningful to whites who encounter it through a significatory practice that both destabilizes the significance of Harlem as synchrony of lifeless waste, and gives evidence of a subcultural presence, largely covert and apparently illegal, whose identity, meaning, and precise location turn out to be undiscoverable.

It's exactly in relation to this subcultural "signification" that the humor of the scene resides as well. That humor is an ambitious affair, whose full ex-plication will have to wait until we've placed the issues just raised more fully in the context of the book's larger meanings. What's appropriate and possi-ble to say now is this: that the eruption-into-vision of Harlem by way of a contemporary (if indeterminate) subcultural practice is funny—for the reader, I mean—because the sign that's thus produced reveals a hodgepodge of stereotypically "black" identities and intentions. "Fertile womens, lovin God": where is the joke supposed to reside here if not in the image of two white men encountering the surprisingly living expression of their jumbled

THE WASTE OF WHITE MASCULINITY

projections of blackness? If the sign is in part an illegible utterance that requires the interrogation of law, what makes it funny is that it's also immediately recognizable as a comic conjuncture of the kinds of activities that
whites imagine blacks really engage in. African Americans cannot spell, according to the racist imagination—or else they misspell on purpose. They
speak and write in any case in some subversively furtive dialect that whites
can't understand, and that also expresses the comic "truths" concerning the
funkiness of a black religion whose sentimental and naive credulity is inseparable from monstrous sexual license. Black women may well "love God," in
other words; they "love," in this fantasy, everything that moves, because
they're looser, more willing, less frigid than white women. They're also
alarmingly fertile women, who seem unable or unwilling to stop the ceaseless issue from their loins of still more savage little lovers of God. And any
God whom African Americans worshiped would, within this racial fantasy,
want to be "loved" by such women. Like the hundred-year-old Sam who put
up the sign and has sired "fifty . . . pickaninnies" (9, 11), that God would
have to be literally omnipotent: impressively virile, eternally erect—fucking,
fucking all the time.[7] The humor of the sign resides in the way it combines
these stereotypically "familiar" elements of African American life into a
deeply *un*familiar utterance. It resides, that is, both in the comically disturbing suggestion that the incredible thing implied by the sign is perfectly be-
lievable of "them," and in the implication that the placard so thoroughly
confuses its stereotypes as to dupe and perplex the cops who encounter it, as
they confront their projections in the form of a radical racial opacity.

I'm suggesting that the ruin with which we begin is a self-presentation
of the book's own waste, and that to read the novel itself is somehow analogous to reading that ruin. *Blind Man*, in other words, at least in part addresses
readers it constructs as white. Its invocation of racial stereotypes speaks complexly to white fantasies of blackness, and its formal rubble is meant to ap-
proximate the historical rubble of a Harlem that the book knows has been
produced by whites. In encountering that novelistic rubble, then, the book's
white readers are asked to confront a sight from the position of the scene's

white cops: to encounter a waste in which they will turn out to be uncon-
sciously implicated, and to see that waste through the lens of stereotypes that
have been worked over—have been rendered strange—by the inscrutability
of a black intention that renders those stereotypes opaque and resistant by
promiscuously affirming them.

This is not to suggest that the novel doesn't speak to African American
readers at all. My sense is that it addresses them in complex and not wholly
inviting ways. On one hand, it asks those readers to take a kind of absurdist
pleasure in the humor directed at how white people misinterpret the meaning of blackness. On the other hand, this pleasure arises from the deploy-
ment of stereotypes to which, as we'll see, the novel offers no authentic alternative—and which construct African Americans less as reading subjects
than as a part of the objectal "waste" that the novel equates with its formal
rubble.

The significance of this strategy for the book's larger project is clear
from the second scene that centers on signs:

> *Motorists . . . saw a speaker standing . . . in front of a sign which read:* CHICKEN
> AUTO INSURANCE, Seymour Rosenblum. *None had the time or interest to investigate
> further. The white motorists thought that the Negro speaker was selling "chicken auto
> insurance" for Seymour Rosenblum. They could well believe it.* "Chicken" *had to do
> with the expression,* "Don't be chicken!" *and that was the way people drove in
> Harlem.*
>
> *But actually the "chicken" sign was left over from a restaurant that had gone
> bankrupt and closed months previously, and the sign advertising auto insurance had
> been placed across the front of the closed shop afterwards.*
>
> *Nor was the speaker selling auto insurance. . . . He had merely chosen that par-
> ticular spot because he had felt he was least likely to be disturbed by the police. The
> speaker was named Marcus Mackenzie, and he was a serious man. (21)*

The humor in this passage is once more bound up with waste's relation to
stereotypes and signs. As in the last scene, the sign itself both signifies and
"is" an emblem of such refuse. "CHICKEN AUTO INSURANCE, *Seymour Rosenblum*"

refers only complexly to the sight that the white motorists (and white readers) encounter. It is, again, a palimpsest made up of the detritus that Harlem no longer remembers, even months after sloughing it off, but that also persists within that culture by way of its endless resignification. This palimpsestial character of Harlem is marked in the sign itself, which is quite literally made up of a past scrap resignified by a more recent one. The result is once more an excessively superficial legibility-by-contiguity combined with a radical indeterminacy. Marcus seems to be explained by the sign precisely by virtue of appearing in its vicinity. Indeed, to white people, the juxtaposed elements of sign and man add up to a kind of stereotypical sense. They can "well believe" that a black man in Harlem would be selling "chicken auto insurance," since they know irrefutably (which is not to say truthfully) that in Harlem the natives are dangerous people whose style of driving is designed to provoke and requires a lot of financial protection. The humor works by declining to refute the stereotype itself while showing us that the sign doesn't actually mean this. Just as, in the previous scene, "FUNERALS PERFORMED" turns out to be at once a true and false statement of fact (the building is no longer a funeral parlor, but Sam has indeed performed burials in its basement), so here Marcus may not be selling chicken insurance, but that doesn't mean we're meant to believe that doing so would be a bad idea. The motorists who believe in this literal reading are no more the object of the joke than are the blacks of whom it's possible to believe this.

But they're also no less the object of that joke. In the context of the tableau with which the passage begins, the sign doesn't mean what they think it does—doesn't, in fact, "mean" at all—but points only to its monumental incoherence. Marcus is a race leader not a salesman; he stands in no apparent relation to any "Seymour Rosenblum," and "selling auto insurance [is] farther from his thoughts than chicken" even is (21). The comedy thus resides in the tension between our knowledge that the motorists are wrong and our belief that they're nonetheless somehow right—a belief that the novel itself encourages. Since, moreover, the book again structures the scene around whites reading black signs, the joke is in part on how Himes's white readers themselves believe in stereotypical projections that the scene yet declines to refute.

What are we to make of this unsettling procedure? Why does Himes implicitly affirm the stereotypes he exposes as white misreadings of blackness? And why does he both refuse to give authentic alternatives to these stereotypes and encourage his readers to laugh at such racist evocations? The first thing to say is that the humor of these scenes cannot be divorced from their deadly seriousness, which resides in their exploration of what I have called the historical character of waste. The second passage is particularly instructive in this regard. By referring explicitly to the bankruptcy of the chicken restaurant, it insists more forcefully than before that if Harlem presents itself to whites illegibly, as a kind of pastiche of historical refuse, this is not for "aesthetic" reasons but rather because of the enforced degradation of black inner-city life, in which narratives of success are materially thwarted, shops repeatedly go out of business, and people often no longer care enough to remove the old sign before pasting up a new one. The failed ephemera of old projects and aspirations persist alongside desire's recent incarnations, and change is a fluid synchrony of waste rather than a narrative of progress or success.

Such a description helps us to grasp the relation between ghettoization and the stereotype. It suggests that for Himes the thwarting of self-making reduces identity to a kind of waste matter, which is both comically rigid in that it can only recycle and patch together the remnants of past "identities," and infinitely fluid in that it's unmoored from the narrative constraints of consistency, development, continuity, and progress.[8] Himes's refusal to refute black stereotypes is in this sense an attempt to insist upon their psychic and cultural reality. It marks his effort to expose the process by which African Americans are increasingly forced to become the stereotypical things that whites project onto them—to be, precisely, *reduced* by a lack of cultural and economic opportunity, even as this reduction produces an almost infinite multiplication of stereotypical possibilities.

The affirmation of multiple images that confuse and baffle those who project them will thus turn out to represent a complex mode of resistance. That resistance entails exploding the stereotypes from within—forcing them back on white readers in the form of not just a cultural but a *psychic* waste. In order to see how this works, however, we need to pursue in greater detail the temporal-historical dilemma I'm describing, and to link that dilemma explicitly to the novel's treatment of black politics.

For the experience of history as nonprogressive transformation accounts for a certain problematic of belief in Himes's representation of the African American experience. Take the novel's persistent refrain: "It was Harlem, where anything might happen" (37; see also 47, 64, 99). Harlem becomes here the site of a belief in the infinitely possible that is rooted in despair. If anything might happen there, this is only because nothing is *certain* to happen, since the narrative certitudes of progress and accomplishment are replaced with the atemporal uncertainties of waste. The people of Harlem therefore *believe*—in almost everything and anything at all. The comic credulity of whites who give credence to stereotypes that they invent is countered by the tragic pathos of an almost bottomless black gullibility. "Niggers'll believe anything" (39) is how one (black) character puts it—and the novel goes on to prove the claim true.

Marcus "believe[s]" that "brotherhood" will "save the world" and "solve the Negro Problem" (21). The parishioners at the Temple of Black Jesus "believe . . . in a Prophet named Ham. They welcome . . . the Black Jesus to their neighborhood" because "[t]he white Jesus [hasn't] done anything for them" (75). Anny, the white wife of an African American musician, "believe[s] in" the rejuvenation serum: "I have come to believe in a lot of things most people consider unbelievable," she says (64). And some of the people of Harlem are said to

believe . . . in Black Power. . . . They filled the collection baskets with coins and bills. It was going anyway, for one thing and another. . . . [W]hy not for Black Power? What did they have to lose? And they might win. Who knew? The whale swallowed Jonah. Moses split the Red Sea. Christ rose from the dead. Lincoln freed the slaves. Hitler *killed six million Jews. The Africans had got to rule—in some parts of Africa, anyway. The Americans and the Russians have shot the moon. Some joker has made a plastic heart. Anything is possible. (47)*

The interpretive frame here is one of the extraordinary ripped from the narrative contexts that explain it—reduced to its bare miraculous magnificence—and robbed altogether of any moral valence (Hitler's monstrosity is comparable to black rule only on an amoral scale of the fantastic). People believe in the prospect of Black Power precisely because it's unbelievable. Their desperate circumstances breed desperate desires, desperate faith in improbable schemes for personal gain and social transformation. The improbable becomes, in fact, the most probable of outcomes in a world where literally *"[a]nything* is possible," especially for those who've been deprived of even the most basic "certainties"—who are, for example, improbably expected to make a life in rat-infested slums, only to be evicted from them when they're condemned for being slums (chapter 22).

The crushing of rational hope in such cases produces the fiercest of irrational longings. Life becomes a series of blind wagers ("What did they have to lose? And they might win") on the chance of miraculous transfiguration. The infinite variety of Harlem's "vices"—"sex perversions, lesbians, pederasts, pot smokers, riders of the LSD, street hustlers," and so on (85)—is simply the underside of this "anything" that's possible. And the converse of black gullibility in the novel is the incapacity to believe in a violence whose aberrance makes it the most likely of life's outcomes: "'Mother-raper stood still and let his throat be cut,' Grave Digger observed. 'Wasn't that,' Coffin Ed corrected. *'He just didn't believe it'*" (62; my emphasis). Or again, from a later scene: "'*He didn't believe it*,' Coffin Ed said. 'Someone he knew and trusted stuck a pistol against his temple, looked into his eyes and blew out his brains'" (169; my emphasis).

This desperate desire to believe is obviously ripe for exploitation. Where there are believers there are would-be suckers, and where there are suckers there are bound to be cons. In this regard, *Blind Man with a Pistol* extends a pattern from Himes's earlier crime novels, all of which are structured in part through an opposition between cons and squares.[9] But two things make the treatment here special. First, there's a deepened sensitivity to how these figures arise historically from the deprivations and consequent longings produced by racial ghettoization. Second and most remarkably, the novel seeks to map a black politics onto this sucker/con opposition.[10] Here, black politics *is* the scam, "the confidence game in which everyone is conned."[11] The novel thus goes out of its way to expose how each of its political leaders manipulates a desire for belief in equality to deceive and exploit the people of Harlem for some kind of personal gain.

Dr. Moore, for example, dispenses Black Power while filling a keg with donated money. He's then chauffeured in his Cadillac limousine to a middle-class housing development on Lenox Avenue, where the Black Power sign across the car's back is "[m]iraculously" changed to proclaim "BROTHERHOOD"; where "[t]he residents [hold] him in high esteem" for his "nonviolent" "efforts at integration"; and where he turns out to be a pimp who indicates to one of his whores that he "could make a mint" off "these Harlem folks" if he just had a corpse to "get them mad" (51, 54). The "Prophet named Ham" is similarly shown to be engaged in political deceit. Purveying a militantly separatist religion at the Temple of Black Jesus, he then sneaks off from the Temple's gates in the Cadillac of an elderly white woman who's clearly implied to be keeping him (79). Even the resolutely "sincere" Marcus turns out to be a sham, in that he's not only too stupid to have any real political ideas, but also so drunk with his newfound power that the purity of his commitment to "brotherhood" is compromised by a desire to see his "name . . . in all the papers" (28). Politics is thus here a kind of con whose (sometimes unconscious) aim is no more than cynical self-gratification: sex, fame, power, money—and the "vices" that go along with them.[12]

One effect of this vision of politics is no doubt the endorsement of political cynicism—a cynicism, that is, about black politics. Just as the novel offers no complex images of African Americans to counter its stereotypical representations, so it declines to offer an alternative to the politics of stupidity, despair, and exploitation. Political intentions are as inescapably corrupt as the stereotypes of blackness are existentially inescapable. We might also note, in this regard, the extraordinary descriptive nastiness of the novel, which far exceeds Himes's previous books in its evocation of bodily repulsiveness. Almost every character here is disgustingly fat, smelly, and/or ugly, oozing sweat from dirty pores and reduced to a kind of human waste that cannot quite contain itself.[13] The characters who aren't represented like this and who retain some dignified control over their bodies are dehumanized in a different way, since they're invariably those most committed to the inhumane exploitation of others. The result of these combined strategies is a general yet detailed assent to the stereotype of Harlem as "jungle" (46) or "Congo" (10): a place where the natives are visibly subhuman (the animal trope is not far away), where apparently decent and sincere motivations are merely masks for the most heinous of crimes, and where each is engaged in a ceaseless struggle to cheat and butcher his brothers and sisters in the self-serving drive toward cultural suicide.

Denning is thus in some sense right to speak of Himes as "walking on the brink of a . . . violent minstrel show."[14] *Blind Man*'s treatment of African American politics contributes centrally to that show, generalizing the local instances of stereotypes into a stereotypical condition whose comedy cannot in the end be separated from the bloodshed of racial fratricide. But to condemn this too quickly is, I think, to miss what's politically most interesting about the novel. The astonishing feat of *Blind Man with a Pistol* consists in its making this stereotypical spectacle part of a larger attempt to expose the "postmodern condition" of Harlem—depthless instability of identity, superficiality of meaning, breakdown of narratives of self-making—as the price that African Americans pay for our culture's commitment to the boundaries constituting racial identity. The hypostatization of stereotypical identities will turn out to be a paradoxical expression of the novel's hostility to identity itself. That hostility is clear already in the book's critique of black politics. The problem, that is, with Dr. Moore and Prophet Ham is that they grasp the fictitiousness of black identity well enough to exploit it personally—both of them "perform" their various identities without in any sense "being" who they "are"—but use that knowledge to enforce racial purity and secure the hierarchies of racial difference. Militant religious and cultural nationalisms seek here only to preserve the status quo. The race leaders can't stand to level such hierarchies, since their politics exploit the despair of inequality in the name of getting rich, getting off, or becoming famous. To achieve equality would therefore be to kill the goose that lays the golden eggs. Identity becomes the political alibi for oppressive social relations, and the politics of racial identity turns out to serve the ends of the larger culture by declining to overthrow—or even to question—the status of identity itself.

The refusal of purity that *Blind Man* enacts at the level of form is both an indictment of such a politics and the deepest "meaning" of the novel. By confronting us with a literary ruin that cannot be cognitively integrated, and by equating that waste with a blackness reduced to the fixed yet fluid rubble of the stereotype, Himes in essence asks his readers to assimilate the inassimilable. He repeatedly figures those readers as white by incorporating whites as readers of blackness into his representation. And he then asks those readers to take back in the stuff that their sense of racial identity has had to eliminate. If that stuff is first given form in the novel's temporal and characterological impurities, and if the encounter with it is then repeatedly staged in the book's representation, the dominant metaphor for the assimilation of such waste concerns the figuratively oral encounter with an excremental projection:

Sitting on top of a charcoal fire in the firebox was a huge iron pot, filled with some sort of stew which had a strong nauseating smell. . . .

"It smells like feces," the second cop said. . . .

One of the nuns entering the kitchen at just that moment said indignantly, "It is feetsies. Everybody ain't rich like you white folks." (9–10)

"Shit!" [cried Johnson X]. "Shit! . . . Shit! Does anyone in their right state of mind . . . believe that shittt?" [He] pronounced the word "shit" as though he had tasted it and spat it out—eloquent, logical and positive. (39)

"Can you tell me if [the dead man has] had sexual intercourse—recently, I
mean?"

. . . "Anyway, it wasn't with a woman," the assistant M.E. said, reddening un-
controllably. "At least in a normal way." (55–56)

"We ain't gonna ask the Black Jesus for no mercy," General Ham declared. . . . "We
just gonna take him and feed him to whitey in the place of the other food we been putting on whitey's table since the first of us arrived as slaves. . . . We're gonna keep feeding [whitey] the flesh of the Black Jesus until he perish of constipation if he don't choke
to death first." (77–78)

The examples obviously aren't identical, and we shall return to them later
with the patience required to differentiate them. For now it's enough to state
the hypothesis: in each of these cases, in complex ways, white readers are
asked to incorporate what amounts to an identificatory excretion: the shit,
the refuse, the detritus of white identity, which shows up as externalized
blackness and results from the moment whites find in the image of a human
"other" a darkness they cannot own in themselves. Beneath the stereotypes
of blackness we've examined, beneath the entire constellation of images
defining Harlem as detestably non-white, there lies an excremental fantasy
that equates African Americans with the defecated portion of a white self
that "knows" it is not colored waste.[15] Shit thus becomes the most concrete
embodiment of the novel's formal approximation of refuse, as well as of the
various representations of ruin with which the book confronts us.

The process, moreover, works in reverse: the book whose formal ruin
makes it indigestible, unincorporable—finally, unreadable—is redefined by
the defacatory metaphor as itself a kind of shit.[16] The (re)incorporation of
this "excrement" is precisely what the affirmation of stereotypes is meant to
achieve. Himes requires white readers to own their waste by having his blacks
assume the degraded images through which whites habitually "see" them—
not in order to subvert those stereotypes by way of a performative resignification, nor as a kind of liberatory mimicry that keeps its distance from the
image that it mimes,[17] but rather in order, with deadly seriousness, to affirm

the waste of black identity and force it back on the "race" who made that waste by eliminating it to begin with. Blacks "are" feces in the white imaginary—and they eat feces. Whites must in turn be forced to eat them if such projections are to be undone. This is the psychological sequence that we need now to start to trace. The fact that the encounter with excremental blackness literally kills Richard Henderson—the white sexual tourist who, in a passage just quoted, is implied to have had anal sex with a black man immediately prior to his death—suggests that it's finally white *masculinity* that's at stake in this process: law, vision, psychic singularity—and thus, the capacity of even the book's black detectives to enforce a law that institutes difference by equating purity and power with white men.

"Blind Man with a Pistol"

The ruin I'm describing first takes place in the case of Grave Digger and Coffin Ed. The detectives belong, as I have suggested, both to the (black) community they police and to the (white) power structure they serve. They therefore help to expose the ways in which Harlem's borders have already been broached, help us to see that the principles governing life in the ghetto are not in any simple sense "black." I'd even argue that this racial impurity accounts for the doubling that produces two detectives in the first place. The liminal status that characterizes even a figure like Chandler's Marlowe—poised uneasily between cops who think of him as an outlaw and criminals who identify him with the law—has in Himes the representational effect of cleaving the hero in two. It renders him a doubled unit that's neither one nor two, in that the heroes are both separate people and insufficiently differentiated as characters.[18] And it does this in order to express a deeper and more significant inner rupture, by which the detectives are black *and* white in a way that disturbs the racial distinctions with which Himes's work is concerned.

 Blind Man's treatment of this "doubled unit" is special in two ways. First, it makes exceptionally clear how masculinity is at stake in Himes's explorations of race. Second, the novel demonstrates this by moving toward a refusal of the distance that places the detectives outside and "above" their community—a separation that's figured largely through metaphors of vision and visibility. We can start to grasp how both these points work by turning to the scene in which the novel introduces Digger and Ed:

The Negro detectives, Grave Digger Jones and Coffin Ed Johnson, were making their last round through Harlem in [their] old black Plymouth sedan. In the daytime it might have been recognized, but at night it was barely distinguishable from any number of other dented, dilapidated struggle buggies cherished by the citizens of Harlem; other than when they had to go somewhere in a hurry it went. But now they were idling along . . . with the lights out as was their custom on dark side streets. The car scarcely made a sound; for all its dilapidated appearance the motor was ticking almost silently. It passed along practically unseen . . . its occupants invisible.

This was due in part to the fact that both detectives were almost as dark as the night, and they were wearing lightweight black alpaca suits and black cotton shirts with the collars open. Whereas other people were in shirt sleeves on this hot night, they wore their suit coats to cover the big glinting nickel-plated thirty-eight-caliber revolvers they wore in their shoulder slings. They could see in the dark streets like cats, but couldn't be seen. (29)

This is in many respects a remarkable passage, not least in the way it plays on the relations among masculinity, race, vision, and visibility. The black detectives are "as dark as the night" and therefore "[cannot] be seen." Their "alpaca suits" intensify and extend a black skin that renders them nocturnally invisible. Their car is visually unremarkable because it's hard to tell it apart from the other "struggle buggies" in Harlem, as well as because, with the headlights doused, its darkness and the quiet of its motor dissolve it into the Harlem night. The passage in this way seeks to suggest that it's the detectives' racial qualities that make them optically inconspicuous. It's because of a darkness that Himes imagines as both epidermal and complexly cultural that Digger and Ed are able to become almost literally inaccessible to sight.

This inaccessibility has a striking resonance in the African American literary tradition. For where one strand of that tradition associates invisibility with ontological erasure and social disempowerment, Himes *empowers* his black detectives by rendering them invisible.[19] Empowerment is here a matter of seeing, not of being seen. It concerns the death of the visible body and its resurrection as an invisible eye, so that Himes's black men become detectives—become socially empowered beings—precisely inasmuch as they can "*see* in the dark," but cannot themselves "be seen."

Their access to such visual power complicates the meaning of their blackness, since it is at once the sign and result of an identification with white law. Because they're identified with that law, Jones and Johnson's "struggle buggy" "goes" when they want it to, unlike those of the disempowered; its "dilapidated" appearance disguises its capacity to become a successfully phallic embodiment of their lawful virility and power. Unlike the book's other African American men, moreover, whose masculine inadequacy is signaled by their repeated reduction to the bodily (sweat, fat, penises, corpses[20]), the detectives' suits veil their actual bodies, which are then recovered in sublated form in "the big glinting nickel-plated thirty-eight-caliber revolvers [that] they wear in their shoulder slings."[21] The unseen seers are thus here also the phallic masters of law. They're masters, indeed, to the exact extent that they're also unseen seers. They're masters because their participation in white power liberates them from the social erasure threatened by African American invisibility, while also countering the vulnerability of being seen with the symbolic power of an invulnerable (because disembodied) vision and masculine law.

The novel in this way tightly intertwines the elements that make up its detectives' identity as "black," "police," and "men." Digger and Ed wield power because they're cops. This wielding of power is in part facilitated by the fact that they're African American: their blackness, that is, helps them become a trusted part of the community they police. But blackness on its own would make them resemble too closely the other people in Harlem: disenfranchised, emasculated, powerless. So being cops also requires an identification with white manhood, which in turn means being sanctioned to participate in a symbolic and scopic register from which African American masculinity is habitually excluded—and excluded in the name of the biological stereotype with which we're already familiar (all penis, no phallus).

This set of associations (white/masculine/looking/power vs. black/not fully masculine/looked at/powerlessness) is absolutely pervasive in *Blind Man*. When, for example, Henderson dies on a night-lit Harlem sidewalk, a crowd gathers round to look because "[a] dead man was always good to see. It was reassuring to see somebody else dead. Generally the dead men were also colored. A white dead man was really something. . . . Just look at him, baby. And feel good it ain't you" (33). Looking is here the mark of not being the object of vision itself. The pleasure of seeing is inseparable from the knowledge that, at least this time, you've escaped the prospect of a "being seen" that makes a person vulnerable to violence. The fact that the dead man isn't "colored" facilitates this disidentification. It enables black people to occupy the position of whites who usually escape violent death, rather than risking the identificatory slide into racial solidarity with a corpse.

Similarly, in the scene in which a TV is delivered to the woman who may or may not be Dr. Moore's whore, Slick "look[s] around at the gaping [crowd] and sneer[s] with contempt. 'You people! A man can't open his fly in this town before you nosy people crowding about to see what he gonna pull out.' A man chuckled. 'Can you blame us? He might pull out a knife.'" And Slick replies: "Well, I ain't got no knife in mine" (121–22). The desire to see is here once more associated with the need to defend against violence. Who knows, after all, how many knives you might miss if you're not sufficiently visually attentive? It's only by way of such optical vigilance that the dangers of Harlem can be exposed and kept at a maximum physical distance. The flip side of such a structure, meanwhile, is again the violence of being seen. Penile exposure to the sight of others is equated with the threat of castration, as Slick says not "mine ain't no knife," but "I ain't got no knife in mine."

Such connections are made more explicit by the serum in the rejuvenation scene. The purpose of that serum is to make Mister Sam young again, so that—as his chauffeur puts it—he can continue "diddling" women. It's thus a fluid designed to render the black man immortal and infinitely virile. The serum itself is a hilarious concoction of thematically serious substances: albumin, baboon testicles, "sperm elixir," "mating organs of rabbits, eagles and shellfish"—this much perhaps makes a certain sense. But also: the "concupiscent eye" of a "fighting rooster what could fertilize eggs from a distance of three feet," reminding Sam of "a man [he] knew what could look at womens and knock 'em up" (42). The relation between seeing and masculine power could hardly be more explicit. Though Himes leaves unstated the half of the opposition by which visibility means powerlessness and death, the scene might be read as a comic revision of the narrative I described in relation to Ed and Digger: the transformation of bodily vulnerability (to age, to death) into a masculine invulnerability associated with sight and bodily transcendence. Perhaps the reason for this narrative's failure—Mister Sam does not get rejuvenated—is the social inaccessibility of whiteness for the characters in this scene, so that unlike in the case of the two detectives, the black identification with vision is merely the decidedly untranscendent ingestion of one more detachable body part.

Finally, two scenes indicate with special clarity the relation of visionlessness to lack of power. The first occurs when Ed and Digger approach Michael X in an effort to determine who's inciting the youths to riot. They find him, to begin with, "master of the situation," his "[s]harp eyes that didn't miss a thing glint[ing] from behind rimless spectacles" (174). But then something remarkable happens. "Michael X took off his already glistening spectacles. Without them he looked young and immature and very vulnerable: like a young man who could be easily hurt. He looked at them, barefaced and absurdly defiant" (175). It's as if the glasses, by marking and securing Michael's visual mastery, magically transform him from "Billie Holiday's kid brother" into a man of leadership and strength (174). Simply remove the glasses, and the vulnerable child reappears—the knowing glint in the eyes having been discarded with the spectacles themselves, revealed as a mere trick of vision produced by the "glistening" glass of the eyewear. Without that eyewear his defiant manner becomes nothing less than "absurd"; his

197

face is visually exposed and rendered unprotected, bare. So it's unsurprising that, by the end of the scene, Grave Digger is prophesying Michael's death. In response to the latter's insistence that the detectives ask their boss who's behind the riots, Digger says: "You keep on talking like that you won't live long." "You think someone is going to kill me?" Michael asks. And Grave Digger: "People been killed for less" (175). It's in this book a very short step from loss of vision to loss of life.

The second scene I have in mind goes further than this one to stress the toxic character of male commitments to vision as power. I'm talking, of course, about the scene from which the novel takes its title—the one in which a blind man with a pistol terrorizes a subway car full of passengers before being gunned down by white policemen. The scene is clearly intended as an allegory. Himes offers a reading of that allegory in his preface to the novel (5). Here he writes that "all unorganized violence is like a blind man with a pistol," suggesting thereby that the blind man in *Blind Man* represents all those "vulnerable soul brothers" who are led into self-destruction by an irresponsible leadership. That leadership is irresponsible, on this account, not for urging violence, but for offering a structure for insurrection that can only destroy those who participate in it because of its insufficiently organized character. In the context of the book's treatment of black politics, this irresponsibility issues from the fact that the leaders don't want to end racial hierarchy, but rather to perpetuate it. The violence they promote has as its aim the enrichment or increased pleasure of the leadership, not the liberation of those they purport to lead. The blind man thus figures the duped of Harlem—the losers in the most deadly of those con games we examined in the first section.

Illuminating and interesting though this account is, it seems to me inadequately attentive to the complex function of vision in this scene. For the blind man's relation to visual power subversively echoes that of Grave Digger and Coffin Ed in the scene where Himes introduces them. Like the African American detectives, the blind man lays claims to masculine power through an identification with its symbol: the pistol. Like them also, and paradoxically enough, this identification is inseparable from a commitment to omnipotent vision. The blind man precisely *refuses to recognize* himself as a man who is blind. It isn't just that he "[does not] want anyone to know" about his blindness and so "trie[s] to act like anyone else" (176), but that he doesn't himself identify with the designation "blind man." He repeatedly "stares" and "looks" around him with the "menacing" eyes of "a heat-blind snake" (179, 177, 176). When a "soul sister" starts screaming "BLIND MAN WITH A PISTOL" after he has shot and killed a passenger, he "wav[es] his pistol as though it [has] eyes" and cries "Where? Where?" (186). The eyes in the pistol suggest once more an identification of male power with vision, even as the blind man's "Where?" indicates an almost insane disavowal of his visual impairment.

The scene's disturbing and critical function in relation to the black detectives resides here. Himes seems to be trying to decouple masculinity from visual power, and to be stressing the toxic illegitimacy of *any* claims to "have" the phallus. By linking the blind man to Digger and Ed while showing the derangement of the visual commitments through which the three are linked, Himes suggests that the blind man embodies a psychic truth that the detectives disavow. To be is in essence to be seen; to claim to see omnipotently and omnisciently is to refuse to know oneself as blind; to insist on vision and phallic power is to perpetrate a crazy violence that can't but rebound upon oneself. Digger and Ed's accession to such power through an identification with whiteness is no more legitimate or sane than the blind man's, since visual power is here revealed as a defense against the masculine recognition of an insurmountable insufficiency.[22]

It should not surprise us, then, that Himes moves gradually to divest Grave Digger and Coffin Ed of the power with which he initially invests them. In the first extended representation of the riot, their vision becomes less an instrument of power than a sign of aestheticized impotence. The "rioting [looks] like a rehearsal for a modern ballet"—and the uniformed policemen seem to be "dancing a cop's version of *West Side Story*"(136)—as the detectives themselves are reduced to spectators, prevented from either actively intervening or pursuing their hunches elsewhere. They then lose even this visual distance to enter the blinded zone of the visible. "[T]he black face of a grizzly-bearded rabbi peep[s] furtively at them" from "a storefront synagogue," but "[t]hey [don't] see him because some heavy object land[s] on top of their car and sudden flame [pours] down all windows" (141). This gasoline fire, presaged by blindness (they "don't see" the grizzly-bearded man), collapses the detectives into the space of the spectacle itself. "The tenement windows . . . suddenly fill . . . with Harlem citizens watching the spectacle" of their fire (142), and Ed must do "a grotesque adagio dance" (141) that links him to the aestheticized theatrics of the riot he's been watching.

With this reduction to the status of spectacle, the two are subjected to the violent consequences that the novel associates with blindness and the visible. Both men's clothes catch fire. Though neither is seriously injured, and though the scene is in part run through the comic mill of the stereotype,[23] it's clear that *Blind Man* is here suggesting the susceptibility of Digger and Ed to the specular violence that their identification with vision is meant to surmount. The scene stresses this susceptibility by requiring Coffin Ed to take off his burning pants—an act that, by exposing his body, insists on his failure to transcend the corporeal through symbolico-visual identification, and that does so by threatening to expose the distance between the all-too-visible penis and the invisible majesty of the phallus.

The consequences of this exposure are not far to find. The dying man whom Ed and Digger discover toward the beginning of the novel is, we will recall, missing his pants. His penis is apparently stained with excrement in a way that indicates he's been having anal sex. So the visual exposure of the penis would seem to undermine the immutable pretensions of the phallus—to signal a masculine vulnerability to death—and to do so by bringing the masculine organ into proximity with the anus.

This movement into visibility and mutability extends to the final chapters of the novel, marking the basic telos of Digger and Ed's "development." When the detectives enter a nightclub called the Five Spot with

THE WASTE OF WHITE MASCULINITY

John Babson, the gay black suspect they've coerced into helping them investigate Henderson's murder, the manager gives them "a ringside seat under the gong. The seat was so conspicuous they knew instantly it was reserved for suspect people. They smiled to themselves, wondering how [the manager] figured their little friend. Did they look that much like the kind, they wondered" (143). There's a discernible ambiguity about this last line—an ambiguity that stems from Digger and Ed's uncertainty about just what makes them seem suspicious. Does the manager mistake their "friend" for a cop, or does he take them all to be "pansies" (145)? It's clear that Himes wants at least to open this second possibility, and to connect it once more to the dangers of visibility. The threat is precisely that Digger and Ed might turn out to "*look* . . . like [Babson's] kind." The violent proclivities of the visible now include the danger of sexual ambiguation. No sooner do the detectives stop being mere seers, no sooner are they physically framed and embodied as objects of visual attention, than they become subject to an interpretive suspicion that threatens to expose their virility as a mask. A phallic ideal of heterosexual manhood cannot withstand the scrutiny entailed in its visible incarnation. And so, as if in defense against being thought gay, the detectives allow their mortal desires to be ensnared by a mini-skirted dancer, causing them to lose sight of their suspect as he wanders off to get himself killed (142–44). Becoming the objects of visual attention means at once risking emasculation and losing a visual capacity to police that is here central to the meaning of manhood.

Babson's death reiterates this equation in displaced but hyperbolic fashion. He's sliced, to begin with, across the buttocks in a way that reminds us of the mutual borders conjoining visibility, anality, and death (146). While his killer is "chivving his ass like beating time," Babson "danc[es] about like an adagio dancer" (146)—a detail that homosexualizes the meaning of the earlier "adagio" with which Ed removes his burning pants. And Babson in death is "curled up like a foetus," cut so much "he [bears] little resemblance to the exhibitionist pansy of a few minutes before" (145). "Exhibitionist" and "pansy" are here practically interchangeable; to be the first is to risk being seen as the second, and both lead inexorably, by way of the anus, to a deadly fetal return of the feminine—in and as the womb.

Himes's residual attachment to the hardboiled novel's conventions requires that Digger and Ed turn out to escape John Babson's literal fate. But their professional and masculine effectiveness is severely undermined by the novel's end. In the final pages, their guns have been reduced to mere playthings, instruments useful only for the violent eradication of rats. This eradication is staged, at one point, as a figurative bullfight: one of the rats "paw[s] the sidewalk, snorting," Ed calls to it "like a toreador," and the spectators cry "Olé" when he kills it (189). But the lack of genuine personal risk makes this test of strength ridiculous, just as Coffin Ed's visual mastery—his bullet strikes the rodent in "the center of its forehead" (189)—is reduced to a meaningless, pyrotechnic exhibition that has nothing to do with solving crimes.

The spectacular nature of this scene, in which the detectives are watched by spectators as they exercise visual power, further indicates the distance they've fallen from their initial position as unseen seers successfully enforcing the Law. They're now caught up in a dialectic of vision that annuls the position of transcendent seer. Even the rats threaten visually to subject them, as it's precisely when one "look[s] up through murderous red eyes" that Ed shoots and kills it (189). The fact, moreover, that the bullet goes through the center of the animal's forehead links Coffin Ed to the blind man's toxic disavowal of blindness in the name of male power.[24] When that man comes out of the subway amidst the pandemonium he has caused, he fires his gun in the direction of the passenger he had tried to shoot before, only to kill a white cop with a bullet that hits him "in the middle of the forehead" (190–91). Given that the shooting spree is motivated in part by a rage against white racism, one can only assume that this is in some sense a spectacularly successful shot—that he has hit his intended target. The novel thus erases the distinction between unlawful and lawful vision. To shoot straight, and in the name of the law, is to shoot in a manner that's indistinguishable from the frenzied absurdity of shooting blindly. One is merely the legalized version of the other's attempt to deny through violence the truths of power-lessness and objectification, as the success of blind vision perfectly comple-ments the castrating reduction of legalized sight to a species of sporty ver-min-control. No wonder, then, that the novel closes with a riot the detectives are powerless to prevent. *Blind Man* has by this point subverted the equation of manhood with vision and power, in a way that compromises the dicks' ef-fectiveness—as policemen and as men.

Excremental Spectacles

Himes once more employs a specifically racial vocabulary for the process I'm describing. He suggests, that is, that his heroes' transformation entails a disidentification with white power—a disidentification motivated by what Digger calls "compassion" for the African American rioters (154). But such a vocabulary does not signal a simple movement from identification with whiteness to identification with blackness—a narrative that would leave in-tact the racial categories themselves. The black detectives' insistence that "[y]ou got to enforce law to get order" (154) makes clear that something more complex is at issue. Digger and Ed make this statement while explain-ing to their boss why African American youths riot. It means in this context that, in order to prevent riots, one would have to give blacks the social means to realize the freedom and equality that have already legally been granted them.[25] "Law" is thus here the product of a mutually intertwined history. No longer the promise of masculine empowerment by way of a visually figured transcendence, it's rather the effect of a history made by blacks and whites "on the ground." The commitment to vision and white Law (capital "L") could in this sense be thought of as a psychotic[26] and socially destructive in-sistence on an impossible racial purity, which seeks to deny the mutual and often violent intertwining of identities that makes up (African) American his-tory. The breakdown of Digger and Ed's effectiveness results from the ruin of this delusional purity—not from an embrace of blackness as opposed to ide-alized whiteness, but from a leakage of racial borders that issues in chaos because it lays waste to a phallic manhood that is at once the sign and guarantee of such impermeable boundaries.

The novel's concern with the piercing of these borders has first to do with the physical transgression of the ghetto's own perimeters. Both of the passages that deal with signs—passages examined in detail earlier—can be thought of as meditations on this transgression. Both suggest the ways in which whites who travel into Harlem confront their projections of blackness in an essentially illegible form, causing a kind of interpretive meltdown that parallels the novel's own effect on readers it addresses as white. The scene of Babson's death explores the inverse of this crossing. Here the detectives *exit* Harlem in an effort to solve Henderson's murder. Though this exit is imagined as the traversing of a racial border, Digger and Ed find in the Village, not a world of white purity, but an interracial world of malaise, where the white girls look like "spaceage witches" and "[e]ven the soul brothers . . . seem . . . to be wandering around in a daze" (131, 134).

The novel thus appears to suggest that the instability of racial borders results in a kind of existential despair. The club to which the investigation leads is, in fact, a microcosmic figuration of a space whose dangers consist in the way its borders are at once marked and crossed. One of its walls contains "irregular-sized elliptic openings, giving Picasso-like glimpses of the interior," but on the inside these openings are "covered by see-through mirrors, in which the guests [can] see nothing but reflections of themselves." The narcissistic self-enclosure of this inside thwarts the visual transaction that seems to be promised from the outside. Similarly, though passers-by can see the performing musicians through these openings, the flawless soundproofing of the club seeks to prevent any sonic permeation: "Not a dribble of noise leaked in from the street unless the door was opened. And no one outside could hear the expensive sounds that were being made within" (142). The statements point again to a kind of incessantly pierced insularity, as the door both completes the club's aural armor and offers a site for that armor's broaching, while shifting the terms of exclusion and hierarchy from black/ white to rich/poor.

Such a shift suggests that the club's insularity is inseparable from a racial contagion. On the inside are both blacks and whites, "like in the Assembly of the UN." The African American patrons who, as the detectives recognize, would in Harlem talk while listening to music, have here "caught . . . from the white people" a tendency to "[dig] jazz in . . . silence" (142–43)— caught it like a disease that equates by "civilizing" those it infects. And with the death of the black man whom the detectives have brought from Harlem, the borders containing both race and space effectively collapse: "the loud urgent screams of police sirens pour . . . into the room," and "[f]rom many throats [comes] a wail like a cry of anxiety—a new sound" now of grief and mourning that knows no racial confines (145). The breakdown of racial borders once more issues in pain and suffering, which become the occasion for a strangely utopian bonding through racially unmarked sorrow.

One could extend these examples of border-leakage considerably. Virtually every scene in *Blind Man* concerns the entry of a "foreign" element into an apparently closed system, the juxtaposition of black and white in the same geographic or psychic space. Such leakage portends the ruin of identities based on racial purity. Though Himes on one hand indicates the genuine dangers of this ruin, he ultimately shows it also to be both necessary and beneficent. He does this by thinking that ruin persistently through metaphors of waste and shit—metaphors that expose the expulsive dynamic that underlies racist exclusions.

When, for example, the white cops in the opening enter the ruin that Reverend Sam inhabits, the harelipped man is cooking something that to them "smells like feces." "It is feetsies," says one of Sam's "nuns." "Everybody ain't rich like you white folks" (10). The reply suggests the projective character of the scene that the white men see. It says that African Americans are forced by poverty to eat things white people find disgusting, things that those people experience as the most abject of inassimilable matter. The confrontation with blackness becomes in this sense a nasal imbibing of shit. And the reason for this is that Himes is exploring how whites see epidermal difference through the lens of a primal bodily fantasy, in which excrement has

205

become emblematic of a dark, expelled, and inassimilable "non-self" that threatens white purity and psychic integrity.

The encounter with racial darkness in essence reactivates this equation. It incites in whites a rejection of those who figure for them the substance whose always fragile expulsion founds the social or properly civilized self. And it leads them to institute social exclusions and economic deprivations, which produce a ghetto whose dirtiness psychically authorizes the racial hatred at its origin—so that ghettoization is a process whose purpose is to make reality conform to a fantasy in order to "prove" the fantasy true and justify racism itself.[27]

The entire constellation of stereotypes in this scene is underpinned by this excremental fantasy. The black family's squalid living conditions, Sam's hyper- but socially impotent virility, the women's excessive fertility, the animalization of children who are forced to eat out of troughs (10)—all are material expressions of a fantasy that, in linking African Americans to a bodily waste they also putatively consume, reduces them to some variant of the impure and the not-human. The white man's olfactory ingestion of this waste marks the enforced reinternalization of such stereotypes. It does so by breaching the bodily borders preserving the white self's purity—borders that are here metonyms for the boundaries surrounding the ghetto itself.

A comparable if more utopian dynamic structures the integration march that Marcus leads with his girlfriend, Birgit. Here we once more have a scene in which the boundaries of Harlem have been broached; blacks and whites come together to march for the end of racism through "Brotherhood." The explosive potential of this conjunction is marked by the fact that, as the marchers march, "the black against the white and the white against the black [give] the illusion of nakedness. The forty-eight orderly young marchers [give] the illusion of an orgy" (27). It's as if the physical juxtaposition of the races can't but visually conjure forth the specter of interracial sex. "The black and white naked flesh in the amber light fill[s] the . . . onlookers with a strange excitement" (27), and even the "citizens of Harlem [are] scandalized" by what "look[s] like a segregationist nightmare" (99). Himes, of

THE WASTE OF WHITE MASCULINITY

course, brings this fantasy into the vicinity of shit. Behind the marchers sits Marcus himself "with the strained expression of a man moving his bowels. With him [sits] a middle-aged white woman . . . who look[s] similarly engaged, with the exception that she [has] constipation" (98). To come into contact with another race here is not just to induce a sexualized breakdown of racial purity. It's also to render explicit thereby the anal-expulsive genesis or origin of racial purity itself—and to say that the pleasures of interracial sex are experienced as inseparable from a regressively excremental excitement.[28]

Two other scenes mentioned briefly earlier help to establish such connections. In the first, Reverend Sam's chauffeur replies to Mubuta's proclamation that, since his rejuvenation serum will enable blacks to "outlive the white folks," it represents "the one and only solution for the Negro problem." "Shit!" cries Johnson X. "Shit! . . . Shit! Does anyone . . . believe that shittt?" The chauffeur's "loose lips punctuate . . . each word with a spray of spit," and he "pronounce[s] the word 'shit' as though he [has] tasted it and spat it out" (39). Such details would seem inconsequential in a novel less concerned with the excremental. But in this novel, they suggest that the invocation of racial purity—the expression of a fantasy that knows the borders between the black and the white—induces expressions of disbelief that take an essentially excremental form. The utopian narrative of purity triumphant provokes a verbal eruption of shit as that story's repressed underside. And this profane exclamation astonishingly materializes the thing it names, calling shit into being in order to thwart the purifying gesture, as well as to mark shit's correlation with the organ of introjection/projection ("as though he had tasted it and spat it out").

The second scene I have in mind concerns the religious nationalism of Prophet Ham. That figure proposes to solve the Negro problem by "feeding whitey . . . the flesh of the Black Jesus." "I don't have to tell you," he informs his followers, "[that] the flesh of Jesus is indigestible. . . . And that, brothers . . . is how we're going to fight whitey and beat him at last. We're gonna keep feeding him the flesh of the Black Jesus until he perish of constipation if he don't choke to death first. . . . We're gonna march with the statue of the Black

Jesus until whitey pukes" (77–78). Here, the novel comes remarkably close to offering an internal representation of its strategies—the forced reincorporation of an indigestible black substance, which induces a kind of spiritual vomiting in the whites who are made to consume it. Ham would even appear to intuit a connection between this process and the undermining of white racist stereotypes. The fantasy construct of blacks as cannibals, which is perhaps a projected version of white culture's tendency to devour other cultures, is in his sermon turned back on itself. "Whitey" himself becomes the cannibal, ingesting an indigestible flesh. Black subjection to white cultural cannibalism is thus at once affirmed and rewritten as a form of black resistance.

If Himes nonetheless distances himself from Ham in ways described earlier, this is because the Prophet remains unconscious of his intuition's profoundest consequences. The Black Jesus is, on his account, a proclamation of essential difference, a symbol of radical separation, rather than the result of a complex entanglement between psyches and cultures that have never been pure. Ham fails to grasp that the flesh he'll serve whitey is already saturated with white fantasy projections. He does not see that its meaning emerges in the confrontation between dark skin and the white man's memory of a repudiated blackness he can't stand to own in himself. The conspicuous absence of excrement in Ham's discourse—the absence of any reference to the psychobiological meaning of "black flesh"—is perhaps the most prominent sign of this unconsciousness, and certainly a mark of Himes's distance from this figure and his "solution."

But finally, the plot that most fully brings together these concerns—excrement, the transgression of borders, masculinity, and race—is the one that charts the death of Henderson after he has crossed into Harlem. A passage toward the novel's beginning is crucial to that plot. For it prepares the theme of white death by extending the issues we've been pursuing into the realm of an interracial and disintegrative sexuality. "If white citizens wished to come to Harlem for their kicks," Himes writes, "they had to take the venereal risks and the risks of short con or having their money stolen. [The black detectives'] only duty was to protect them from violence" (29–30). This is a more striking statement than is perhaps first evident. It suggests, once more, the *inevitability* of violence for whites who cross this border. To enter the space of white projections is here to run the inherent risk of being somehow undone—so much so that the Harlem police would seem to exist for the sole purpose ("Their only duty") of "protect[ing] white people" from African Americans. But the passage also insists that this violence is inseparable from sexual contact. What brings white citizens to Harlem in the first place is the wish to "get their kicks": the wish for access to the "primitive" desires that they disavow and project into Harlem. Contact with such desires can only lead to a kind of self-dissolution, since one main function of the boundary around Harlem is to mark the distinction between a "civilized" sexuality and the rampant concupiscence of those desires that a white sense of self cannot abide. The quoted passage is thus the beginning of a remarkable social analysis. It suggests both the sexual basis of racism and the violence that comes when whites cross over to enjoy their disavowed desires—while nevertheless, and quite impossibly, continuing to disavow them.

Blind Man's main instance of such a desire is of course that of the (repressed) homosexual. Its second chapter traces the meandering of an ostensibly straight white man, who is at once attracted and repelled by the "wanton, indecent" movements of the black "sissies" he encounters on 125th Street (15). Himes ultimately names this man Henderson. The sissies are, as it turns out, his reason for coming to Harlem:

The white man watched [the black sissies] enviously. His body twitched as though he were standing in a hill of ants. His muscles jerked in the strangest places, one side of his face twitched, he had cramps in the right foot, his pants cut his crotch, he bit his tongue, one eye popped out from its socket. . . . He couldn't control himself. . . . [He] couldn't help acting guilty and frightened. He slithered [toward the African American men] like a moth to the flame. (15–16)

The passage suggests the extraordinary degree of repression involved in white male sexuality. Each of its details indicates the revolt of homosexual desire against a male body that defines itself as straight and white. Muscles "jerk" and "twitch" and "cramp," with the surreal precision of somatic displacement, in the face of a disciplined effort at "control." The extremity of violence in this conflict is marked by a turning of the body against itself: biting one's tongue bespeaks the regression of an oral sadism turned back on itself, while an eye that literally "pop[s] out from its socket" portends a kind of entropic fragmentation, a projective dispersal of a body that the straight man cannot keep together.

When compared with the "naked" (15, 16, 17) and unembarrassed exhibitionism of the sissies, this conflict becomes all the more striking. It's as if Himes were saying that, in a racist society, white men achieve a "normal" sexuality by denying their homosexual urges, projecting them onto black men in a way that frees those blacks from sexual repression even as it subjects them to oppression and racial ghettoization. The price that African American men must pay for this is obvious—besides the forms of disempowerment I've just mentioned, *Blind Man* clearly wants to suggest that the projective homosexualization of black men emasculates them (it's black gay men who are feminized in the novel, whom the book calls "sissies" and "pansies"), and that this is an essential ingredient of racism. The price that white men pay is that described in the passage I've quoted: a kind of grotesque mutilation of self that, though our culture calls it normal, entails a bereavement for lost desires that lead one to "env[y]" those who express them. Such a bereavement is structurally insurmountable, precisely because those desires are now felt to portend the death of the masculine self that's founded upon their exclusion.[29]

One thing that should be clear from such statements is a disquieting tendency in Himes's novel to equate white racism with homosexuality—his claim for the racist's "gayness," in this sense, harboring a hidden assertion that the homosexual is a racist. Diana Fuss and Lee Edelman have recently traced this homophobic equation in writers as diverse as Frantz Fanon, Toni Morrison, and, in some respects, James Baldwin.[30] My argument suggests that Himes belongs in this group of figures as well. But it also seems to me important to push the analysis further. For if the sissy figures in part the unnatural implantation in blacks of a properly "white" desire, Himes nonetheless allows us to see how that figure functions as a site of exchange that ruins the distinctions (white/black, straight/gay, masculine/feminine) on which this homophobic understanding rests.

The most significant element of this process concerns the death of Henderson himself. That death is, as I have indicated, associated with the act of anal sex, as if to make as explicit as possible the relation between penile contact with the anus and the ruin of phallic masculinity. The sexualized power relations that white racism requires are in this way broken by their enactment. Far from being the extension or expression of white domination over blacks, the penetration of the African American man's anus destroys the illusion of invulnerable white manhood. This ruination expresses the precariousness of the boundaries that separate Harlem from its outside—and that distinguish the extroverted black pansy from the neurotic normality of the white hysteric. For if the journey into Harlem wastes white manhood through the excremental, this is because that manhood turns out *already to be the anus it encounters*. The cops who try to solve the crime discover a trail of blood: "The trail wasn't hard to follow. It had a pattern. An irregular patch of scattered spots that looked like spots of tar in the artificial light was interspersed every fourth or fifth step by a dark gleaming splash where blood had spurted from the wound" (59–60). The "dark[ness]" of this blood, its resemblance to "spots of tar," suggests the excremental character of the dead white man's insides. Indeed we know that it's blood that gives excrement its dark color, blood that is the only dark-colored substance in the human body. Himes is in this sense staging again the fantasy on which white racism rests. The black man is repudiated for an epidermal difference that takes its meaning from the shit whose expulsion marks a primal attempt to establish the difference between white self and other. This shit, in turn, takes its color from blood. If its darkness makes it on one hand a symbol in the white imaginary for the not-me—the dirty, the impure—that darkness nonetheless connects it back to the inside of the white body, precisely inasmuch as blood is something that all of us have inside. Racism thus entails a rejection of the anal that constructs the black man as "pansy" ("feminine" because anally receptive), even as this scene insists on the breakdown of all the distinctions I've elaborated. The excrement turns out to be "inside"; the white man comes into contact with himself, in and as the pansy's anus; and penetrating that anus entails a kind of figural reincorporation of shit, which then is splattered out on the sidewalk in a literal and self-destructively "successful" repetition of the initial projection.

This wasting of white manhood is, I'd suggest, the novel's ultimate subject. The process is even in some sense the cause of Digger and Ed's acquired impotence, since their power derives, as I have shown, from identifications with an invisibly white ideal of transcendent potency and vision. Henderson's hysterics expose from the start the distance between this masculine ideal and the actual men who ought to incarnate it. His death, moreover, serves to undo the distinctions upon which white manhood rests—not least of all by turning him into the corpse that Harlem's residents look at, in order to feel glad that it isn't them who are dead and on display. We know that by the end of the novel the two detectives will themselves be subject to such visibility, impotence, and death. The suggestion seems to me clear enough: that Digger and Ed's vulnerability results from the incarnate ruin of a white masculinity with whose ideal they're at first identified, and which can survive as white and male only by escaping such incarnation—by transcending its ruinous and blind implication in the waste matter of the body. The greatest virtue of *Blind Man with a Pistol* is that it refuses this escape. Indeed, the novel would seem to suggest that the greater the insistence on purity, potency, and lawful vision, the more toxic the results. When the detectives' superior ties their hands because their investigation "might uncover an interracial homosexual scandal that nobody wishes known" (159), an explosive ceremony of racial impurity in Harlem starts to take place. Blacks begin to riot and loot, to incarnate the excessive bodily fantasies that whites have projected onto them, and so to insist on their right to sully a world that tries to reduce them to the dirt that whites don't want to acknowledge. The very attempt to impose racial purity results in this return of waste. The toxic assertion of white power and Law—the effort to hide a "scandal" that threatens the basis of such power—leads to the breakdown of Law itself.

And this, of course, is what *Blind Man* seeks to effect through its formal disruptions as well. By striving to be a "literary ruin," the novel refuses the epistemological certainties that would enable one simply to read it. It denies readers it constructs as white the internalization of a meaning that can be integrated without disturbance. It prevents those readers from finding in it an uncontaminated image of self, just as it multiplies and confuses black stereotypes to the point of rendering them inescapable yet collectively unrecognizable. In this way the novel asks white readers to ingest it as waste, rubble, shit—an inassimilable and impure materiality, unredeemed by aesthetic sublimation, which *Blind Man* equates in its content with the waste that white men refuse to avow.

Afterword

I have argued that the crime novel is a place in our culture where a range of dominant fantasies about gender are at once hyperbolically elaborated and contested. Those fantasies are concerned above all with woman as threat to the bounded male self. They're rooted in infantile experiences of psychic and bodily indistinction—experiences in which the fledgling self, in first beginning to distinguish itself, feels at once the pleasure and terror of dissolution into the not-me. The chapter on *Sanctuary* explicitly argued that this dissolution is associated with the mother through the accident of her role in parturition; that men repudiate the appeal of this state in the name of autonomy and an impermeable male armor; and that later experiences of boundary confusion, including those that center upon the ejection of bodily waste, are coded feminine and reviled by men in the masculinist culture in which we live. I have also shown how *Blind Man with a Pistol* explores a similar set of fantasies that constitute white masculinity in relation to racial otherness. If one of the political limitations of the crime genre is that it extends this conflation of femininity (and blackness) with the abject, its strength lies in

214

the way it also opens the possibility for undoing that conflation by disturbing the binaries that support it.

Indeed, one thing that it means for crime fiction to *be* a genre is that it consistently holds open the possibility of this subversion of binaries. In part because of the single-mindedness with which it pursues the meanings of manhood (a single-mindedness that's both cause and result of the genre's marginalization), male abjection is one of crime fiction's enduring generic tendencies—one that's perhaps only rarely actualized, but that asserts its appeal across the genre's historical and subgeneric transformations. It appears even in the most toxic of crime texts as the traces of a repression by which the invulnerable male hero is defensively constituted. And it shows up in the books I've analyzed as a more explicitly realized, and more self-consciously explored, experience of psychic ruin. These books could in this sense be said to body forth what the genre more commonly includes by repressing. One of the purposes of focusing on them has been to isolate what we might call a "generic unconscious" within the more conventional masculinism of the genre—an unconscious whose continued critical repression has made it difficult to take these books as seriously as I think we should take them.

Readers may have noted, perhaps even been troubled by, two significant omissions in my treatment. First, I have ignored altogether contemporary developments in American crime writing. Second, I have focused exclusively on what I've called the "negative moment" of psychic dissolution, without attempting to trace the reconstitution of masculinity along less toxic lines. One question that arises in conclusion is whether addressing the first of these might also address the second—that is, whether contemporary crime writers imagine a manhood that has emerged from the state of effaced or perforated borders, and whether this emergence enables their men to engage in more fully intersubjective and more equitable gender relations.

I have found it useful, in pursuing these questions, to move away from the conceptual reference points of my central arguments, and to draw instead on the remarkable theoretical work of the analyst Marion Milner. Milner is one of the few object relations theorists whose claims for the psychic value of dissolution remain in touch with the scariness of that state. She speaks, for example, of a "total letting go of . . . faeces, urine, vomit, saliva, noise, flatus, . . . a state of blissful transcending of boundaries, which, to the conscious ego, would be identified with madness." This state of madness is for Milner crucial to psychosocial health; the "plunge into no-differentiation . . . results (if all goes well) in a . . . new division of the me-not-me, one in which there is more of the 'me' in the 'not me', and more of the 'not-me' in the 'me.'"[1] Milner makes this argument in the context of a discussion of creativity, without pursuing its implications for the psychic construction of gender. But given the fact that she roots the experience of "no-differentiation" in maternal fusion, it's easy to see the link between her claims and the ones I've been making—to suggest that a non-misogynist culture would be one in which it's *men* who have passed through this state of madness, men who've emerged in a "new division" between the self and not-self, and men who are therefore newly able to build relations with women that don't require the demonization of a reviled and feminine otherness.

Is this a vision of manhood that contemporary crime novels offer? The recent swelling in the ranks of crime writers makes a comprehensive answer difficult. There are more practitioners of the genre now than ever, and the multiplication of subgeneric categories is vast. This increase in production has been accompanied by an increased diversity in both characters and writers. There are now not only African Americans (most recently, Walter Mosley) but women (Sue Grafton, Sara Paretsky) writing in the hardboiled style, and as Robin Winks has pointed out, we can now find books in which the detective is "a Navajo (Tony Hillerman), an Africaner working with a Bantu (James McClure) . . . a Chicano (Rex Burns), a male homosexual (Joseph Hansen), a lesbian (M. F. Beal), a dwarf, a child, a machine."[2] To survey this literature adequately would obviously require a separate study. I'd like, therefore, to start by making some general but provisional remarks, and then to turn to one crime writer whom I believe holds out the promise of something genuinely moving and progressive with respect to gender.

·   ·   ·

Much contemporary American crime fiction is in at least implicit dialogue with that most revolutionary and influential moment in the post–World War II era—the 1960s. In particular, that fiction engages the gains of feminism and multiculturalism by stressing, on one hand, the hero's greater capacity for emotional connectedness, and on the other, a greater range of "others" with whom to connect. The first of these is marked most clearly in those novels that transform the detective into a woman, a gay man, a lesbian, and/or a person of color. For almost without exception, this transformation is part of an explicit attempt to humanize the detective—to give her, for example, a personal history, a social group with which to identify, a commitment to the interpersonal that's rarely found in at least the hardboiled strain of classic American crime fiction. Thus Sue Grafton's Kinsey Milhone evinces an unusual self-consciousness about what it means to identify as a woman, while maintaining both long-standing friendships and intermittent romantic entanglements. Walter Mosley's Easy Rollins is acutely aware of the tension between his personal and social identities—his commitment to personal space and private property marking (for Mosley) an effort to succeed within the terms of white society, and conflicting with Easy's social identification as a member of the black community. Tony Hillerman's Chee and Leaphorn seek to sustain a Navajo community incessantly subject to the rapacious divisiveness of white capitalism and greed. And Barbara Wilson's Pam Nilsen, perhaps the most compelling of the new lesbian sleuths, is not only an amateur detective who makes her living in a printing collective, but also a figure who becomes aware of the intersubjective imperatives of sleuthing. As a social worker says to her in *Sisters of the Road*: "You can't just walk into . . . Trish's life and walk out again. Too many people have done that already. Once she trusts you, if she ever does, you've got a responsibility."[3]

This heightened sense of connection and responsibility makes the new crop of alternative detectives in many ways more appealing than their predecessors. Certainly, in terms of conventional politics, they stack up well against the classic hardboiled detective, with his official commitment to an autonomy that repudiates inner and outer otherness. And yet from a psychic point of view I have some reservations. The multicultural detective novel remains intensely committed to the singularity of the self. That self may have been traditionally marginalized, and may be capable of having a range of relations with other selves. But what remains intolerable is any experience of infirm ego-boundaries—which is, perhaps, another way of saying that these texts' visions can seem naive because they're insufficiently aware of the need to reinvent the self as part of the project of imagining less exclusionary social relations.

An instructive example of this difficulty occurs in Grafton's *"A" Is for Alibi*. Here, the villain turns out to be a precise rewriting of the *femme fatale* as male. Charlie Scorsoni, it's hard not to feel, is at the origin of the novel's evil because in making love to him Kinsey feels that "all [her] walls [are] reduced to rubble," and that this reduction offers her a practically uterine and regressive return to a "cave of heat and flesh."[4] The final confrontation with Charlie takes place with Kinsey hiding in a garbage can; she's there reminded of herself as a "kid" who "hated hide-and-seek," and feels on the brink of wetting her pants in terror at being found (252). The correlation of this moment with the sex scene seems to me hard to resist. It's as if the novel were suggesting that sexual connections entail an experience of psychic dissolution, which returns one to the infantile state of terrifying, disgusting, yet desirable fusion—and to which one can only respond with acts of toxic self-assertion that obliterate the object of love and fear:

He lifted the [trash can's] lid. . . . In his right hand was a butcher knife with a ten-inch blade.
    I blew him away. (253)

It's perhaps unsurprising that the novel ends with both a mournful account of the pain produced by this necessary violence ("I'll never be the same" [253]), and the melancholic assertion that "in the end all you have . . . is yourself" (253).

I realize that this commitment to the self is a complicated matter for members of marginalized and excluded social groups. It reflects the need to claim an integrity and sense of agency that racism and sexism have rendered extremely difficult to achieve. I want, therefore, merely to open the question of the political value of these books, rather than coming down against their versions of self and relation: to wonder aloud if the commitment to psychic autonomy is commensurate with the stress on emotional relatedness, or if these novels' visions represent incoherent attempts to retain a destructive singularity while seeking to promote various levels of community and solidarity.

This question seems to me less open when we turn to white male authors since the seventies. For as Fred Pfeil has recently argued, these writers' "soft-boiled dicks" celebrate a "neo-masterful masculinity-in-relation." They "define . . . masculinity . . . as an ongoing negotiation between the feminine and . . . the 'hypermasculine': between sensitivity and enforcement, emotional openness and an even more brutal violence than that in which their [hardboiled] forefathers indulged."[5] Pfeil is talking in particular about the work of three contemporary authors: Jonathan Kellerman, Robert B. Parker, and James Lee Burke. The apparent "softening" in their works is for him compromised by this hypertoxic masculinity, which is often split off and deposited in a sidekick who saves the hero from excessive taint while increasing the orgiastic violence that's imagined as necessary for social cleansing. The feminization of the hero in this sense turns out to be purely appropriative; it marks for Pfeil an attempt to arrogate sensitivity (as well as cooking skills and a "feminine" sensuality) to the man, as a way of enriching and inflating the male self, increasing his inviolable autonomy and the self-sufficient display of his narcissism.

I'm largely persuaded by such claims, though I must confess that I find it hard to read these authors through to the end—so smug and self-congratulatory have I found their treatment of the "new" masculinity. Nor do these books exhibit either the formal inventiveness or the implicative power that I've traced in the novels I want to celebrate. They tend instead to formalize, even to domesticate, a Chandlerian narrative strategy promoting a kind of wounded lyricism, in which the first-person voice guarantees at once the legibility of events, the sensitive receptivity of the hero, and that hero's invulnerability. In this sense, the work of Burke, Kellerman, Parker, and others signals a striking historical irony: that the gains of feminism have led in part to the closing down of possibilities in crime fiction, to a betrayal of the promise contained, paradoxically, in books less directly engaged with women's concerns for equality and masculine responsiveness.

There is, however, at least one exception to this general rule: K. C. Constantine's remarkable series of Mario Balzic novels. Pfeil himself has persuasively argued for Constantine's difference from the figures just mentioned. He suggests that the pleasures of Constantine's books reside less in the narcissism of "neo-mastery" than in a dialogism that gives voice to ethnic, gendered, class, and even generational particularity (134). This dialogism is highly inventive and formally ambitious; it works in conjunction with a third-person style that details the hard facts of historical contingency, in order to stress the mutually determining relations between the personal and the political (159–61). The result of these strategies in Balzic's case is "an unfinished . . . and unmastering masculinity-in-process" (161)—a manhood imperfectly making itself within specific sociohistorical limits to, and opportunities for, a burgeoning non-sexist and non-racist consciousness.

Like Pfeil, I find this vision especially moving and compelling. It marks a much more thoroughgoing effort than those mentioned earlier to embed autonomy in community—and to question the value of psychic singularity by stressing the constant impingements upon consciousness that require Balzic to *change*. Such impingements become especially acute in *Cranks and Shadows* (1995), where Balzic is forced to change in the most professionally significant of senses: by quitting his job as chief of police. I want to close by offering a brief analysis of this novel. My aim is not to give a comprehensive account of its vision of masculinity, but rather to extend Pfeil's observations by focusing on a book to which he did not have access—a book that seems to me darker, funnier, and more politically promising even than Constantine's earlier work.

·   ·   ·

Cranks and Shadows is structured along what looks at first like a conventional trajectory: the movement from blindness to insight. Balzic gradually becomes aware, over the course of this long novel, of just how much he does not know. He comes to see the inadequacy of his initial conceptions about the book's mystery, and this goes hand in hand with the inexorable unveiling of corruption: with his discovery that fire chief Eddie Sitko is in political cahoots with Orville Householder and Lyman Dunne, and that these men in essence own the city of Rocksburg in which Balzic works. The book's basic gesture is thus commensurate with any number of conventional detective stories. It moves toward a moment in which the mystery or enigma is solved, and in which the detective, as well as the novel's reader, is placed in a position of greater knowledge than at the book's beginning.

But to describe the novel in this way is to miss almost everything of interest in it. For the movement from blindness to insight here is less about the triumph of mastery than about the discovery of mastery's limits—and indeed, its ultimate dangers. These limits are signaled most clearly by the fact that the solution to the central mystery results in no arrests, no climactic confrontation, no narrative closure at all. It results instead in Balzic's awareness that he has lived his life in total ignorance of how the world works. "I thought I was better'n" Sitko and his kind, he says at one point in the novel.

I thought they were doin' politics. And I was fucking determined that politics was never gonna get into my department. . . . And now I'm in a jackpot. 'Cause it turns out I don't understand a goddamn thing that's goin' on around here. I'm walkin' around here thinkin' there's something wrong with my memory. There's nothin' wrong with my memory. My memory's fine. But you can't . . . see somethin' if you never looked at it. . . . I heard the . . . words, but I didn't pay attention. I didn't pay attention. . . . Right under my goddamn chin and I wouldn't look down.[6]

The passage is one of several in the novel that make a similar point. Most centrally, that point concerns Balzic's inadequate responsiveness: his inability to "see" because he hasn't really been "looking," hasn't been fully receptive to the social facts of life. The facts in question are in this case inescapably

221

political. They've been invisible because of Balzic's willful refusal to see the extent to which political currents shape both him and the climate in which he works. Constantine stresses this willful ignorance by having Balzic's men say to him, over and again when stating a political fact of which Balzic is ignorant: "Mario, I can't believe you don't know about this" (94). And unlike, say, Chandler, whose individualism leads him to make corruption endemic to any *polis*, Constantine directs Balzic's dawning consciousness toward a specific political imposthume: toward a Reaganite Republicanism whose effects on personal and communal living are imagined as deeply corrosive.

The novel's critique of this political culture consists of several related strands. The first is an attack on the privatization policies that, as the novel opens, have led to countless layoffs in Rocksburg and produced a city government so emaciated, so understaffed, that it consists entirely of "the Electrical Department, the Street Department, the Police Department," and the mayor's office (2).

Second and more significantly, the corruption Balzic uncovers concerns the tax shelters that enable people like Sitko, Dunne, and Householder to live lives of enormous luxury while providing kickbacks to their cronies and deforming local democratic institutions. Constantine stages the discovery of these shelters in characteristic fashion. It takes place not in a private moment that highlights Balzic's detecting wizardry; it happens, instead, conversationally, when Detective Carlucci reports it as something he has discovered almost by accident, while trying to find out for Balzic what the Conemaugh Foundation is. Carlucci's tone in this discussion is bewildered, troubled, astonished. He has been forced to see that the world doesn't work as he thought it did, that the real thieves aren't those one can catch in possession of something that belongs to someone else. Rather, they're those who can't be caught because they have mastered the legal trick of owning as little as possible: of putting their money into private foundations that relieve them of taxable titles, but that pay for their cars, their meals, their travel, their houses, even their life insurance—and so enable them to "do what [they] want, whenever [they] wanna do it" (168). This is, of course, at some deep level, precisely what Balzic wanted to know in asking about the Conemaugh Foundation. But his preoccupation with that precise question makes him again unable to hear. When Carlucci gets up to go, Balzic asks: "You okay? You don't look so good." And Carlucci: "Course I don't look good, what've I been tellin' ya? You don't get it, do you?" To which Mario can only at this point respond with the question, "Get what?" (169).

The third aspect of the book's critique resides in the link it makes between this legal criminality and the toxic character of conventional masculinity. This strand weaves its way most clearly through the story of Julie Richards, the idealistic councilwoman whose request that the firemen open their account books sets in motion the book's central plot. The firemen respond to this request in part by stirring up public resentment against Richards; they draw on the public's romance with firemen to stifle and defy her. But they also begin to threaten and harass her, throwing a rock through her window with a note that says, "Fireman need hose and bunker suits. Maybe you need firemans hose" (145). They send her "shoeboxes full of dog crap" and "pictures of . . . penises" on which they've inscribed, "This is what you need" (147). The point here seems to be that the threat of a puerile yet dangerous masculinism is central to the meaning of Rocksburg's corruption—that the legalized criminality of Sitko and his men at once supports and is supported by their equally virulent misogyny, as well as by their complacent sense of masculine entitlement.

This connection extends, moreover, beyond the firemen themselves. There's an officer in Balzic's own department who turns out to moonlight for Sitko—who's hired himself out to the fire chief's right-wing, private parapolice force (the Special Weapons and Emergency Response Team or SWERT). The officer's name is Yesho; Constantine describes him in the following terms:

He was the most dedicated weight lifter in the department among the male officers. He weighed 220 pounds, stood just slightly over five feet nine inches . . . and spent at least three hours every day in the weight room in the basement of City Hall. Balzic worried long and often about the emotional stability of police officers who seemed to believe they were never strong enough to do what they had to do. . . . [H]e never felt comfortable with the illusion of physical strength. Maybe it was because he was older and wasn't as strong as he once was; more likely it was because he had taken some of the worst beatings in his life from women who didn't look capable of lifting more than a basket of wet clothes or a pot of soup. (51)

I like to think of this passage as in part a critique of the male body's fetishization in contemporary crime writers such as Parker and Burke—each of whom describes his hero's workouts in loving and lavish detail, as a way of demonstrating that hypervirility has not been compromised by male sensitivity. In the context of *Cranks and Shadows*, the critique may be even sharper. For Constantine is here trying to suggest, through the conjunction of Yesho's relation to Sitko with his impeccably hard body, that the commitment to male invulnerability is structurally homologous to the politics of selfishness and greed. The belief that you can "never" be "strong enough" is like the belief that you can't ever be rich enough—and both are more or less dysfunctional attempts to defend oneself against the knowledge of an insurmountable insufficiency. Yesho's weightlifting is in this sense precisely a sign of "emotional [in]stability"; it reflects the "illusion" that "physical strength" can enable you "to do what [you have] to do," whereas in truth no amount of muscle can save you from beatings by "women who [don't] look capable of lifting more than a basket of wet clothes or a pot of soup." The reason for this is that there's a kind of structural limit to physical strength, an almost foundational vulnerability to violence against which one cannot defend oneself. To believe in the invincibility of the body is merely—and dangerously—to deny the reality of this structural limit.

The effects of this denial extend beyond the danger to those who engage in it. Mario at one point tells his wife, Ruth, about a domestic dispute in which he has tried to intervene. "You know," he begins, "how everybody says all we need is more cops on the streets. . . . Well, . . . I was right there between [the quarreling couple] and I couldn't do a thing about it. . . . I just catch a flash of somethin' comin' around, and before I can make a move she catches him . . . behind his ear with this ashtray" (247). The sense of impotence is once more palpable, and part of the passage's point is that to deny this impotence—to behave as if all we need is more cops, a stronger police force (a SWERT), or a harder body—is to put not only oneself but also others at risk of harm.

It's in this context instructive that the book's political plot is interwoven with a domestic one, in which Balzic is forced to confront a growing sense of masculine inadequacy. This plot is once more structured in terms of a movement from blindness to an insight that functions to reveal the limits of insight itself. When, for example, Mario reports to his wife that they are out of milk, she says: "Make some. . . . You know where the Sanalac is." "The what?" Balzic replies. And it turns out that they've been using powdered milk for the past fifteen years, though Balzic isn't aware of this despite having made it "[l]otsa times" (177, 178). Constantine's point is not, I think, that Balzic is growing senile. The couple have been using Sanalac "since the first time [Balzic had his] cholesterol checked" (177), so the implication is that "forgetting" this fact is a way for Mario to disavow the fragility of his own body. There's little more moving to me in the novel than those moments at which this disavowal is undone:

[F]irst it was . . . gettin' glasses, you know, first you're holdin' the phone book out to there. Then you get the bifocals. Then before you know, it's trifocals. And you start havin' all these close calls when you're drivin' and you're never really really sure whether they're close calls or whether they just look close because of the goddamn glasses. 'Cause everything you see when you turn around in the seat . . . is like three pictures. Four with the trifocals. And you know from right then, right at that moment, you know there's a part of you you can't really ever completely trust anymore. . . . Then you start not hearin' things. People are talkin' to you and pretty soon . . . you're startin' to ask people, "Huh? What did you say?" And you're doin' it all the time. . . . And . . . each new thing you gotta get used to, you say, hey, there's one less thing I can depend on, one less thing I'm absolutely positively sure

about. I can't be . . . sure I'm seein' what I think I'm seein' [or] hearin' what I think I'm hearing'. (133)

If, in the context of the political plot, what it means for Balzic to "know" is less to conquer a criminal adversary than to face the limits to his policing power imposed by tax laws that legalize crime, what it means in the personal realm is to acknowledge the carrion limits of a body one cannot fully control. Such an acknowledgment differs both from the psychic disasters I've traced in this study and from the displays of male sensitivity in other contemporary crime novelists. It differs from the latter in that it registers the costs of sensitization: the pain and suffering of an investigative consciousness coming to realize the limits of its capacities, becoming aware that the senses most central to masterful policing cannot but betray you. And it differs from the former in that it traces the process of a new integration: Balzic is not destroyed by his encounter with forms of fragility that the male self conventionally codes as "other"; the psychic pain this causes works instead to enrich with darkness a mind that then becomes increasingly responsive to the vulnerability of others—and even, remarkably, to the potential pleasures of fragility itself.

This potential for increased pleasure is central to the novel's concerns. It becomes perhaps most obvious in the place where public and private plots meet: in Balzic's refusal to quit his job, despite the fact that (1) he's ten years past retirement age; (2) he knows Ruth's happiness depends on it; and (3) he's rightly convinced that Sitko will get him voted out of office in the upcoming election. His reasons for declining to retire are complex and needn't be traced in detail. What's central is that, for all his sensitivity throughout the series, Balzic remains fundamentally committed to an image of himself as powerful, as someone engaged in the masterful gestures of goal-oriented activity. He's therefore unable to face a life that would require him to be experientially "present" here and now: to open himself to the pleasures of the body and of intersubjective intimacy. He is, in fact, so afraid of these pleasures that he comes to justify his refusal to retire by denying his capacity for them. He tells

Ruth he doesn't know how to "loaf" or to "do nothing" as retired people do. Ruth then asks him "about all the time [he] spend[s] in Muscotti's" bar: "Don't you ever think of that as loafing? Hangin' out? Just goofin' off?" Balzic responds with denials that he knows to be preposterous:

"No. Hell no. That's not what I'm doin'. . . . I'm talkin' to people. I'm workin'. . . . I'm findin' out what's goin' on." He was saying the words and he heard himself saying them . . . but he couldn't believe what he was saying. He sounded pathetic. He was *pathetic. These words were the lamest excuses for doing something he'd ever heard. (175)*

Balzic is of course right about this—these are "lame . . . excuses for doing something." But the point is that he makes such excuses because he can tolerate drink and talk only once they've been subsumed under the rubric of instrumental activity: as part of the project of masculine mastery, of "findin' out what's goin' on."

   Such a description is perhaps surprising in the light of Balzic's capacity for enjoyment in the earlier novels. Those books often catch him indulging the sensuous pleasures of taste and smell, in a way that Constantine explicitly imagines as subordinating the visual sense.[7] They also stress Balzic's enormous capacity for sympathetic listening: for a kind of responsiveness that may in part be crucial to his work, but that entails a pleasure in speech that exceeds the requirements of that work—and that's central to the powerful sense of relatedness these books communicate. It is, in this sense, as if in this novel the specter of upsetting the balance between such pleasure and the drive toward mastery—of increasing one's sensuous receptivity while recognizing the limits to masterful activity—inspires a defensive recommitment to power, as well as the refiguration of pleasure as part of the drive toward it.

   One of *Cranks and Shadows*'s great strengths is that it charts this recommitment while tracing the process of its undoing. In a remarkable scene at the book's center, Balzic sits in Muscotti's bar, listening to the owner recount a story that's intended to illuminate Balzic's dilemma. Muscotti was once a local gangster, a wise guy of considerable importance. The story he tells concerns his experience of losing that sense of importance. "I used to think I loved power," he says:

When I was young, it used to give me a hard-on. . . . And when [the mob] took it away from me, I thought I was gonna die. . . . I remember thinkin' . . . You lost your power, you lost your dick, you're gonna lose your heart. Hey, who's kiddin' who—I lost my dick about twenty years ago. . . . And I thought, you jerk, what did they take from you? Huh? If they could take it from you that easy, you never had anything to begin with. . . . And I said to myself, you jerk, they didn't take noth-ing. What they did was give you a gift. They gave you your friggin' life back. Handed it to me on a big platter. And there I was, mopin' around, gettin' ready to croak out. Remember when I quit drinkin' there for about six weeks? . . . I found out I didn't have to drink. . . . You know what that told me? Huh? . . . That told me I drank all those years 'cause I had to. Not 'cause I wanted to. 'Cause when they retired me? I found out I didn't have to drink. . . . I found out I didn't have to play the friggin' role either. . . . All those years I drank it was nothing but a friggin' act. Tough guy drinks whiskey, drinks everybody under the table. . . . How friggin' stupid can you be?" (120–21)

What's most important for me in this passage is the way it thinks of power as something inseparable from masculine sexual conquest (it gives you a hard-on), while also elaborating the constraining character of this commit-ment to mastery. Power is, in its very essence, nothing more or less than an "act"; it entails a kind of doubled conformity to what Herbert Marcuse has called the "performance principle,"[8] in that it requires you to play the role of being perpetually able to perform. Such a performance is "stupid" because it alienates you from your desire. It issues less from an interior space of cre-ativity and responsiveness than from an external standard of manhood that's been disastrously internalized.

The tragedy of this internalization is that it leads you to live a life that's indistinguishable from death. The pleasure you think you take in power is merely someone else's pleasure—the pleasure of some mysterious Other with whom your manhood requires you to identify. It's only by having this power removed—and this is literally imagined as castration, as Muscotti's loss of his "dick"—that you can reclaim your life by turning toward the question of your desire. The loss of power is in this sense a "gift" because it relieves you of the need to perform the play of powerful manhood, and so enables you to discover for the first time what it is that you want.

It's fitting, then, that the book should end with that most communal and festive of pleasurably non-performative activities—a party. Balzic has made the decision to retire along with three of his men, and the party is meant to celebrate their careers and launch them into their new lives. Constantine stages this ending partly in terms of Balzic's capacity to open himself up to Ruth's desire—to take her into account in a way that, far from impoverishing or diminishing him, is the condition of his newly heightened sense of self in relation. That sense is in turn linked to the pleasures and terrors of coming to know. The party's tone is set by the announcement that Joseph Royer, one of the retirees, has changed his name to Royanowics after finding out that his parents hid from him his Polish ancestry. This announcement has momentous effects that repeat in the "domestic" sphere those of Balzic's investigation: just as "Rocksburg's not Rocksburg anymore" since "everything [Balzic] ever knew about . . . who protects who and why and how, is . . . not what" he thought it was, so "Royer ain't Royer anymore" now that he has embraced his ethnic identity (297).

Constantine's emphasis on this catastrophic knowledge—on a knowledge that cannot be integrated into existing cognitive and epistemological structures—is central to the power and meaning of this scene. It suggests again the limits of mastery, the ways in which knowing is a process that requires one over and again to admit the strangeness of people and things one tries to take in. It suggests as well the provisional character of our efforts to assimilate experience; when Ruth tells Mario to enjoy the party because "the hard part [of retiring is] just starting," Constantine writes: "'I know,' he said. 'I know.' But he knew that he didn't" (304)—a statement suggesting the importance of knowledge not as mastery, but as the fraught and conflicted self-admission of the limits to what one can master.

But at the same time, the novel declines to code the unknown as a radical opacity. Royer's reinvention as Royanowics requires him to pass through the recognition that *he* is one of those "others" about whom he's told "dumb Polack jokes [all his] life" (294). He has, in short, been forced to experience himself in the other and the other in himself—has emerged in that state I alluded to earlier in relation to Milner's work: a "new division . . . in which there is more of the 'me' in the 'not me', and more of the 'not-me' in the 'me.'" Constantine charts this emergence more than once in the novel's closing pages. It happens, for example, when Royanowics's wife agrees with Ruth that "Raviolis're nothin' but dago pirogies" (292). For here what's crucial is again the tension between similarity and difference, a capacity to find oneself in the other without obliterating either one. Raviolis may be Italian pirogies, but this still makes them, precisely, Italian, even as it asserts a similarity that's the basis of inter-ethnic relations.

Perhaps most moving in this regard is the way this discovery of self in the other plays itself out in the book's central couple. Balzic's renewed relationship with Ruth concerns accepting the blurriness of their boundaries, the meaning of an "us" that continually negotiates its unity in and through division, and in which Balzic is de- and remasculinized, precisely inasmuch as the masculine is here imagined as a movement toward pleasure, relation, vulnerability—and away from the drive toward mastery. The retirement party is intended to celebrate just this psychic movement. It culminates, in the book's final passage, with an invitation to the pleasurable making of selves in a kind of improvisatory relation—that is, an invitation to dance. I'd like to close by passing this invitation on in turn to my readers. To do so is to end on a note that is for me the most moving in Constantine—a note whose serious levity surprises no one, I suspect, as much as it does me:

"Oh quit your bellyachin' and let's do it," [Ruth] said, pulling [Balzic] onto the floor. "There'll never be another night like this one. Not for us. So just do it. Just dance!"

And they did. Until the sun came up. (311)

Notes

Notes to the Introduction

1. See, for example, Leo Bersani, "Is the Rectum a Grave?" in *AIDS: Cultural Analysis/Cultural Activism*, ed. Douglas Crimp (Cambridge: MIT Press, 1988), 197–222, and Kaja Silverman, *Male Subjectivity at the Margins* (New York: Routledge, 1992).

2. There are, of course, crime authors besides those I treat who could help extend my argument—were there but space enough and time! Cornell Woolrich, David Goodis, and Patricia Highsmith come immediately to mind, as they seem to me intensely concerned with the exploitation of crime conventions for the subversion of masculinity.

3. The claims of my project here intersect with a larger contemporary rethinking of gender—and also race—in modern American literature. See, for example, Houston A. Baker, Jr., *Modernism and the Harlem Renaissance* (Chicago: University of Chicago Press, 1987); Suzanne Clark, *Sentimental Modernism: Women Writers and the Revolution of the Word* (Bloomington: Indiana University Press, 1991); Sandra M. Gilbert and Susan Gubar, *No Man's Land: The Place of the Woman Writer in the Twentieth Century*, 3 vols. (New Haven: Yale University Press, 1988–1994); Andreas Huyssen, "Mass Culture as Woman: Modernism's Other," in *After the Great Divide: Modernism, Mass Culture, Postmodernism* (Bloomington: Indiana University Press, 1986), 44–62; Frances Kerr, "Feeling 'Half-Feminine': Modernism and the Politics of Emotion in *The Great Gatsby*," *American Literature* 68.2 (1996): 405–31; Walter Benn Michaels, *Our America: Nativism, Modernism, and Pluralism* (Durham: Duke University Press, 1995); and Joseph Allen Boone, *Libidinal Currents: Sexuality and the Shaping of Modernism* (Chicago: University of Chicago Press, 1998).

4. To note just a few of these developments: Immigration reached staggering new proportions during this period (a million for the first time in 1913), producing anxieties about the nation's ethnic purity that culminated in the Immigration Acts of 1921 and 1924. The Federal suffrage Amendment was passed and ratified in 1920, after a decade of newly intensified feminist agitation that sometimes included explicit demands for greater sexual freedom. And African American anger at white racism exploded in the years following the First World War, leading most dramatically and convulsively to a rapid succession of urban race riots in the summer of 1919.

5. This vision of modernism is, of course, largely Eliotic. See especially the essay on James Joyce, where Eliot praises the use of myth in *Ulysses* as "a way of controlling, of ordering, of giving a shape and significance to the immense panorama of futility and anarchy which is contemporary history" (*"Ulysses*, Order, and Myth" [1923], in *Selected Prose of T. S. Eliot*, ed. Frank Kermode [London: Faber and Faber, 1975], 177). If I make such arguments central to my understanding, it's because they seem to me to capture the ambition (if not the actual achievement) of many modernist texts, and because I am persuaded by Michael Levenson's claims about Eliot's centrality in defining this ambition. See Levenson, *A Genealogy of Modernism: A Study of English Literary Doctrine 1908–1922* (Cambridge: Cambridge University Press, 1984).

6. David Glover argues that authors of hardboiled detective fiction sought to redefine crime writing as a masculine activity, rejecting what they thought of as the aristocratic effeminacy of analytic detective stories in favor of the grittiness of hardboiled "realism." There are obvious parallels here with the modernist revolt against gentility—that is, with modernism's attempt to reclaim aesthetic production as a space for the redemptively manly virtues of craft, experimentation, and disciplined labor. Raymond Chandler makes this connection himself in "The Simple Art of Murder" (1944). See Glover, "The Stuff That Dreams Are Made Of: Masculinity, Femininity and the Thriller," in *Gender, Genre and Narrative Pleasure*, ed. Derek Longhurst (London: Unwin Hyman, 1989), 74; and Chandler, *The Simple Art of Murder* (1950; New York: Vintage, 1988), 14.

7. See John G. Cawelti, *Adventure, Mystery, and Romance: Formula Stories as Art and Popular Culture* (Chicago: University of Chicago Press, 1976); Dennis Porter, *The Pursuit of Crime: Art and Ideology in Detective Fiction* (New Haven: Yale University Press, 1981); Julian Symons, *Bloody Murder: From the Detective Story to the Crime Novel: A History* (London: Faber and Faber, 1972); Tony Hilfer, *The Crime Novel: A Deviant Genre* (Austin: University of Texas Press, 1990); Stephen Knight, *Form and Ideology in Crime Fiction* (London: Macmillan, 1980); and Marty Roth, *Foul and Fair Play: Reading Genre in Classic Detective Fiction* (Athens: University of Georgia Press, 1995).

8. The most recent and ambitious variant of this argument is Jopi Nyman, *Men Alone: Masculinity, Individualism, and Hard-Boiled Fiction* (Amsterdam and Atlanta: Rodopi, 1997).

Notes to Chapter 1

1. Though I'm less concerned with generic boundaries than with what the texts I examine have to say, a brief note on my terminological choices may help forestall confusion. I use "crime novel" as a capacious term that refers to texts conceived, written, and/or marketed as genre fiction centrally preoccupied with crime. Within this category, I distinguish between the hardboiled detective novel and the "inverted detective novel" or roman noir. The former is represented here primarily by Hammett and Himes (with some attention to Raymond Chandler in the current chapter); it's a genre that cannot do without the figure of the detective, for reasons having intimately to do with the erotics and libidinal politics of its form. The inverted detective novel is a historical mutation of this first form, whose primary concern is with the psychological effects of crime on the criminal himself. The detective is therefore structurally dispensable and is, in fact, often dispensed with. Cain and Thompson are the representative figures of this form in my study, with Faulkner offering something of a hybrid between a hardboiled and a noir sensibility.

2. See, for example, D. A. Miller, "Language of Detective Fiction, Fiction of Detective Language," in *The State of the Language,* ed. Leonard Michaels and Christopher Ricks (Berkeley: University of California Press, 1990), 483–85; James Guetti, "Aggressive Reading: Detective Fiction and Realistic Narrative," *Raritan* 2.1 (1982): 136; and John G. Cawelti, *Adventure, Mystery, and Romance: Formula Stories as Art and Popular Culture* (Chicago: University of Chicago Press, 1976), 143.

3. William Marling, "The Hammett Succubus," *Clues* 3 (1982): 67. See also, on hardboiled misogyny, Cawelti, *Adventure, Mystery, and Romance,* 146–60; David Herman, "Finding Out about Gender in Hammett's Detective Fiction: Generic Constraints or Transcendental Norms?" *Genre* 24.1 (1991): 1–24; and Bethany Ogdon, "Hardboiled Ideology," *Critical Quarterly* 34.1 (1992): 71–87.

4. For versions of this point, see to begin with Raymond Chandler's famous claim that the ideal hardboiled story is "one you would read if the end was missing" (quoted in Frank Krutnik, *In a Lonely Street: Film Noir, Genre, Masculinity* [London:

Routledge, 1991], 39–40). Fredric Jameson draws on this statement to argue that the Chandlerian novel merely "passes itself off as a murder mystery," since the evanescent temporality of its mystery plot is counterposed by the more lasting and affecting spatial organization of what he terms the "search" ("On Raymond Chandler," in *The Poetics of Murder: Detective Fiction and Literary Theory*, ed. Glenn W. Most and William W. Stowe [New York: Harcourt Brace Jovanovich, 1983], 143). Martin Priestman speaks as well of this "decentering of . . . plot" in Chandler, suggesting that "an enhanced sense of *dis*unity . . . is the main effect of [the author's] 'cannibalization'" of his short stories as material for his novels (*Detective Fiction and Literature: The Figure on the Carpet* [New York: St. Martin's, 1991], 171, 170). And similar claims have been made about Hammett and other hardboiled writers. See especially James Naremore, "Dashiell Hammett and the Poetics of Hardboiled Detection," in *Art in Crime Writing: Essays on Detective Fiction*, ed. Bernard Benstock (New York: St. Martin's, 1983), 63; Dana Polan, *Power and Paranoia: History, Narrative, and the American Cinema, 1940–50* (New York: Columbia University Press, 1986), 324; and Steven Marcus, Introduction to Dashiell Hammett, *The Continental Op* (New York: Vintage, 1975), xxi.

5. Tzvetan Todorov, "The Typology of Detective Fiction," in *The Poetics of Prose*, trans. Richard Howard (Oxford: Blackwell, 1977), 51.

6. Marty Roth, *Foul and Fair Play: Reading Genre in Classic Detective Fiction* (Athens: University of Georgia Press, 1995), 89–90, 91.

7. Gertrude Stein, *Everybody's Autobiography* (New York: Vintage, 1973), 4.

8. Freud, *Beyond the Pleasure Principle*, in *The Standard Edition of the Complete Psychological Works of Sigmund Freud*, trans. James Strachey, vol. 18 (London: Hogarth, 1955), 15.

9. Since I'm arguing that Freud must repress the pleasurable potential of compulsive repetition if he's to succeed in opposing the death drive to Eros, it's important to note that there is also a second movement to his argument. As though in response to the breakdown of its theoretical oppositions, *Beyond the Pleasure Principle* moves irresistibly toward a monism that makes Eros not the opposite but an *expression* of death. It reinscribes pleasure within compulsive repetition, renders the "*urge . . . to restore an earlier state of things*" "a universal attribute of instincts," and insists that *all* instinctual activity—whether death-tending or Erotic—is ultimately and radically conservative (36). It would nonetheless be easy to show that

it's pleasure that again pays the price for this move. Far from allowing us to revel in the detonative unpleasures of egoic ruin, the "compulsification" of pleasure merely tames enjoyment into the calm of a different style of extinction—the extinction of unpleasurable tension through a discharge that now approximates death. It's perhaps worth noting that, though Freud exhibits this ambivalence toward pleasure in pain from his earliest texts on sexuality, those texts tend to be far more open about the conflict I'm describing. See the explicit claims in *Three Essays* concerning the *increase* of tension and excitation as "undoubtedly pleasurable," and of "sexual excitation" itself as the "by-product" of any intense feeling, "even though it is of a distressing nature" (*Three Essays on the Theory of Sexuality* [1905], *Standard Edition*, vol. 7 [1953], 209, 233).

10. Jean Laplanche writes that, "[i]f we accept the definition 'the pleasure of unpleasure,' the *paradox [of] masochism* lies in the very contradiction of those terms" (*Life and Death in Psychoanalysis*, trans. Jeffrey Mehlman [Baltimore: Johns Hopkins University Press, 1976], 103). This terminological difficulty designates for Laplanche a split within Freudian pleasure that corresponds to the one my argument describes: on one hand, Freud understands the German *Lust* in a highly biologized manner, as "the allaying of vital tensions"; on the other, he understands that term, in a properly psychoanalytic sense, as a mad and "frenetic enjoyment" (105) in the increase of psychic tension, and in an unavoidable submission to trauma that is the condition of sexuality's emergence.

11. My argument here owes a general debt to Leo Bersani's *The Freudian Body: Psychoanalysis and Art* (New York: Columbia University Press, 1986). "Sexuality," Bersani writes, "[is] that which is intolerable to the structured self" (38). And again, on the next page: "sexuality . . . could be thought of as a tautology for masochism."

12. Two of the many critics who discuss the centrality of first-person voice in the genre are Slavoj Žižek (*Looking Awry: An Introduction to Jacques Lacan through Popular Culture* [Cambridge: MIT Press, 1991], 62) and Julian Symons (*Bloody Murder: From the Detective Story to the Crime Novel: A History* [London: Faber and Faber, 1972], 135).

13. Dashiell Hammett, *The Glass Key* (New York: Vintage, 1989), 3.

14. Quoted in Naremore, "Poetics of Hardboiled Detection," 54.

15. Gilles Deleuze and Félix Guattari, *Kafka: Toward a Minor Literature*, trans. Dana Polan (Minneapolis: University of Minnesota Press, 1986), 20.

16. The process I'm describing here is similar to that which Lacan elaborates in his discussion of anamorphosis (*The Four Fundamental Concepts of Psycho-Analysis*, trans. Alan Sheridan [New York: Norton, 1981], 79–90).

17. In his early short story "The Tenth Clew," Hammett plays deliberately upon the capacity of language to do violence. The murder weapon in this case is "a small portable typewriter," which the police discover to be "matted with hair and blood." The link between this instrument and more conventional weapons is made explicit when the narrator says that "[t]he serial number of the typewriter . . . had been removed . . . apparently filed out of the frame." This is, of course, a conventional way in which killers in detective stories thwart efforts to trace the origins of their guns. See "The Tenth Clew," in *The Continental Op*, 6, 14.

18. Georges Bataille, *Erotism: Death and Sensuality*, trans. Mary Dalwood (San Francisco: City Lights, 1986), 189.

19. These moments are especially marked in Chandler, and I return to them in more detail later in this chapter.

20. Here is perhaps the place to discuss how Hammett's *The Maltese Falcon* (1930; New York: Vintage, 1984) fits into the argument I'm making. That novel poses some difficulties to my reading, in that it, too, is written in the third person, yet appears to make its hero a figure of the phallic potency that I claim *The Glass Key* undercuts. The first thing to say about this is that I don't wish to overstate my point—there is no *necessary* relation between a third-person style and the undermining of conventional masculinity. It's just that that style holds open possibilities that I'm suggesting are more fully foreclosed in first-person hardboiled narratives.

That much said, it seems to me that, with a slight shift in the present terms, *The Maltese Falcon* can be seen to partake of a project that's commensurate with the one I'm describing. The novel dramatizes nothing so much as the impossibility of possessing the phallus and the democratic distribution of castration—of physical and psychic vulnerability. As long as the falcon "belongs" to no one, it succeeds in imparting the illusion that it *can* belong to someone and, accordingly, in articulating moral difference along the axis of sex: the good guys are the men and the manly (but not too manly) women; the bad guys are the women who act too much like they "have it," along with the men who obviously don't. It's thus the transcendental inaccessibility of the falcon that facilitates socio-symbolic (albeit criminal) circulation in the novel, enabling its world to "work." Money and women can change hands, the plot can continue smoothly to unfold as a quest for an elusive object, and the falcon itself can be imagined as that which confers a fullness of being on its owner and meaning on the quest to obtain it.

No sooner, however, does the bird fall into Spade's hands than things begin to fall apart. First, Spade comes into literal contact with death, stepping on the hand of the dead man who has just brought him the bird (184). Second, he's lured to a hotel where Gutman's daughter scratches him with a pin, marking him as one of the castrated as well (189). Third, the falcon, once stably possessed, turns out to be a fake (238), so that "it" has never circulated at all and no one in the novel has ever really been in possession of it. And fourth, this exposure means that all socio-symbolic exchanges are retroactively annulled, all circulation finally deauthorized: Spade must give up both the money and the "girl," returning most of his cut to Gutman, handing over the rest to the cops who suspect him, and exchanging Brigid, one final time, in order to put her definitively out of circulation.

Indeed, with this annulment it turns out that the only thing that's really "gone around" in this book is castration itself. *Everyone* here has his or her skin broken, his or her blood drawn, at least once (save Brigid, who takes the fall instead). So if the novel appears to end with Spade's sadistic triumph at the expense of the woman, this is only because we so often forget the novel's actual ending, in which Effie Perine criticizes Spade for his phallic inhumanity, and Spade is shown to pay an intolerable price for his commitment to invulnerability.

21. Though Ned is not a professional private eye, but rather "a gambler and a politician's hanger-on" (149), he plays the role of detective in a way that's crucial to the book's exploration of masculinity.

22. See especially p. 90, where one of O'Rory's thugs says excitedly "I got something to try," "tumble[s]" Ned onto the bed, then makes his "hands busy on Ned Beaumont's body" until "Ned Beaumont's body and arms and legs jerk . . . convulsively."

23. Freud's earliest full treatment of the primal scene is in the Wolf Man case history, "From the History of an Infantile Neurosis" (1918), *Standard Edition*, vol. 17 (1955), 29–47.

24. Hartman, "Literature High and Low: The Case of the Mystery Story," in *Poetics of Murder*, 215.

25. Penderson-Krag, "Detective Stories and the Primal Scene," in *Poetics of Murder*, 15, 16, 18–19.

26. Freud, "Infantile Neurosis," 45.

27. "In the end there were to be found in [the Wolf Man] two contrary currents . . . of which one abominated the idea of castration, while the other was prepared to accept it and console itself with femininity as a compensation" (ibid., 85). Such a consolation leads to what Freud elsewhere calls "feminine masochism"—a masochism that "places the subject in [the] characteristically female situation [of] being castrated, or copulated with, or giving birth to a baby" ("The Economic Problem of Masochism" [1924], *Standard Edition*, vol. 19 [1961], 162). This form of masochism is rooted in an unresolved *negative* Oedipus complex—in the boy's desire for the father and identification with the mother—and is therefore pathological for men in a way it isn't for women. For a lucid discussion of these matters see Kaja Silverman, *Male Subjectivity at the Margins* (New York: Routledge, 1992), 189–90.

28. Several recent thinkers reconceive the primal scene in ways that have influenced my argument. See especially Silverman, who draws on the work of Laplanche to suggest that the child's helpless submission to the primal moment requires us to rethink it less in terms of a triumphant voyeurism than as a kind of visual trauma: a "voyeurism with a difference" that's "conducive . . . of passivity and masochism" rather than sadistic mastery (*Male Subjectivity*, 171, 164).

29. Priestman, *Detective Fiction and Literature*, 171.

30. Raymond Chandler, *The High Window* (1942; New York: Vintage, 1976) 131–32; *Playback* (New York: Ballantine, 1977), 78–79.

31. Žižek, *Looking Awry*, 66.

32. The term is Laplanche's; see *Life and Death*, 105.

33. Theodor Reik, *Masochism in Modern Man*, trans. Margaret H. Beigel and Gertrude M. Kurth (New York: Grove, 1941), 312.

34. Raymond Chandler, *Farewell, My Lovely* (1940; New York: Vintage, 1988), 172–74.

35. Gilles Deleuze, *Coldness and Cruelty*, trans. Jean McNeil, in *Masochism* (New York: Zone, 1991), 71.

36. "In sadism and masochism there is . . . no direct relation to pain: pain should be regarded as an *effect* only" (ibid., 120–21).

37. David Savran, *Taking It Like a Man: White Masculinity, Masochism, and Contemporary American Culture* (Princeton: Princeton University Press, 1998), 189, 205. Reflexive masochism, on Silverman's account, is one in which the masochist becomes

both subject and object of his own violation, thereby "indulg[ing] his appetite for pain without . . . calling into question either his virility, or his paternal lineage" (*Male Subjectivity*, 326).

38. Tania Modleski, *Feminism without Women: Culture and Criticism in a "Postfeminist" Age* (New York: Routledge, 1991), 149.

39. Nick Mansfield, *Masochism: The Art of Power* (Westport, CT: Praeger, 1997), xi, xii.

40. Savran is the most judicious in this respect. He argues compellingly for the radical potential of a kind of Christian masochism, which he sees as synonymous with Huey Newton's concept of "revolutionary suicide" (*Taking It Like A Man*, 157).

41. Naremore suggests in a similar spirit that "the failed key is an appropriate image for a novel . . . preoccupied with symbolic castrations." See "Poetics of Hardboiled Detection," 66.

42. Naremore (ibid., 52) remarks upon the intensely passionate nature of Ned's relation to Paul, which he contrasts with the passionlessness of heterosexual relations in the novel.

43. Herman makes an especially compelling case for Janet's complexity. See "Finding Out about Gender," 18.

Notes to Chapter 2

1. W. M. Frohock, *The Novel of Violence in America*, 2nd ed. (Dallas: Southern Methodist University Press, 1957), 21.

2. Joyce Carol Oates, "Man Under Sentence of Death: The Novels of James M. Cain," in *Tough Guy Writers of the Thirties*, ed. David Madden (Carbondale and Edwardsville: Southern Illinois University Press, 1968), 110.

3. Frohock, *Novel of Violence*, 15.

4. Oates, "Man Under Sentence," 117.

5. Since my analysis will be more concerned with the fantasy underlying the fear of befoulment than with tracing that fear's class politics, it's perhaps worth marking my agreement with Raymond Williams's claim that "there are in fact no masses, but only ways of seeing people as masses" ("Culture Is Ordinary" [1958], in *Resources of Hope* [London: Verso, 1989], 11). Williams would no doubt have been wary of my psychoanalytic predilections. But I like to think that the present essay contributes to an understanding of just what underwrites, psychically speaking, the possibility of such a seeing. On the emergence of an olfactory discourse of class, meanwhile, see Alain Corbin, *The Foul and the Fragrant: Odor and the French Social Imagination*, trans. Miriam L. Kochan, Roy Porter, and Christopher Prendergast (Cambridge: Harvard University Press, 1986).

6. As many of his critics have noted, Cain's decisive innovation as regards the crime novel was to abolish the figure of the detective and to narrate from the point of view of—indeed, through the mouth of—the criminal. See Richard Bradbury, "Sexuality, Guilt and Detection: Tension between History and Suspense," in *American Crime Fiction: Studies in the Genre*, ed. Brian Docherty (New York: St. Martin's, 1988), 89, and Paul Skenazy, *James M. Cain* (New York: Continuum, 1989), 157–58.

7. Cain, *The Postman Always Rings Twice* (1934; New York: Vintage, 1992), 114, 115.

8. Frohock, *Novel of Violence*, 19.

9. Oates, "Man Under Sentence," 124. James Baldwin also makes this connection between sentimentality and brutality, in an essay that sees Cain's *Postman* as a direct descendant of *Uncle Tom's Cabin*. See "Everybody's Protest Novel," in *Notes of a Native Son* (Boston: Beacon, 1955), 14.

10. Frohock, *Novel of Violence*, 19.

11. *Selected Letters of Raymond Chandler*, ed. Frank MacShane (New York: Delta, 1981), 22–23.

12. Sigmund Freud, "The 'Uncanny,'" in *The Standard Edition of the Complete Psychological Works of Sigmund Freud*, trans. James Strachey, vol. 17 (London: Hogarth, 1955), 236. Freud uses "animistic," "narcissistic," and "savage" more or less interchangeably, since for him "each one of us has been through a phase of individual development corresponding to [the] animistic stage in primitive men" (240). He can thus write in *Totem and Taboo* (1912–1913) that "[t]he animistic phase [in human history] would correspond to narcissism both chronologically and in its content," and it's clear that narcissism must for him be sacrificed if the child is to be properly socialized (*Standard Edition*, vol. 13 [1953], 90).

13. Cf. Mikkel Borch-Jacobsen, *Lacan: The Absolute Master*, trans. Douglas Brick (Stanford: Stanford University Press, 1991), esp. 43–45. My reading of mimetic violence is indebted to Borch-Jacobsen's remarkable body of work.

14. We might here recall Cain's own assertion of independence—his claim that he "belong[s] to no school, hard-boiled or otherwise"—and suggest that this represents a blow in the mimetic war I'm describing. See James M. Cain, Preface to *The Butterfly* (1946; New York: Vintage, 1979), ix.

15. Freud seems dimly aware of this logic when, in a remarkable passage from "The 'Uncanny,'" he describes a "silly" story that produced in him a powerfully "uncanny" effect: "In the middle of the isolation of war-time . . . I read a story about a young married couple who move into a furnished flat in which there is a curiously shaped table with carvings of crocodiles on it. Towards evening an intolerable and very specific smell begins to pervade the house; they stumble over something in the dark; they seem to see a vague form gliding over the stairs—in short, we are given to understand that the presence of the table causes ghostly crocodiles to haunt the place, or that the wooden monsters come to life in the dark, or something of the sort" ("'Uncanny,'" 244–45). The passage on the *unheimliches Heim* of the female genitals follows immediately upon this, so that we might risk the following, albeit speculative, reading: the couple's move into their new home represents a return to the primal womb-*Heim*, which smells precisely inasmuch as it portends a primitive and animal assimilation of self. For what is the fear of the crocodile if not a fear of being devoured? The womb in this sense augurs not merely one's death but also one's murderousness: the incorporative assimilation of the self to a bellicose, pre-egoic, and animal (in)humanity. And though the predominant psychoanalytic tropes for this destructiveness are metaphors of orality (I eliminate the other by eating him), passages like this one enable us to hypothesize that the psychic vestiges of this being-the-other are primarily—archaically—olfactory. See Freud, *Group Psychology and the Analysis of the Ego* (1921), *Standard Edition*, vol. 18 (1955), 105, and *Totem and Taboo*, 142 and passim, for the association of identification with devouring orality.

16. I'm indebted to Leo Bersani (*The Freudian Body: Psychoanalysis and Art* [New York: Columbia University Press, 1986], chap. 1), Jane Gallop (*The Daughter's Seduction: Feminism and Psychoanalysis* [Ithaca: Cornell University Press, 1982], chap. 2), and Herbert Marcuse (*Eros and Civilization: A Philosophical Inquiry into Freud* [New York: Vintage, 1955], chap. 2) for helping me to conceptualize the olfactory dimension of my argument.

17. James M. Cain, *Serenade* (1937), in *Three by Cain* (New York: Vintage, 1989), 9.

18. James M. Cain, *Cloud Nine* (New York: Mysterious, 1984), 8.

19. Immanuel Kant, *Anthropology from a Pragmatic Point of View*, trans. Victor Lyle Dowdell (Carbondale and Edwardsville: Southern Illinois University Press, 1978), 45.

20. Skenazy, *James M. Cain*, 46. See also Oates, "Man Under Sentence," 111, and Frohock, *Novel of Violence*, 20–21.

21. Oates, "Man Under Sentence," 111.

22. James M. Cain, *Double Indemnity* (1936; New York: Vintage, 1992), 5.

23. Sigmund Freud, "On Narcissism: An Introduction" (1914), *Standard Edition*, vol. 14 (1957), 85.

24. It may here be helpful to anticipate by remarking that, at least as the late Freud imagines it, the difference between love and identification is one of peace versus war. While both processes fantasmatically "internalize" the object, identification assimilates it to the ego and therefore abolishes it as such. Love, on the other hand, puts the object in the place of the ego-ideal, preserving its autonomy in an internally differentiated part of the self. Love is thus the antidote to identification in that, where the latter can't but kill the object, the former tries to let it live. See Freud, *Group Psychology*, esp. chaps. 7 and 8.

25. Mikkel Borch-Jacobsen, *The Freudian Subject*, trans. Catherine Porter (Stanford: Stanford University Press, 1988), 228, 230.

26. The representation of the gay man's over-refined character might seem incommensurate with this devolutionary figuration, but the novel imagines that excessive culture as itself a form of decay. Just as, in the terms of emotional responsiveness, the brute is merely the flip side of the sentimentalist, so the doctrine of aestheticism is somehow less than human in its abundant and narcissistic commitment to the cultivation of selfish pleasure. The novel plays on this coincidence most explicitly when Winston returns from Mexico with a sculpted Aztec "cricket" that's "at least five hundred years old": "If Manship had done it," he vaunts, "they'd have thought it was a radical sample of his work. The line of that belly is pure Brancusi. It's as modern as a streamlined plane, and yet some Indian did it before he even saw a white man" (149).

27. Sigmund Freud, *Civilization and Its Discontents* (1930), *Standard Edition*, vol. 21 (1961), 80.

28. My point here is not that the love Freud places at the source of sociality is genital through and through. Quite the contrary. *Civilization and Its Discontents* argues centrally that man must sublimate part of his directly sexual libido into aim-inhibited or "brotherly" love, in order to overcome a "natural aggressive[ness]" that opposes the binding work of civilization (122). This sublimation entails a severe "restriction upon sexual life" (109); it's part of the reason for the civilized individual's almost metaphysical unhappiness, since there is, alas, only so much libido to go round, and if I must distribute it inhibitedly to everybody, I'll have little left for an uninhibited indulgence that provides me with the greatest happiness of all. Nevertheless, civilization does allow at least one location for that satisfaction—in the familial couple—and this explains the importance Freud grants to directly sexual trends in this social genesis. For what must above all be accounted for in such a genesis is the movement from a narcissistic and animal asociality to that "first" social unit called the family. If that movement is to be effected, the human animal must come to desire satisfaction repeatedly from the same object, and it's the sight of that object's genitals that, on the somewhat repressed logic of Freud's reading, makes this continuity conceivable. The problem of inhibiting that urge arises only secondarily, as a problem of binding both within and beyond the now-instituted familial unit.

29. Freud makes this connection between vision and objectal distance in "Instincts and Their Vicissitudes" (1915), *Standard Edition*, vol. 14 (1957), 132. See also Christian Metz's claim that "[i]f it is true of all desire that it depends on the infinite pursuit of its absent objects, voyeuristic desire, along with certain forms of sadism, is the only desire whose principle of distance symbolically and spatially evokes this . . . rent" (*The Imaginary Signifier: Psychoanalysis and the Cinema*, trans. Celia Britton et al. [Bloomington: Indiana University Press, 1982], 60).

30. Freud, *Group Psychology*, 102.

31. Cain's own, extratextual account of the homosexual "disease" and its cure is at this point worth quoting in detail: "The lamentable sounds that issue from a homo's throat when he tries to sing are a matter of personal observation, and if I could have stopped there I could have been completely persuasive. . . . But the theme demanded the next step, the unwarranted corollary that heavy workouts with a woman would bring out the stud horse high notes. Right there is where it goes facile and I suppose silly. Several doctors . . . assured me that they could believe it, and pleaded with me to write the book . . . ; [but] I have . . . serious doubts" (quoted in Roy Hoopes, *Cain: The Biography of James M. Cain* [New York: Holt, Rinehart and Winston, 1982], 283–84).

32. Cornel West has a name for the "rationality" of this type of racism: "The

'scientific' racist logic which promotes the observing, measuring, ordering and comparing of visible physical characteristics of human bodies in light of Greco-Roman aesthetic standards associates racist practices with bodily ugliness, cultural deficiency and intellectual inferiority" (*Keeping Faith: Philosophy and Race in America* [New York: Routledge, 1993], 269).

33. Sigmund Freud, *The Interpretation of Dreams* (1900), *Standard Edition*, vol. 4 (1958), 322–23.

34. See Oates, "Man Under Sentence," 124, and Skenazy, *James M. Cain*, 62.

35. My brief discussion of dreams is indebted to the first chapter of Borch-Jacobsen's *Freudian Subject*, which indeed bears the title "'Dreams Are Completely Egoistic.'"

36. Skenazy, *James M. Cain*, 159.

37. Peter Brooks, *The Melodramatic Imagination: Balzac, Henry James, Melodrama, and the Mode of Excess* (New York: Columbia University Press, 1985).

38. Tania Modleski, "Time and Desire in the Woman's Film," in *Home Is Where the Heart Is: Studies in Melodrama and the Woman's Film*, ed. Christine Gledhill (London: British Film Institute, 1987), 330.

39. On hysterical aphonia, see Breuer's case history of Anna O. in Sigmund Freud and Josef Breuer, *Studies on Hysteria* (1895), *Standard Edition*, vol. 2 (1955), 21–47, as well as Freud's "Fragment of an Analysis of a Case of Hysteria" (1905), *Standard Edition*, vol. 7 (1953), esp. 22–41. On the centrality of the mute role in the history of melodrama, see Brooks, *Melodramatic Imagination*, chap. 3.

40. We might here suggest that the novel supplements the "scientific racist logic" described by Cornel West with what Joel Kovel has called an "aversive racism": "The nuclear experience of the aversive racist is a sense of disgust about the body of the [racial other] based upon a very primitive fantasy: that it contains an essence—dirt—that smells and may rub off onto the body of the racist. Hence the need for distance and the prohibition against touching" (*White Racism: A Psychohistory* [London: Free Association, 1988], 84).

41. I'm differing here with Skenazy and Frank Krutnik, both of whom understand the transgression against Oedipus as serving ultimately to reinforce oedipal Law. See Skenazy, *James M. Cain*, 160–67, and Krutnik, "Desire, Transgression and James M. Cain," *Screen* 23.1 (1982): 31–37.

42. See, for example, the remarkable formulations in Freud, *The Ego and the Id* (1923), *Standard Edition*, vol. 19 (1961), 34.

43. See in particular *Civilization and Its Discontents*, 123–33, where Freud insists that the father's love and the fear of its loss underlie the resolution of oedipal hostilities. The problem is that the text is here supposed to be *explaining* the transformation of hate-identification into sociable love, so an argument that begins by assuming that love is bound to disappoint.

44. Freud, *Group Psychology*, 113.

Notes to Chapter 3

1. Henry Seidel Canby, "The School of Cruelty," *Saturday Review of Literature*, 21 March 1931, reprinted in *William Faulkner: The Critical Heritage*, ed. John Bassett (Boston: Routledge and Kegan Paul, 1975), 108.

2. Review of *Sanctuary*, *Times Literary Supplement*, 24 September 1931: 732.

3. Granville Hicks, "The Past and Future of William Faulkner," *Bookman*, September 1931, reprinted in *Critical Heritage*, 120, 123–25.

4. A. C. Ward, from *American Literature, 1880–1930* (1932), reprinted in *Critical Heritage*, 134.

5. The cinematic comparison has remained especially current. See Gerald Langford, *Faulkner's Revision of* Sanctuary: *A Collation of the Unrevised Galleys and the Published Book* (Austin: University of Texas Press, 1972), 7, and Joseph W. Reed, Jr., "The Function of Narrative Pattern in *Sanctuary*," in *William Faulkner's* Sanctuary, ed. Harold Bloom (New York: Chelsea House, 1988), 16.

6. Canby, "School of Cruelty," 108–9.

7. Hicks, "Past and Future," 126.

8. The novel's mode in large part emerged in Faulkner's revisions to the original galleys. By increasing the violence of that earlier version, practically eliminating the stream-of-consciousness techniques, and developing in general a style that appears objective and easily assimilable, he turned a bizarre but recognizably modernist experiment into his only popular success. He himself has said something like the opposite of this. The original, he once wrote, was "a cheap idea . . . deliberately conceived to make money," and the revisions were intended "to make out of it something that would not shame *The Sound and the Fury* and *As I Lay Dying* too much" (Introduction to the Modern Library edition of *Sanctuary* [New York, 1932], v, vii). It's clear from even the most cursory comparison, however, that the revisions make the novel *more* sensational, even as they produce an experiment that's to my mind unique in the Faulkner corpus. For analyses of the novel's textual history that stress these transformations, see Noel Polk, Afterword, *Sanctuary: The Original Text*, ed. Noel Polk (New York: Random, 1981), 293–306; Gerald Langford's Introduction and collation (cited above); and Michael Millgate, "*Sanctuary*," *The Achievement of William Faulkner* (New York: Random House, 1966), 113–23.

9. Sigmund Freud, "Negation," in *The Standard Edition of the Complete Psychological Works of Sigmund Freud*, trans. James Strachey, vol. 19 (London: Hogarth, 1961), 236–37.

10. Jacqueline Rose makes a similar point when, in a remarkable essay on negativity in Klein, she argues that "[t]he lost object is not . . . only the hallucinated object of satisfaction" but also "an object which . . . is required—is actively sought after— *in order to be bad*." On this reading "the genesis of the . . . Kleinian bad object is nothing less than the genesis of the object itself." "The persecutory object-relation rises up as the first defence against something without 'definite name and shape,'" and "[o]bject-relations are 'improvements on' . . . primordial . . . anxiety" to the exact extent that "distrust of the object is better than despair" (*Why War? Psychoanalysis, Politics, and the Return to Melanie Klein* [Oxford: Blackwell, 1993], 151–52).

11. See "Instincts and Their Vicissitudes" (1915), *Standard Edition*, vol. 14 (1957), where Freud argues that "[h]ate, as a relation to objects, is older than love. It derives from the . . . ego's primordial repudiation of the external world" (139)—a repudiation which, in this essay too, Freud describes as a fantasy of oral expulsion.

12. I'm here elaborating on Klein's basic claim that "[t]he fear of the destructive impulse seems to attach itself at once to an object," and that this "destructive impulse projected outwards is first experienced as oral aggression." It is, from here, just one short step to the further speculation I derive from Faulkner: that the "first" experience of the death drive *within* is also bound up with oral fantasy, and that the thing "I" originally spit up is a mouth that seeks internally to devour me. See Klein, "Notes on Some Schizoid Mechanisms" (1946), *The Selected Melanie Klein*, ed. Juliet Mitchell (New York: Free Press, 1986), 179–80.

13. Hicks, "Past and Future," 126.

14. R. E. Sherwood, review of *Sanctuary*, *Scribner's Magazine*, April 1931: 13 (advertising insert), my emphasis.

15. My thinking on some of the points here enumerated is indebted to three especially fine essays on the novel: André Bleikasten's *Sanctuary* section in *The Ink of Melancholy* (Bloomington: Indiana University Press, 1990), 211–71; George Toles's "The Space Between: A Study of Faulkner's *Sanctuary*," in *Twentieth Century Interpretations of* Sanctuary, ed. J. Douglas Canfield (Englewood Cliffs, NJ: Prentice-Hall, 1982), 120–28; and John T. Matthews's "The Elliptical Nature of *Sanctuary*," *Novel* 17.3 (1984): 246–65.

16. It will have struck some readers by now that the "(no)thing" to which Faulkner's text has led us could also be thought through two more current psychoanalytic concepts: Jacques Lacan's "*das Ding*," which we might define as an originarily expelled portion of the real that shapes yet resists symbolization; and Julia Kristeva's conceptions of the abject and abjection—states of defiling indistinction, in which identity is disturbed by the polluting interiority of bodily substances that the socialized self must exclude as not-self. There are differences between these concepts, of course, and I don't mean to conflate them. What leads me to bring them together is that the repudiated objectal non-object is in both of these cases maternally connoted. Lacan: "[M]other/child interpsychology . . . is nothing more than an immense development of the essential character of the maternal thing, of the mother, insofar as she occupies the place of . . . *das Ding*" (*The Seminar of Jacques Lacan, Book VII: The Ethics of Psychoanalysis*, trans. Dennis Porter [New York: Norton, 1992], 67). Kristeva: "[D]evotees of the abject . . . do not cease looking . . . for the desirable and terrifying, nourishing and murderous, fascinating and abject inside of the maternal body" (*Powers of Horror: An Essay on Abjection*, trans. Leon S. Roudiez [New York: Columbia University Press, 1982], 54).

17. Hicks, "Past and Future," 127, 126.

18. The case for the novel's sadism is made most forcefully by Canby and Ward; Sherwood is the most explicit proponent of its masochism, and the language throughout his review suggests a strong readerly identification with Temple.

19. I borrow this term from Leo Bersani and Ulysse Dutoit's extraordinary chapter on Alain Resnais in *Arts of Impoverishment: Beckett, Rothko, Resnais* (Cambridge: Harvard University Press, 1993), 147–48.

20. William Faulkner, *Sanctuary: The Corrected Text* (New York: Vintage, 1993), 3–4.

21. Cf. Toles, "Space Between," 120.

22. This is a particularly good example of how Faulkner's revisions to the original manuscript contribute to the confusions I'm describing: the early version has Horace explicitly "listen to" the singing, and makes the entire auditory cluster a less ambiguous function of his consciousness. See *Sanctuary: The Original Text*, 21–22. Subsequent citations to passages deleted by Faulkner that appear in this edition are given by page number in the text, accompanied by the abbreviation *SO*.

23. Lacan contrasts the imaginary visual plenitude of the mirror phase with "a background of organic disturbance and discord, in which . . . we should seek the origins of the image of the 'body in bits and pieces'. . . . This illusion of unity, in which a human being is always looking forward to self-mastery, entails a constant danger of sliding back again into the chaos from which he started" ("Some Reflections on the Ego," *International Journal of Psychoanalysis* 34 [1953]: 15). I'm suggesting that *Sanctuary* may be thought to effect precisely such a "sliding back" within the realm of the visual.

24. It's for this reason irrelevant that the scene of Horace's failed reflection takes place "before" Popeye spits in the spring. From the moment that the latter's image touches the water's surface, he has in fact already spit into it because he is the "object" he expels.

25. See the discussion of mouths in Bleikasten, *Ink*, 247–48.

26. It would not be difficult to show here that Freud's account, in "Instincts and Their Vicissitudes" (94–95), of the "scopophilic instinct" corroborates this breakdown, even though the essay itself tries to insist that vision represents the surmounting of oral proximity.

27. Walter J. Slatoff's *Quest for Failure: A Study of William Faulkner* (Ithaca: Cornell University Press, 1960) performs a brilliant analysis of this oxymoronic pattern in Faulkner's work. My essay owes a general debt to his arguments, though I hope it's clear that, at least in *Sanctuary*, the use of oxymoron is for me less reprehensible than Slatoff suggests (see esp. 264–65). It would also be possible to use this trope in an effort to give some speculative content to the common critical claim for *Sanctuary* as a "modern gothic": the gothic is, as Rosemary Jackson suggests, a historical instance of a more capacious mode that she calls "fantasy," and "[w]hat emerges as the basic trope of fantasy is the *oxymoron*, a figure of speech which holds together contradictions and sustains them in an impossible unity" (*Fantasy: The Literature of Subversion* [London: Methuen, 1981], 21).

28. Jacques Derrida has argued, in a different context, for the repressed and ruinous centrality of vomit to Enlightenment aesthetics. See "Economimesis," *Diacritics* 11 (1981): esp. 22–25.

29. Here I am in partial agreement with Cleanth Brooks's claim that the masculine "discovery of evil [in *Sanctuary*] is bound up with [Horace's] discovery of the true nature of woman." The difficulty is that Brooks—like many critics before him—complies with the novel's misogyny in a way that blinds him to its critique, since he himself declines to step outside of the book's gynophobic equations. See *William Faulkner: The Yoknapatawpha Country* (New Haven: Yale University Press, 1963), 127–28. For a critique of this tendency in Faulkner's male critics, see Judith Bryant Wittenberg, "William Faulkner: A Feminist Consideration," in *Modern Critical Views: William Faulkner*, ed. Harold Bloom (New York: Chelsea House, 1986), 233–45.

30. Matthews's "Elliptical *Sanctuary*" is a brilliant account of nature's relation to culture in the novel, focusing on the figure of ellipsis as what both marks and effaces their boundary.

31. On the role of these two moments—the account of Popeye's voyeuristic "sexuality" and the description of his childhood suffering—in revealing a new dimension to Popeye, see T. H. Adamowski, "Faulkner's Popeye: The 'Other' As Self," in *Twentieth Century Interpretations*, 32–48.

32. Recent critics often behave as if to say this is to endorse the novel's misogyny. My point is rather that *Faulkner* invented a character who satisfies the male fantasy that female sexuality is incipiently depraved and women are responsible for their own violation. To miss this is to miss something crucial about the novel, and thus to cripple attempts to get at what might be less politically disturbing—indeed, more politically promising—in it.

33. Eric Sundquist makes this point in his *Faulkner: The House Divided* (Baltimore: Johns Hopkins University Press, 1983), 53.

34. See Aubrey Williams, "William Faulkner's 'Temple' of Innocence," in *Twentieth Century Interpretations*, 59–69, for an extended treatment of the theme of childhood in *Sanctuary*. His treatment of Popeye, to which my own discussion is indebted, appears on 66–67.

35. See Matthews, "Elliptical *Sanctuary*," 253–54, 262–63.

36. Matthews also makes this observation (ibid., 263).

37. Bersani and Dutoit's discussion of Resnais's Holocaust documentary, *Night and Fog*, is worth quoting here. "Far from having to warn us," the authors write, "that we may have the same impulses as the Nazis . . . Resnais [makes] the images of Nazism an active part of our contemporaneity. *We move within them easily.* The Nazi past is already being repeated inside our sensory collaboration with this film, a collaboration that Resnais encourages us to feel as a kind of self-identification and, consequently, as an inescapable complicity" (*Arts of Impoverishment*, 187). While I am obviously not suggesting that *Sanctuary* is a documentary, this argument has implications for any art that, like Faulkner's, seeks to embroil us (anti-)realistically in the very real horrors it describes.

38. See Rose, *Why War?*, 174: "It is the advantage of [scientific] theories like that of the black hole or the Big Bang that they are so apocalyptic. The drama of their imagining compensates for what scares. The idea of something negative as explosion or pure inexplicable force [is] more manageable or acceptable than the idea of something negative which . . . seems to wipe out the conditions through which it can . . . be known."

Notes to Chapter 4

1. Robert Polito, *Savage Art: A Biography of Jim Thompson* (New York: Vintage, 1996), 7.

2. See especially R. V. Cassill, "*The Killer Inside Me*: Fear, Purgation, and the Sophoclean Light," in *Tough Guy Writers of the Thirties*, ed. David Madden (Carbondale and Edwardsville: Southern Illinois University Press, 1968), 231–32; Tony Hilfer, *The Crime Novel: A Deviant Genre* (Austin: University of Texas Press, 1990), 137; and Geoffrey O'Brien, "Jim Thompson, Dimestore Dostoevsky," Afterword to Thompson, *Savage Night* (1953; Berkeley, CA: Creative Arts/Black Lizard, 1985), 149.

3. I share Max Allan Collins's sense that Thompson "is seldom at his best in the third person": first-person writing brought out in him something singularly inventive and terrifying. See Collins, "Jim Thompson: The Killers Inside Him," in *Murder Off the Rack: Critical Studies of Ten Paperback Masters*, ed. Jon L. Breen and Martin Harry Greenberg (Metuchen, NJ: Scarecrow, 1989), 42.

4. O'Brien, "Dimestore Dostoevsky," 150.

5. Barry Gifford, Introduction to Thompson, *Savage Night*, vi.

6. Cassill encloses this phrase in quotation marks, but I have been unable to locate its source.

7. My discussion of such matters in Freud is deeply indebted to Samuel Weber's arguments concerning many of the same issues. See *The Legend of Freud* (Minneapolis: University of Minnesota Press, 1982), 84–117.

8. Freud, *Jokes and Their Relation to the Unconscious*, in *The Standard Edition of the Complete Psychological Works of Sigmund Freud*, trans. James Strachey, vol. 8 (London: Hogarth, 1960), 97.

9. For a discussion of male degradation of women, see Freud's "On the Universal Tendency to Debasement in the Sphere of Love" (1912), *Standard Edition*, vol. 11 (1957). Here Freud traces sexual degradation to unresolved incestuous wishes in men, which split libidinal trends excessively into "tender" and "sexual" feelings, so that "virtuous" women resemble the mother so closely that men remain "psychically impotent" with them. What's most remarkable about this argument is the universality with which Freud endows it. "I shall put forward the view," he writes, "that psychical impotence is much more widespread than is supposed, and that a certain amount of this behaviour does in fact characterize the love of civilized man" (184). Such an argument is important because it indicates that the very process of oedipalization produces in men a distaste for women, even as it positions them to take women as their sexual objects.

10. See Weber, *Legend*, 107–8, for a full discussion of this connection.

11. Freud, *The Ego and the Id* (1923), *Standard Edition*, vol. 19 (1961), 34.

12. Freud, "On Narcissism: An Introduction" (1914), *Standard Edition*, vol. 14 (1957), 96. This essay once more pre-dates Freud's explicit conceptualization of the superego, but even in *The Ego and the Id* Freud talks of "ego ideal" and "superego" without distinguishing them. The distinction in fact corresponds to the dilemma I posed earlier: the ideal is that in the paternal imago to which the ego aspires, while the superego is that which chastens and punishes that aspiration. For a reading of Freud that distinguishes these functions, see Kaja Silverman, *Male Subjectivity at the Margins* (New York: Routledge, 1992), 192–95.

13. See especially Freud's discussions, in *The Ego and the Id*, of the negative therapeutic reaction (49–50) and melancholia (53–55).

14. See Freud, "On Narcissism," 95.

15. In this sense, Polito seems to me right to think of Thompson's work as a displaced and often angry dialogue with his father. See *Savage Art*, 41–42, 55–56, 60–62, and 350.

16. This claim for primacy may seem surprising in the light of my arguments in chapter 3 concerning the primacy of oral expulsion. My point is in part the Freudian one that the anal phase is more proto-oedipal than is the oral phase: it's more directly linked to the identity crisis surrounding the castration complex, because it is structured by social prohibition in a way that the oral relation is not (or comes to be only secondarily). I'm also, however, trying to create an ambiguity around this concept of primacy, in order to indicate the deep relation between the various substances that figure the danger of failed differentiation. Each of these substances can be experienced as "first" or psychically primary. Vomit, in short, is primary for Faulkner in a way that excrement is for Thompson and olfactory residues are for Cain.

17. See, for example, Polito, *Savage Art*, 452.

18. Jim Thompson, *Pop. 1280* (New York: Vintage/Black Lizard, 1990), 36–37.

19. John Brenkman is one of several recent thinkers who speak movingly of the costs exacted by this pathology. See *Straight/Male/Modern: A Cultural Critique of Psychoanalysis* (New York: Routledge, 1993), esp. 122.

20. Kenneth Payne makes a version of this point. See his "Moral Indistinguishability in the Crime Fiction of Jim Thompson," *Arkansas Review* 5.1–2 (1996): 125.

21. See also the earlier scene in which Nick addresses Jefferson in the diminutive, as "Robbie Lee" (130).

22. On the historical and cultural conjunctions between incest and interracial desire, see Werner Sollers, *Neither Black Nor White Yet Both: Thematic Explorations of Interracial Literature* (New York: Oxford, 1997), 285–335, and Michael Rogin, *Ronald Reagan, the Movie, and Other Episodes in Political Demonology* (Berkeley: University of California Press, 1987), 190–235.

23. Gaddis is said, for example, to have killed his wife and fed her to the hogs, and to have stolen his dead grandmother's gold teeth. Both suggest a kind of creepily regressive awfulness. They indicate a capacity to do the worst, especially within the family's bosom, and therefore form a psychically convincing series with the more explicitly oedipal crimes attributed to him.

24. The key texts and scenes here are *Savage Night*, 2, 13, and *The Killer Inside Me* (1965; New York: Quill, 1983), 25–26. *A Hell of a Woman* (1954) offers perhaps the most detailed and drastic description of splitting in Thompson's work, but is less concerned with how that splitting pivots upon the father.

25. See especially Jacques Lacan, "The Mirror Stage as Formative of the Function of the I as Revealed in Psychoanalytic Experience," in *Écrits: A Selection*, trans. Alan Sheridan (New York: Norton, 1977), 1–7.

26. The dialectic I'm describing has important resonances with Jean-Paul Sartre's phenomenology of shame, which he finds most fully exemplified in the figure of a self caught looking through a keyhole. Shame arises precisely from the consciousness of being objectified as "he who looks" in this way. See *Being and Nothingness: An Essay on Phenomenological Ontology*, trans. Hazel E. Barnes (New York: Philosophical Library, 1956), 257–61.

27. See note 16 above for a discussion of this primacy.

28. This argument relies on a theory in which the Oedipus complex and the castration complex are mutually intertwined: oedipal desire is resolved for the boy through the mechanism of castration, by which he comes (1) to recognize sexual difference in terms of castration or not; (2) to fear his own castration if he persists in a desire for the mother; and (3) to accept a definitive loss of the mother as the condition of an individuated identity based upon an incorporation of the father as ideal and prohibitive function. See Freud, "The Dissolution of the Oedipus Complex" (1924), *Standard Edition*, vol. 19, 173–79.

29. On the turning around of masochism into sadism, see Freud, "Instincts and Their Vicissitudes" (1915), *Standard Edition*, vol. 14 (1957), 126–30.

30. The novel contains numerous scenes like this one, which stress Nick's sympathy for the downtrodden and the socially marginalized. See esp. 76, 94–95, 172, and 198.

31. On the concept of the abject, see Julia Kristeva, *Powers of Horror: An Essay on Abjection*, trans. Leon S. Roudiez (New York: Columbia University Press, 1982).

32. See Payne, "Moral Indistinguishability," 124.

33. It's here worth distinguishing my argument from that of Christopher Metress, who also argues that Thompson's work is concerned with the failure of conventional masculinity—that "the images of masculinity inscribed in [that work] reflect . . . not the common fantasies of masculine prowess and domination but the common nightmares of impotence and ineffectuality" ("Living Degree Zero: Masculinity and the Threat of Desire in the *Roman Noir*," in *Fictions of Masculinity: Crossing*

Cultures, Crossing Sexualities, ed. Peter F. Murphy [New York: New York University Press, 1994], 182). This seems to me true enough; but in part because it lacks any detailed treatment of femininity in Thompson, Metress's argument begs the question of whether this anatomy of impotence has a politically progressive component, or whether it once more lays the blame for the nightmare of masculinity at the door of women. The current section is intended to address this question in detail.

34. Freud, *Jokes*, 97–98.

35. On this paranoid-schizoid logic, see Melanie Klein, "Mourning and Its Relation to Manic-Depressive States" (1940), in *The Selected Melanie Klein*, ed. Juliet Mitchell (New York: Free Press, 1986), 146–74.

36. This association of holes with the gap between ego and ideal is especially evident in a scene toward the middle of the novel. Here, Rose is expecting Nick to sleep with her immediately after he has, unbeknownst to her, been to bed with Amy. Nick is sure that his recent activities will make it impossible to get an erection, and that Rose will therefore "shoot [him] right through the offendin' part." "I drove on into the barn," he continues, "wondering how much it would handicap a fella having a hole where I was going to have one" (105). The anxiety here is perhaps commonplace enough. What seems to me less common is that the scene exposes the origin of this anxiety in a phallic ideal of which one must fall short—the fantasy of perpetual erection, of a penis always and ever engorged and ready to do one's manly bidding. The distance between this impossible ideal and the actual limitations of flesh is itself a kind of hole, which the fantasy of genital violence merely makes literal and explicit.

Notes to Chapter 5

1. The story of how Himes, who first drew critical attention in the forties as a writer of naturalist protest fiction, came to write what he called his "Harlem domestic" novels is fairly well known by now. Nelson and Denning give brief descriptions (see citations below). For Himes's own account, see his remarks to John A. Williams ("My Man Himes: An Interview with Chester Himes," *Amistad* 1 [1970]: 25–93), and the second volume of his autobiography, *My Life of Absurdity: The Later Years* (New York: Paragon, 1976), 102–6.

2. Raymond Nelson, "Domestic Harlem: The Detective Fiction of Chester Himes," *Virginia Quarterly Review* 48 (1972): 260.

3. Michael Denning, "Topographies of Violence: Chester Himes' Harlem Domestic Novels," *Critical Texts* 5.1 (1988): 17, 16.

4. Chester Himes, *Blind Man with a Pistol* (New York: Vintage, 1989), 21.

5. Compare the more leisurely and traditional introductions of Marcus in Chapter 3 and Dr. Moore in Chapter 6. Himes knows full well what he's doing here.

6. Another version of this epistemological difficulty concerns the book's tendency to recount an identical moment in different ways. When, for example, Anny describes the events of the rejuvenation scene (66–67, 69), she adds all kinds of details that the "objective" narration fails to mention. We have no reason to believe she's lying—indeed, she's portrayed with unusual sympathy. We're therefore left uncertain about the trustworthiness of the objective eye.

7. Frantz Fanon elaborates on this familiar fantasy when he says that "the Negro is only biological" and that, within the white imaginary, "one is no longer aware of the Negro but only of a penis; the Negro is eclipsed. He is turned into a penis. He *is* a penis" (*Black Skin, White Masks* [1952], trans. Charles Lam Markmann [New York: Grove Weidenfeld, 1967], 165, 170).

8. Homi Bhabha describes a similar tension between fixity and change in his discussion of the colonial stereotype. He argues that the colonizer anxiously repeats the fantasies and stories that constitute the meaning of the colonized other, in a way that both seeks to fix that meaning and undermines the assumption that it's already fixed ("The Other Question . . . ," *Screen* 24.6 [1983]: 18). What's striking about Himes is the shift in perspective. Practically eliminating from his purview the white agents of this fantasy, he gives us blacks who themselves perform the "daemonic repetition" (18) it requires—who fluidly repeat the fixed identities that are foisted upon them from without. The results of this strategy are politically disquieting—but also politically promising—in ways I pursue below.

9. See Denning, "Topographies," 12.

10. *Cotton Comes to Harlem* (1965) performs a similar mapping of the confidence game onto a political plot, and one could read that novel as a transitional document between the earlier work and the final extravagance of *Blind Man*.

11. Denning, "Topographies," 14.

12. Even the rejuvenation con fits this basic pattern: Mubuta claims his serum is "the one and only solution for the Negro Problem," since it will enable black people simply to "outlive the white folks" (39).

13. Coffin Ed and Grave Digger are complicated exceptions, and I treat them at length in this chapter's second section.

14. Denning, "Topographies," 16.

15. See Joel Kovel's remarkable speculations concerning the excremental character of the fantasies underlying white racism: "We have been talking of dirt, which represents a set of peculiar fantasies based upon bodily experience. The central aspect of bodily experience upon which this tissue of daydreams rests is . . . the act of defecation, and the central symbol of dirt . . . is feces, known by that profane word with which the emotion of disgust is expressed: shit. Furthermore, when contrasted with the light color of the body of the Caucasian person, the dark color of feces reinforces, from the infancy of the individual in the culture of the West, the connotation of blackness with badness. . . . Thus the root symbol between the idea of dirt and the blackness of certain people is that highly colored, strongly odored, dispensable and despised substance which the human body produces so regularly" (*White Racism: A Psychohistory* [London: Free Association, 1988], 87).

16. Leo Bersani makes a similar claim when he argues that the work of Jean Genet "invit[es] us to view literature . . . not as epistemological and moral monuments but . . . as cultural droppings" (*Homos* [Cambridge: Harvard University Press, 1995], 181).

17. In what follows, I shall be contesting the political value of distance advocated by most theorists of mimicry. See especially Joan Riviere, "Womanliness as a Masquerade" (1929), in *Formations of Fantasy*, ed. Victor Burgin, James Donald, and Cora Kaplan (London: Methuen, 1986), 35–44; Mary Ann Doane, "Film and the Masquerade: Theorizing the Female Spectator," in *Femmes Fatales: Feminism, Film Theory, Psychoanalysis* (New York: Routledge, 1991), 17–32; Judith Butler, *Gender Trouble: Feminism and the Subversion of Identity* (New York: Routledge, 1990); Diana Fuss, *Identification Papers* (New York: Routledge, 1995), 141–65; and Homi Bhabha, "The Other Question . . ."

18. See Denning's comment that "[t]he two characters are not 'individuals,' nor does their relationship fit any of the conventional pairings of sleuth and sidekick" ("Topographies," 11).

19. The tradition I have in mind here is perhaps best exemplified by Ralph Ellison, and indeed, the difference of emphasis emerges in the titles of his and Himes's books: *Invisible Man* and *Blind Man*. Both suggest an interest in the relation of masculinity to seeing, and both books explore this problematic in an explicitly racial context. One might then speculate that Himes's novel marks a self-conscious rewriting of Ellison—particularly given several jokes within *Blind Man* itself. The reference to Mister Sam's chauffeur as "the invisible man," for example, is clearly meant as an allusion to the Trueblood incident in Ellison's book—to the scene, that is, in which the novel's narrator (the invisible man) acts as chauffeur to a wealthy white man, bringing him into the rural ghetto and exposing him to Trueblood's recitation of his incestuous rape of his daughter. See Ralph Ellison, *Invisible Man* (New York: Signet, 1952), 36–66.

20. I examine the significance of corpses in relation to race in what follows. For the reduction of black men to penises, see especially the two scenes in which graffiti figures centrally (62, 85). In each, a major component of the picture is the depiction of male sex organs, and one of these pictures "[gives] the illusion of [a] primitive painting of pygmies affected with elephantiasis of the genitals" (85).

21. I'm suggesting that Himes's novel intuits, and complicates through race, the narrative of male subject formation described by Jacques Lacan. See especially "The Signification of the Phallus," in *Écrits: A Selection*, trans. Alan Sheridan (New York: Norton, 1977), 281–91; and "Desire and the Interpretation of Desire in *Hamlet*," trans. James Hulbert, in *Literature and Psychoanalysis: The Question of Reading: Otherwise*, ed. Shoshana Felman (Baltimore: Johns Hopkins University Press, 1982), 11–52.

22. My argument here suggests that Himes anticipates recent developments in African American cultural criticism—that he at least in part understands the destructive character of claims to black humanity that equate such humanity with virile masculinity. See esp. Phillip Brian Harper's exploration of how, "since the dominant view holds prideful self-respect as the very essence of healthy African-American identity, it also considers such identity to be . . . weakened wherever masculinity appears to be compromised" (*Are We Not Men? Masculine Anxiety and the Problem of African-American Identity* [New York: Oxford University Press, 1996], ix).

23. For example: "Lucky for your hair," says Digger to Ed as the latter manages to free himself from his smoldering trousers. "These kinks is fireproof," Coffin Ed replies (141).

24. This connection is strikingly corroborated by the moment in an earlier novel when Ed has acid thrown in his face. Here "Coffin Ed, blinded with the burning acid and a white hot rage, emptie[s] his pistol, spraying the top of the deck and the wall behind it with .38 slugs." See *A Rage in Harlem* (1957; New York: Vintage, 1991), 70.

25. See the Interlude following Chapter 15, where the detectives tell their superior that Abraham Lincoln is responsible for the riot since "[h]e hadn't ought to have freed us if he didn't want to make provisions to feed us" (135).

26. I'm referring here to Melanie Klein's suggestions concerning the "paranoid-schizoid" origins of our most primitive defenses, all of which are meant to preserve the fragile distinction between a good "inside" and an "outside" that threatens destruction. See especially "Notes on Some Schizoid Mechanisms" (1946), in *The Selected Melanie Klein*, ed. Juliet Mitchell (New York: Free Press, 1986), 176–200. My claim is that the normative commitment to racial purity contains this psychotic core, which perhaps paradoxically makes experiences of impurity feel like a kind of madness.

27. Klein's conception of projective identification may offer the most useful theoretical description of this process. See "Notes on Some Schizoid Mechanisms," esp. 183, 186, and 197–98.

28. *Blind Man*'s suspicion of this integrationist solution—a solution based on interracial heterosexuality—rests on Himes's sense of its insufficient alertness to psychic negativity. The marchers are protected from such negativity by their continued obliviousness to the basis of their politics in a desire for the titillation of tabooed flesh. Himes's critique of the marchers is thus bound up with the fact that they're unable to grasp how much would have to be socially worked through—how little of conventional heterosexuality can survive—in the effort to make love triumph over racism.

29. See in this context Judith Butler's claim that heterosexual gender identity is founded on the repudiation of a prior homosexual attachment, whose loss cannot be mourned because the identity resulting from that loss is based on its radical forgetting ("Melancholy Gender/Refused Identification," in *The Psychic Life of Power: Theories in Subjection* [Stanford: Stanford University Press, 1997], 140).

30. See Fuss, *Identification Papers*, 154–61, for a reading of the unexamined homophobia in Fanon's analysis of colonial racism. Edelman's *Homographesis: Essays in Gay Literary and Cultural Theory* (New York: Routledge, 1994) traces a similar dynamic in Fanon, as well as in a range of African American imaginative writers. I have myself been struck by the congruence between *Blind Man* and Fanon's *Black Skin, White Masks*. Both suggest that homosexuality is essentially a white invention; both see racial hatred as the distorted expression of a homosexual love that's foreign to black culture, so that homosexuality emerges in black men only in the form of gay male prostitutes forced by racism to sell themselves in order to survive. See Fanon, 180 and 156, and Himes's portrayal of *all* his gay black men as prostitutes.

Notes to the Afterword

1. Marion Milner, *On Not Being Able to Paint* (New York: International Universities Press, 1957), 150, 155.

2. Quoted in Marty Roth, *Foul and Fair Play: Reading Genre in Classic Detective Fiction* (Athens: University of Georgia Press, 1995), xiv.

3. Barbara Wilson, *Sisters of the Road* (Seattle: Seal, 1986), 58.

4. Sue Grafton, *"A" Is for Alibi* (1986; London: Pan, 1990), 176, 177.

5. Fred Pfeil, *White Guys: Studies in Postmodern Domination and Difference* (New York: Verso, 1995), 161, 149.

6. K. C. Constantine, *Cranks and Shadows* (New York: Mysterious, 1995), 212.

7. See especially *The Man Who Liked Slow Tomatoes* (1982; Boston: Godine, 1993), 126–27, where Balzic's "eyes were only partly open as he ate and drank. The world was visual fuzz, but it couldn't have been clearer to his nose or tongue."

8. See Herbert Marcuse, *Eros and Civilization: A Philosophical Inquiry Into Freud* (New York: Vintage, 1955), 40–49.

Index

Canby, Henry Seidel, 85–86, 247n. 18
Cassill, R. V., 127–28, 250n. 2
Cawelti, John G., 9, 233n. 2, 233n. 3
Chandler, Raymond, 24, 32–35, 49–50,
51–53, 193, 219, 222, 232n. 6, 233n. 1,
233–34n. 4. See also *Farewell, My Lovely*;
The High Window; *Playback*
Clark, Suzanne, 231n. 2
class, 38–39, 239–40n. 5
Cloud Nine (Cain), 54
Collins, Max Allan, 250n. 3
Constantine, K. C., 220–30. See also
Cranks and Shadows
Corbin, Alain, 240n. 5
Cranks and Shadows (Constantine),
221–30; catastrophic knowledge in,
229; commitment to instrumental activity in, 226–27; critique of conventional masculinity in, 223–25; critique
of mastery in, 221–22; critique of Rea-
ganism in, 222–23; difference from classic crime fiction, 226; difference from
contemporary crime fiction, 226; hero's
inadequate responsiveness in, 221–22;
male body in, 223–26; masculinity as
performance in, 228; reinvention of
masculinity in, 229–30; sensuous pleasure in, 227, 228–29
crime novel, 2–3, 126–27, 214–15; and
modernism, 8–9; apparent conservatism
of, 126–27; as worthy of close reading,
9–10; commitment to firm ego-boundaries in, 3, 218–19; contemporary,
215–20; defined, 233n. 1; encourages
male abjection, 4, 7, 215; engagement
with feminism, 217, 220; "generic unconscious" of, 215; hostility to meaning
in, 5–6, 21–22, 102, 192, 213; intersub-
jectivity in, 45, 215; marginalization of,
8, 215; misogyny of, 3, 214–15; subver-

sive narrative strategies in, 5–6. *See also*
individual authors and works

death drive, 6, 14–15, 16, 33, 65,
234–35n. 9
Deleuze, Gilles, 22, 35–36
Denning, Michael, 173, 190, 256n. 18
Derrida, Jacques, 249n. 28
Doane, Mary Ann, 256n. 17
Double Indemnity (Cain), 56, 70, 83
Dutoit, Ulysse, 247n. 19, 250n. 37

Edelman, Lee, 210, 258–59n. 30
Eliot, T. S., 232n. 5
Ellison, Ralph, 257n. 19
Eros, 6, 14–16, 28–29, 65–66, 83,
234–35n. 9
excrement, 7, 132–33, 147, 151–52,
155–57, 158–61, 191–93, 200, 205–12,
252n. 16

Fanon, Frantz, 210, 255n. 7, 259n. 30
Farewell, My Lovely (Chandler), 33, 35
Faulkner, William, 7, 8, 85–86, 89–125,
160, 233n. 1, 252n. 16. See also *Sanctuary*
Federal Suffrage Amendment, 231n. 3
femininity, 3, 7, 27–28, 30, 32, 35, 44–45,
53–54, 62, 69, 71–72, 76–81, 83–84,
103–15, 118–20, 122–25, 160–67,
169–70, 201–2; associated with narcissism, 7, 62; associated with smell,
53–54, 64, 79–81, 82; as threat to
bounded male self, 4, 11, 17, 25, 45,
53–54, 214
femme fatale, 17, 33–34, 218
Freud, Sigmund, 5, 6–7, 16, 17, 83, 111;
Beyond the Pleasure Principle, 13–16;
death drive in, 14–15, 16, 234–35n. 9;
Eros in, 14, 16, 234–35n. 9; "'A Child Is

Skenazy, Paul, 74, 240n. 6, 244n. 41
Slatoff, Walter J., 248n. 27
smell, 7, 46–48, 49–51, 54, 62–70, 79–81,
    157, 167–70, 205–6, 241n. 15, 252n. 16;
    associated with femininity, 53–54, 64,
    79–81, 82; associated with gay man,
    64–69; and vision, 65–68, 69–70
Sollers, Werner, 252n. 22
Sound and the Fury, The (Faulkner),
    245n. 8
space, 74, 92–93, 234n. 4
Stein, Gertrude, 12
Sundquist, Eric, 249n. 33
superego, 128, 130–34, 138, 141, 151–52,
    163; and excrement, 132–33, 151–52;
    pathology of, 131–34, 138, 140–44,
    150–52, 156–60, 161, 165; prohibition
    vs. ideal, 130, 131–32, 144, 150–52,
    251n. 12
Symons, Julian, 9, 235n. 12

"Tenth Clew, The" (Hammett), 236n. 17
Thompson, Jim, 126–28, 132–70, 233n. 1;
    first-person narrators of, 127, 132, 133;
    father of, 133; gender in, 133, 253–54n.
    33; humor in, 127–28, 132–33; inver-
    sion of genre in, 126; oedipal structure
    in, 132–33; scatology in, 132–33, 252n.
    16; vision in, 133. See also *Pop. 1280*
time, 12, 18–19, 22, 35–36, 74–76, 81, 82,
    92–93, 173, 175–76, 177–79, 186–87,
    234n. 4

Todorov, Tzvetan, 12
Toles, George, 247n. 15, 247n. 21

violence, 3, 7, 11–12, 17, 25, 32, 43, 51,
    52, 53–55, 57, 60–64, 68–69, 73, 77–81,
    83, 116, 132–33, 138, 139–40, 143–44,
    150, 152–60, 167–72, 190–91, 196–97,
    198–203, 208–9, 211–13, 219–20; oral,
    99, 118, 119, 162–63, 167–70,
    240–41n. 15
vision, 7, 34–35, 54–55, 59–61, 79, 85–92,
    93–102, 104–6, 108–9, 111, 116–20,
    146–47, 150, 151–52, 181–82, 194–203;
    and smell, 65–68, 69–70; and vomit, 7,
    89–90, 91–92, 95–102; as repression of
    vomit, 91–92, 99–100, 105–6
vomit, 7, 87–90, 86, 104, 112–15, 119,
    120–25, 252n. 16; and vision, 7, 89–90,
    91–92, 95–102; rewritten as blood in
    Sanctuary, 103–5, 107, 111

Ward, A. C., 85, 247n. 18
Weber, Samuel, 251n. 7, 251n. 10
West, Cornel, 244n. 32
Williams, Aubrey, 249n. 34
Williams, Raymond, 239–40n. 5
Wilson, Barbara, 217
Winks, Robin, 216
Wittenberg, Judith Bryant, 249n. 29
Woolrich, Cornell, 231n. 1

Žižek, Slavoj, 235n. 12

ABOUT THE AUTHOR

Greg Forter was born in New York State in 1961 and educated at the University of California, Berkeley. He teaches American literature at the University of South Carolina, Columbia, and is currently working on a book about gender, mourning, and creativity in American literary modernism.